Global Governance

Demonstrations during the meetings of the International Monetary Fund (IMF), World Bank and World Trade Organisation (WTO) continue to grow in intensity; the gulf between rich and poor within and across nations is on the increase; environmental degradation continues unabated; human security is in decline. These issues and many more point to failings in global governance. What are these failings? In what ways have the activities of international organisations contributed to the perpetuation of global inequalities? How might they be addressed? These are some of the questions this book seeks to answer.

Global Governance: Critical perspectives offers a critical examination of the role of international organisations in the management of global affairs. It contains essays by leading scholars in the field, each exploring one aspect of global governance. In doing so, the book explores recent trends and developments in global governance and examines failings in the work of international organisations. Areas covered include:

- The role of international organisations in global governance
- Protests
- Development
- Trade and finance
- Labour and environment
- Culture and human rights
- Human security
- Gender and civil society

Rorden Wilkinson is Senior Lecturer in International Relations and International Political Economy at the University of Manchester. He is the author of *Multilateralism and the World Trade Organisation* (Routledge, 2000).

Steve Hughes is Senior Lecturer in International Business and Director of Graduate Studies at the School of Management, University of Newcastle. He has written extensively on labour and the global political economy and acted as an adviser on international issues to a variety of organisations.

Global Governance

Critical perspectives

Edited by
Rorden Wilkinson and Steve Hughes

London and New York

First published 2002
by Routledge
11 New Fetter Lane, London EC4P 4EE

Simultaneously published in the USA and Canada
by Routledge
29 West 35th Street, New York, NY 10001

Routledge is an imprint of the Taylor and Francis Group

Typeset in Times New Roman by
Graphicraft Limited, Hong Kong
Printed and bound in Great Britain by
TJ International, Padstow, Cornwall

British Library Cataloguing in Publication Data
A catalogue record for this book is available
from the British Library

Library of Congress Cataloging in Publication Data
A catalog record for this book has been requested

ISBN 0-415-26837-0 (hbk)
ISBN 0-415-26838-9 (pbk)

Contents

Illustrations

Figures

Tables

Boxes

Contributors

Paul Cammack is Professor in the Department of Government at the University of Manchester currently seconded as Director of Graduate Studies in the Graduate School of Social Sciences. He is engaged in a Marxist interpretation of the politics of the contemporary global economy, of which the chapter published here is a part. His most recent book is *Capitalism and Democracy in the Third World* (Cassell/Leicester University Press, 1997).

Richard Dodgson is a research officer in widening participation at universities for the North East of England. In this post he has recently completed the first stage of a comparative project that examines the widening access policies on a global scale. Prior to taking up his current post, he received his doctorate for the University of Newcastle, and researched and published in the areas of globalisation, international political economy, and the global politics of health/population control.

Lorraine Elliott is Fellow in the Department of International Relations and Convenor of the Department's Postgraduate Programme, at the Australian National University. She has written extensively on global environmental governance and environmental security. A second edition of her most recent book, *The Global Politics of the Environment* (Macmillan, 1998) is in preparation. She has been a Visiting Fellow at the Asia Research Centre at the London School of Economics and a Visiting Research Fellow at Balliol College, Oxford.

Randall D. Germain teaches international political economy at the University of Wales, Aberystwyth. He is the author of *The International Organization of Credit: states and global finance in the world-economy* (Cambridge University Press, 1997), and the editor of *Globalization and Its Critics: perspectives from political economy* (Macmillan Press, 2000). He has also published in journals such as the *European Journal of International Relations*, *New Political Economy*, *Review of International Studies*, and *Review of International Political Economy*.

Nigel Haworth is Professor of International Business at the University of Auckland, New Zealand. He is currently working in a number of areas, including regionalisation and its impact on labour and labour markets (especially in APEC), the fusion of International Political Economy with Labour Relations theory, SME development in the Asia-Pacific Region, and sustainable Maori commercial development. His main teaching interests are in the political economy of the Asian region, and the nature and impacts of economic internationalisation. He works closely with local and national government in New Zealand around economic development issues and represents New Zealand in a number of international forums.

Steve Hughes is Senior Lecturer in International Business and Director of Graduate Studies in the School of Management at the University of Newcastle. He was Senior Lecturer in the School of Business and Economics at the University of Auckland, New Zealand, Fellow of the New Zealand APEC Study Centre, and Visiting Fellow in the Department of Government at the University of Manchester. He has published work on trade and labour standards, the intersection between industrial relations and international relations, and the political economy of APEC integration. He has acted as an adviser on international issues to a number of labour and non-governmental organisations.

Lucy James was awarded her PhD in International Studies from the University of Birmingham in 1996. From 1997 to 2001 she was Lecturer in International Relations in the Centre for International Politics, Department of Government, University of Manchester. Her research areas were gender, the new security agenda, and International Relations theory. She is co-author (with Terry Terriff, Patrick Morgan and Stuart Croft) of *Security Studies Today* (Cambridge: Polity, 1999). She has since changed career and is currently studying for a Diploma in Counselling and Psychotherapy at Nottingham Trent University.

Stephanie Lawson is Professor of International Relations and Director of European and International Studies in the School of Economic and Social Studies, University of East Anglia. She was previously Fellow in the Research School of Pacific and Asian Studies at the Australian National University. Her present research interests focus on issues concerning culture, ethnicity, nationalism, and democracy, and combine comparative and normative approaches to the study of world politics. She is the author of many book chapters and articles dealing with these issues in the Asia-Pacific region. Her books include *Tradition Versus Democracy in the South Pacific* (Cambridge University Press, 1996) and *The New Agenda in International Relations* (Polity Press, 2001).

Kelley Lee is Senior Lecturer in Global Health Policy, and Co-Director of the Centre on Globalisation, Environmental Change and Health at the London School of Hygiene and Tropical Medicine. She is Chair of the World Health Organisation (WHO) Scientific Resource Group on Globalisation, Trade and Health, and on the Steering Committee of the UK

Partnership for Global Health. Her research interests focus on the impact of globalisation on communicable and non-communicable diseases. Recent publications include *Health Policy in a Globalising World*, co-edited with K. Buse and S. Fustukian (Cambridge University Press, 2002), *Globalization and Health: An introduction* (Palgrave, forthcoming) and *Globalization and Health: Case studies* (Palgrave, forthcoming).

Craig N. Murphy is Professor and Chair of Political Science at Wellesley College and Research Professor at Brown University's Watson Institute of International Studies. His work focuses on international institutions and the political economy of inequality across lines of class, gender, region, ethnicity, and race. He is author of *International Organization and Industrial Change: Global Governance since 1850* (Polity, 1994) and 'Global Governance: Poorly Done and Poorly Understood', *International Affairs*, 76: 4 (2000). He is a founding editor of *Global Governance*, which received the 1996 award of the American Association of Publishers for the best new scholarly journal in business, the humanities, and the social sciences. He is immediate past-president of the International Studies Association (ISA) and Chair of the Academic Council on the United Nations System (ACUNS).

Caroline Thomas is Professor of Global Politics at the University of Southampton. She is interested in the interface between development studies and global politics and has published widely on human security concerns, most recently: 'Where is the Third World Now?', *Review of International Studies*, Volume 25 Special Issue, December 1999; *Global Governance, Development and Human Security* (Pluto Press, 2000); and (edited with Annie Taylor) *Global Trade and Global Social Issues* (Routledge, 1999). She is currently working on human security and the global politics of health.

Heloise Weber is Research Fellow at the Centre for the Study of Globalisation and Regionalisation, University of Warwick. Her interests are broadly in global political economy. Her current focus is on an emerging global development architecture and its embeddeddness in frameworks of global governance.

Rorden Wilkinson teaches international relations and international political economy in the Centre for International Politics, Department of Government, University of Manchester. He is convenor of the International Political Economy Group (IPEG) of the British International Studies Association (BISA); and author of *Multilateralism and the World Trade Organisation* (Routledge, 2000). He is primarily interested in trade, global governance, labour and production. His work has been published in, among others, the *Journal of World Trade*, *New Political Economy*, *Global Governance*, *British Journal of Politics and International Relations*, *Environmental Politics*, and *International Studies Perspectives*.

Foreword

Why pay attention to global governance?

Craig N. Murphy

Why bother studying 'global governance', the very limited 'actually existing world government' that has emerged over the last century and a half? What world government there is, is, after all, both amorphous and morally suspect. Robert Cox sees at its centre a *nebuleuse*, a cloud of ideological influences that has fostered the realignment of elite thinking to the needs of the world market.[1] Much of the scholarship on global governance focuses on the only slightly more concrete international *régimes*, the norms, rules, and decision-making procedures that states (and sometimes other powerful actors) have created to govern international life within specific realms. Most of us who study global governance warn against assuming that the seemingly more real world organisations – the World Trade Organisation (WTO), the United Nations (UN) and its constituent parts – are more than agreements among their state members, even though secretariats can develop as much autonomy from their state members as the managers of large firms can have from their shareholders and corporate boards.

At times, even when 'global governance' becomes the most concrete, it takes forms that political scientists find the most unfamiliar. In the last decade, global-level private authorities have emerged to regulate both states and much of transnational economic and social life. They include bond-rating agencies imposing policies on governments at all levels, tight oligopolies in reinsurance, accounting, high-level consulting that create similar regulatory pressure, and the peculiar combination of *ad hoc* private regulation and non-regulation that governs global telecommunications and the Internet. Environmental and labour standards adopted by companies have private accounting or consulting firms monitor product and workplace compliance. Arguably, these regulations are more significant than some current intergovernmental regimes that have the same purpose. Similarly, much of the impetus for contemporary public international regulation comes from transnational interest groups, including associations of progressive firms attempting to impose the same costs for environmental and social standards on their competitors, and, of course, traditional consumer groups, labour groups, and environmentalists. In addition, as a consequence of neoliberal marketisation, the services once provided by public intergovernmental organisations are now contracted to private, non-governmental, often 'social movement'-style, organisations. Today it is, more often than most of us realise, NGOs who run the refugee camps, provide disaster relief, design and carry-out development projects, monitor and attempt to contain the international spread of disease, and try to clean up an ever more polluted environment. Moreover, most of them do so primarily with *public* funds from major donor governments and intergovernmental organisations, officially enamoured of the efficiency of NGOs and the 'empowerment' that they foster, but also, many analysts suspect, because NGOs provide these necessary international public services on the cheap.

Why then should we study the neoliberal ideology with its world-wide significance, the growing network of both public and private regimes that extend across the world's largest regions, the system of global intergovernmental organisations, and transnational organisations both carrying out some of the traditional service functions of global public agencies and also working to create regimes and new systems of international integration? It is primarily a question of justice.

Some democratic theorists argue that the contemporary growth of unregulated transnational economic activity undermines the democratic gains won over the last century. To restore and further the democratic project, the theorists champion international institutions both ruled by the people and powerful enough to regulate the global markets in labour, money, goods, and ideas that have expanded so rapidly in recent decades.[2] Similarly, analysts linked to the United Nations Development Programme (UNDP) have explored the limited provision of 'global public goods', understood primarily as goods that are unlikely to be provided by unregulated markets.[3] Many of their arguments appeal even to those most affected by the liberal *nebuleuse*; it is hard, for example, to argue against the global monitoring of infectious diseases that could devastate any population in which they are introduced. On the other hand, many of the world's privileged would certainly deny that distributive justice, peace in far away lands, or the protection of the cultural property of the poor constitute 'public goods'. Nonetheless, the debate about what constitute necessary global public goods demands empirical investigations into their provision (or, usually, their non-provision) by the existing institutions of global governance.

For example, some analysts – and many more activists – argue that the most powerful of the public institutions of global governance – the International Monetary Fund (IMF), WTO, and even the World Bank – through their promotion of unregulated economic globalisation, have contributed to the growing numbers of the destitute as well as to the growing privilege of the world's rich.[4] Even more disturbing have been the UN's failures to stop the devastating conflicts after the end of the Cold War, the worst of which have been in Africa. In 100 days from April to July of 1994 more than a half-million people, including at least three-quarters of the entire Tutsi population of Rwanda were systematically slaughtered despite a widely-ratified

UN Genocide Convention and ample early warning provided to the UN Secretariat and the Security Council by its own officers in the field. Analyses of the etiology of the genocide blame not only the Secretariat, the Security Council and its permanent members, but also the entire international aid community, public and private, which for twenty years nurtured a deeply aid-dependent regime that increasingly incited ethnic hatred and violence.[5] The consequences of the failure to avert the genocide have mounted from year to year. The Tutsi military government that seized power to stop the slaughter went on to trigger a cascade of continuing wars across central Africa.

Preventing genocide and the avoidable cascading violence of regional war, finding ways to efficiently provide essential international goods that markets will never provide, and challenging globalisation's sudden reversal of the twentieth-century's democratic gains, are some of the most compelling reasons to try to understand the nebulous system of global governance. This book makes a major contribution to the scholarship that has attempted to provide that understanding. Previously, that literature, like global governance itself, has not been that well developed.

James Rosenau has helped us understand the role of private transnational associations. A world in which transformations in telecommunications have lowered the costs of political education and created opportunities for more and more subgroups to work with one another is a world of increasingly skilful citizens able to act both above and below the levels of traditional national politics.[6] But why, we might ask, has so much of this creative movement in world politics just added up to the supremacy of the neoliberal agenda both within and across states?

Sociologists of the Stanford University-centred 'world polity' school answer that global governance is an expression of liberal norms, a co-evolving social construction based on those norms.[7] Xiaowei Luo has even argued that if one looks at the evolution of technology-focused organisations, we can see a transformation of the global liberal culture away from a free-market fundamentalism characteristic of the nineteenth century and toward 'social development'-style liberalism similar to that underlying the UNDP's broad calls for the improved provision of global public goods.[8]

Other social constructivists, for example, political scientists Martha Finnemore and John Ruggie, might disagree.[9] Significantly, one realist scholar has argued that even some of the most-widely touted regimes formed among the most-privileged nations – North American Free Trade Agreement (NAFTA) and the European Monetary System (EMS) – amounted to coercive impositions upon Canada's Liberals and on southern European governments of the centre and the left.[10] The dean of realist international political economy in the United States, Princeton's Robert Gilpin, is blunter, arguing that if there is anything that looks like liberal global governance it is an expression of the power and preferences of the United States.[11]

Yet, it is certainly not *just* that. Susan Strange devoted much of the end of her life to demonstrating that the US and western European governments shared the responsibility for giving up state power to the global market through a series of 'rational', short-term self-interested decisions with consequences recognised as disastrous by at least some political leaders on both sides of the Atlantic.[12] Moreover, the social forces that have continued to back the neoliberal agenda are truly transnational, which implies that to understand contemporary global governance we need to develop a class analysis that transcends national boundaries, something that the scholars praised by Rorden Wilkinson in the first chapter of this book have attempted. Yet, I doubt that any of us would argue that we have gotten it quite right. If there is an emergent global, non-state specific capitalist class, it is certainly evolving along with American power and the institutions of global governance. Global governance is not simply a superstructure responding to the interests of an already differentiated global ruling class. It is more a site, one of many sites, in which struggles over wealth, power, and knowledge are taking place.

It may be more accurate to argue that contemporary global governance remains a predictable institutional response not to the interests of a fully-formed class, but to the overall logic of industrial capitalism. 'Economic globalisation', understood as industrial capitalism's pressure toward larger and larger market areas, necessarily means that at some points the real economies will escape the boundaries of states, as the global economy has today. Contemporary observers are bound to see such moments as representing 'triumphs of the market' over the state, but, no doubt, at the same time there will be simultaneous pressure to establish new institutions of governance at a 'higher', more inclusive level, at least at the level at which new markets have developed. Historians of intergovernmental organisation and international integration note that for the last two centuries at least, the ideology most-often used to justify new, powerful, and autonomous international institutions has been a kind of 'scientism', the argument that there are socially-beneficial, technical tasks that should be handed over to 'experts' to be done for us.

This brings us right back to questions of democratic theory: Must globalisation inevitably be accompanied by the anti-democratic government of 'expertise' or by the non-government of marketisation at ever more inclusive levels? Is it possible to marshal the egalitarian forces that Rosenau correctly sees as being empowered by the technologies of globalisation to create a democratic system of global governance that would both prevent repetition of the tragedies of the post-Cold War decade and provide essential goods that global markets will not provide?

Since the end of the Cold War, one ubiquitous impediment has been US foreign policy. The US has given rhetorical support to a variety of innovations in global governance from expanded humanitarian operations, to the vast agenda of the Beijing women's conference, to the creation of the International Criminal Court. Yet US action has not matched its words, preventing Security Council action in Rwanda, refusing to adhere to the land mines' ban and criminal court agreements that it had originally championed, and failing, year after year, to pay its UN dues. John Washburn (once the senior US citizen in the international civil service), carefully explains why US political culture and institutions assure that the country will remain an inconsistent leader and, ultimately, an obstruction to the strengthening and democratisation of global governance. Washburn's advice is to ignore the US, to let the UN and those who advocate its strengthening and democratisation to 'look after themselves'.[13]

Arguably, the International Criminal Court Treaty and the Ottawa Convention on Landmines are successful demonstrations of this strategy. Both are significant extensions of international humanitarian law promoted by the political leadership of close US allies and non-governmental movements with deep ties inside the US, but achieved over the opposition of the US government. There is also reason to believe that both innovations can have most of their desired effects even without US adherence. The strategies used to achieve both treaties suggest that it is possible, in some fields, to nullify the impact of the US's separation of powers and history of isolation that gives the US legislators the power and desire to block democratic extensions of global governance.

Unfortunately, few of the conventions needed to establish a more powerful and more democratic form of global governance can be designed that cleverly, as each of the sections of this book makes clear. Where significant corporate interests are likely to be implicated, where real attempts are being made to control lucrative global markets, what some analysts have called the 'indispensability and indefensibility' of US policy, is likely to remain.[14]

Many analysts would leave it at that. If the strengthening and democratisation of global governance are not in US interests, then there is no particular point in pursuing such goals until the US's relative power sharply declines. If the most powerful economic interests oppose such developments, it is difficult to imagine how they can be pursued successfully. In contrast, social constructivists recognise that interests are never given; they are historically embedded, enacted social structures, subject to rethinking and enacting differently. Not surprisingly, much of John Ruggie's work as Assistant UN Secretary General supported Kofi Annan's effort to convince American and global corporate leaders to change what they understand as their own 'interests' relative to the UN's agenda.[15]

Many of the authors in this volume would have us look even further, not only to the ways in which interests are constructed, but also at the ways in which the politics of global governance leads its participants to think in terms of power as the ability to control others – others with competing economic interests, others with different cultural understandings. 'Governance' might also imply a concept of power that emphasises capability, power as the ability to do things, collectively and individually, not through one-sided 'expertise', but democratically. Understood in those terms, the political space created by the real need to re-regulate a larger, more inclusive global capitalist economy, may provide opportunities for creating at least some institutions for collective, global solidarity that would challenge the erosion of democracy, the economic inequality, and the insecurity that have marked the recent remit of global governance.

Notes

1 Robert W. Cox, 'Structural Issues of Global Governance: Issue for Europe', in Robert W. Cox with Timothy Sinclair, *Approaches to World Order* (Cambridge: Cambridge University Press, 1996).
2 See especially, part III of David Held, *Democracy and the Global Order: from the modern state to cosmopolitan governance* (Cambridge: Polity Press, 1995).
3 Inge Kaul, Isabelle Grunberg and Marc A. Stern (eds) *Global Public Goods: international cooperation in the 21st Century* (New York: Oxford University Press, 1999). An important earlier study in this tradition was Ruben P. Mendez, *International Public Finance* (New York: Oxford University Press, 1992). Also see Wolfgang H. Reinicke, *Global Public Policy: governing without government?* (Washington, DC: The Brookings Institution, 1998).
4 One of the most devastating evaluations of the impact of globalisation and the market-promoting practices of the IMF and World Bank on the poor was undertaken by the Department of Social Medicine at the Harvard Medical School. See Jim Yong Kim, Joyce V. Millen, Alec Irwin and John Gresham (eds) *Dying for Growth: global inequality and the health of the poor* (Monroe, NE: Common Courage Press, 2000).
5 Peter Uvin, *Aiding Violence: the development enterprise in Rwanda* (West Hartford, CT: Kumarian Press, 1998); International Panel of Eminent Personalities to Investigate the 1994 Genocide in Rwanda and the Surrounding Events, *Rwanda: the preventable genocide* (Addis Ababa: OAU, 2000); Michael Barnett, *Eyewitness to Genocide: the United Nations and Rwanda* (Ithaca, NY: Cornell University Press, 2002).
6 See especially, James N. Rosenau, *The United Nations in a Turbulent World* (Boulder, CO: Lynne Rienner, 1992); Rosenau, 'Governance in the Twenty-first Century', *Global Governance* 1: 1 (1995), pp. 13–44; and Rosenau, *Along the Domestic–Foreign Frontier: exploring governance in a turbulent world* (Cambridge: Cambridge University Press, 1997).
7 John Boli and George M. Thomas, *Constructing World Culture: international Nongovernmental Organizations since 1875* (Stanford: Stanford University Press, 1999).
8 Xiaowei Luo, 'The Rise of the Social Development Model: Institutional Construction of International Technology Organizations, 1856–1993', *International Studies Quarterly* 44: 1 (2000), pp. 147–75.
9 Martha Finnemore, *National Interests in International Society* (Ithaca, NY: Cornell University Press, 1996); John Gerald Ruggie, *Constructing the World Polity: essays on international institutionalism* (London: Routledge, 1998).
10 Lloyd Gruber, *Ruling the World: power politics and the rise of supranational institutions* (Princeton: Princeton University Press, 2000).
11 Robert Gilpin, *The Challenge of Global Capitalism: the world economy in the 21st Century* (Princeton: Princeton University Press, 2000).
12 Susan Strange, *The Retreat of the State* (Cambridge: Cambridge University Press, 1996).
13 John L. Washburn, 'United Nations Relations with the United States: The UN Must Look After Itself', *Global Governance* 2: 1 (1996), pp. 81–96.

14 Shardul Agrawala and Steinar Andresen, 'Indispensability and Indefensibility? The United States and the Climate Treaty Negotiations', *Global Governance* 5: 4 (1999), pp. 457–82.
15 Kofi Annan, 'The Quiet Revolution', *Global Governance* 4: 2 (1998), pp. 121–38.

Acknowledgements

This volume represents what we intend to be the first in a series of works designed to interrogate contemporary global governance. It has, from the outset, been a collective effort. As a result, we have accumulated many debts. We owe much to the foresight of the Faculty of Social Sciences and Law at the University of Manchester for its decision to fund the initial workshop out of which this project grew – entitled 'Engaging Global Governance: towards a new agenda?', University of Manchester, 3 July 2000.

Institutionally, we are grateful to the Department of Government at the University of Manchester for its support, as well as to the School of Management at the University of Newcastle. Our commitment to take global governance seriously and embark on a programme of interrogation began while we were both at the University of Auckland, New Zealand, and we owe thanks to that institution as well as to those who offered comments on and support for our early endeavours.

Individually, we are indebted to those who presented their work in that initial workshop and have since been key pillars of this project: Richard Dodgson, Lorraine Elliott, Randall Germain, Nigel Haworth, Lucy James, Stephanie Lawson, Kelley Lee, Caroline Thomas and Heloise Weber. Others too have played an important role: Simon Bulmer, Paul Cammack, Norman Geras and Amanda Layne, all of the Department of Government at the University of Manchester. Nicola Phillips provided helpful comments; and we are grateful to Craig Fowlie and all of those at Routledge who have worked on this project from its initial inception through to its completion.

Perhaps more than most, our families have endured something of the burden of this volume. In particular we are grateful to Jacqueline Wilkinson, Ivan Wilkinson, Graham Wilkinson, Vicky, John, Elizabeth and Lucy Singler, and Jackie, Annie, Sarah and Joe Hughes. That said, although our debt is considerable, we alone bear responsibility for what follows.

Rorden Wilkinson and Steve Hughes
Manchester and Newcastle, November 2001

Abbreviations

ACP	African, Caribbean and Pacific states
AIC	Advanced Industrial Country
APEC	Asia Pacific Economic Co-operation
ASEAN	Association of South East Asian Nations
ASEM	Asia–Europe Meeting
BCBS	Basle Committee on Banking Supervision
BIS	Bank for International Settlements
CAS	Country Assistance Strategies
CBD	Convention on Biological Diversity
CCL	Contingent Credit Lines
CDF	Comprehensive Development Framework
CDS	City Development Strategy
CGAP	Consultative Group to Assist the Poorest
CGFS	Committee on the Global Financial System
CIS	Commonwealth of Independent States
CND	Campaign for Nuclear Disarmament
COP 6	Sixth Conference of Parties
CPIA	Country Policy and Institutional Assessments
CSD	Commission on Sustainable Development
CPSS	Committee on Payment and Settlement Systems
CTE	Committee on Trade and Environment
DAC	Development Assistance Committee
DFID	Department for International Development (UK)
EBF	Extra Budgetary Funds
EBNSC	European Business Network for Social Cohesion
EBRD	European Bank for Reconstruction and Development
EC	European Community
ECB	European Central Bank
ECOSOC	Economic and Social Council of the United Nations
EEC	European Economic Community
EC	European Community
ECLA	Economic Commission for Latin America
EMIT	Environmental Measures in International Trade

EMS	European Monetary System
ESAF	Enhanced Structural Adjustment Facility
ESF	Emergency Social Fund
ESW	Economic and Sector Work
EU	European Union
EWC	European Works Council
FAO	Food and Agriculture Organisation
FCCC	Framework Convention on Climate Change
FCTC	Framework Convention on Tobacco Control
FDI	Foreign Direct Investment
FIFA	Federation Internationale de Football Association
FIL	Financial Intermediary Lending
FLA	Fair Labour Association
FSF	Financial Stability Forum
G7	Group of Seven leading industrial states
G8	Group of Eight (G7 plus Russia)
G10	Group of Ten
G20	Group of Twenty
G22	Group of Twenty-Two
G33	Group of Thirty-Three
G77	Group of Seventy-Seven
GAG	Global Architecture of Governance
GATT	General Agreement on Tariffs and Trade
GATS	General Agreement on Trade in Services
GCGF	Global Corporate Governance Forum
GEF	Global Environment Facility
GEMS	Global Environmental Monitoring System
GHG	Global Health Governance
GNP	Gross National Product
GPPP	Global Public–Private Partnerships
GSP	Generalised System of Preferences
HIPC	Heavily Indebted Poor Countries
IAEA	International Atomic Energy Agency
IAIS	International Association of Insurance Supervisors
IBRD	International Bank for Reconstruction and Development
ICC	International Chamber of Commerce
ICFTU	International Confederation of Free Trade Unions
ICJ	International Court of Justice
ICPD	International Conference on Population and Development
IDA	International Development Association
IFI	International Financial Institution
IFTU	International Federation of Trade Unions
IHG	International Health Governance
ILO	International Labour Organisation
IMF	International Monetary Fund

IMFC	International Monetary and Financial Committee
IMO	International Maritime Organisation
IOSCO	International Organisation of Securities Commissions
IPCC	Intergovernmental Panel on Climate Change
ITO	International Trade Organisation
ITS	International Trade Secretariat
ITU	International Telecommunications Union
IUF	International Union of Foodworkers
LDC	Less/Least Developed Country
MAI	Multilateral Agreement on Investment
MDB	Multilateral Development Bank
MEAs	Multilateral Environmental Agreements
MERCOSUR	El Mercado Común del Sur
MNC	Multinational Corporation
NAFTA	North American Free Trade Agreement
NAM	Non-Aligned Movement
NATO	North Atlantic Treaty Organisation
NEP	New Economic Programme
NGO	Non-Governmental Organisation
NIC	Newly Industrialised Country
NIEO	New International Economic Order
OAU	Organisation of African Unity
ODA	Overseas Development Assistance
ODS	Ozone Depleting Substance
OEEC	Organisation for European Economic Co-operation
OECD	Organisation for Economic Co-operation and Development
OIE	Office International de Epizooties (World Organisation for Animal Health)
OIHP	Office International d'Hygiene Publique
OPEC	Organisation of Petroleum Exporting Countries
PECC	Pacific Economic Co-operation Council
PGA	People's Global Action
PRC	People's Republic of China
PRGF	Poverty Reduction and Growth Facility
PRSP	Poverty Reduction Strategy Paper
RIIA	Royal Institute of International Affairs
SAARC	South Asian Association for Regional Co-operation
SAPs	Structure Adjustment Programmes
SBP	Sustainable Banking for the Poor
SDDS	Special Data Dissemination Standards
SICA	Soccer Industry Council of America
SME	Small and Medium Size Enterprise
SPS	Sanitary and Phytosanitary Measures
SSP	Sectoral Strategy Papers
SSR	Social and Structural Review

TBT	Technical Barriers to Trade
TFI	Tobacco Free Initiative
TRIMs	Trade-Related Investment Measures
TRIPs	Trade-Related Intellectual Property rights
TNC	Transnational Corporation
TUAC	Trade Union Advisory Council
UN	United Nations
UNCED	United Nations Conference on Environment and Development
UNCHE	United Nations Conference on the Human Environment
UNCTAD	United Nations Conference on Trade and Development
UNDP	United Nations Development Programme
UNEP	United Nations Environment Programme
UNESCO	United Nations Educational, Scientific and Cultural Organisation
UNFPA	United Nations Fund for Population Activities
UNGASS	United Nations General Assembly Special Session
UNHCR	United Nations High Commissioner for Refugees
UNICEF	United Nations Children's Fund
UNIDO	United Nations Industrial Development Organisation
UNITAR	United Nations Institute for Training and Research
UNO	United Nations Organisation
UNRISD	United Nations Research Institute for Social Development
UNRRA	United Nations Relief and Rehabilitation Administration
WBCSD	World Business Council on Sustainable Development
WCED	World Commission on Environment and Development
WDM	World Development Movement
WEF	World Economic Forum
WFTU	World Federation of Trade Unions
WFSGI	World Federation of the Sporting Goods Industry
WHA	World Health Assembly
WHO	World Health Organisation
WIPO	World Intellectual Property Organisation
WLM	Women's Liberation Movement
WMO	World Meteorological Organisation
WRI	World Resources Institute
WTO	World Trade Organisation
WWF	World Wide Fund for Nature

1 Global governance

A preliminary interrogation[1]

Rorden Wilkinson

Images of violent clashes between drum-beating protestors and robocop-style police in Seattle; water-cannon, firecrackers and tear gas in central Prague; and the crumpled body of a demonstrator shot dead by police in Genoa, have combined vividly and tragically to bring home the tensions underlining globalisation and its system of governance. Though attempts have been made to dismiss the demonstrations out of hand and depict the participants as nothing more than a 'global rent-a-mob', the case for conducting a rigorous interrogation of contemporary global governance has not been weakened. Global inequalities in income and wealth, information provision, education, and life experiences continue to grow; environmental degradation continues to accelerate and appears unlikely to be met with appropriate political solutions; and there remains a marked deficit in the efficacy, democratic accountability and levels of transparency across the broad array of world institutions.

Yet, although the reasons for conducting a wholesale interrogation of global governance are compelling, it is poorly understood in the literature. With the exception of a small, but significant, group of scholars,[2] the disciplines of international relations and international political economy have largely avoided engaging with a phenomenon that appears to challenge the foundations of existing wisdom. Global governance is variously treated as a fad, an oxymoron, or it is dismissed out of hand. The discipline's realist orthodoxy remains wedded to an understanding of world politics that perceives states as the most significant actors, and attributes little to the role of international organisations or non-state actors. Through these lenses, global governance can be understood only as a function of the international distribution of power, or as a result of behavioural practices, norms, rules and decision-making procedures that have developed over time. Even those liberal institutionalists that have sought to qualify realist assumptions by suggesting that international institutions can, at particular junctures, have a significant impact on international interaction, are wary of suggestions that a system of global governance has emerged and is taking form.

In those few instances when global governance is taken seriously, it is commonly deemed synonymous with the development of international organisation: that process of institutionalisation which, since at least the middle of the nineteenth century, has sought to establish moments of authority designed to co-ordinate activities across state boundaries. Here, the emergence of a series of institutions during the nineteenth century is said to have provided the platform for the establishment of two world organisations: the League of Nations and the International Labour Organisation (ILO). From this point onwards, albeit with the odd institutional funeral, the process of international organisation is understood to have evolved through time in a largely linear fashion producing an increasing number of world and regional bodies. The result has been the emergence of a constellation of bodies, many of which are invisible from public view, but which are nevertheless deemed to be largely peripheral to the natural rhythms of world politics.

Though there is much that can be learnt about global governance by exploring developments in international organisation, the synonymity with which these two phenomena are treated does not enable the qualitative dimensions of contemporary global governance to be fully captured. Global governance is distinct in at least two ways. The first is a recognition that it comprises an array of actors, not only those visible aspects of world political-economic authority such as the United Nations (UN), the World Trade Organisation (WTO), the International Monetary Fund (IMF) and the World Bank, but also quasi-formal intergovernmental gatherings such as the Group of 7 (G7) and the World Economic Forum (WEF); combinations of state and non-state actors such as the UN's Global Compact and the ILO; private associations such as the International Chamber of Commerce (ICC); mercenary groups such as Sandline International and Executive Outcomes; non-governmental organisations (NGOs) like the World Wide Fund for Nature (WWF), the World Development Movement (WDM) and Oxfam; transnational religious bodies; international terrorist organisations (however loosely associated); transnational political movements; financial markets; global accountancy and law firms; and transnational business.

The second distinguishing feature is the way in which varieties of actors are increasingly combining to manage – and in many cases, micro-manage – a growing range of political, economic and social affairs. In this way, global governance can be thought of as the various patterns in which global, regional, national and local actors combine to govern particular areas. Global governance, then, is not defined simply by the emergence of new actors or nodes of authority; instead it comprises a growing complexity in the way in which its actors interact and interrelate. Most certainly, some of the agents of global governance are newly emerged; others, however, are much longer established. Nevertheless, key to understanding contemporary global governance is the capacity to identify the range of actors involved in the act of management, as well as to uncover the variety of ways in which they are connected to one another.

That said, it is premature to speak of the existence of a complete and fully coherent system of global governance. Global governance is better understood as emerging. The intensification of global political, economic and social interaction has generated pressures for a concomitant system of governance. Where the demand for such a system is greatest, and where there is a corresponding political-economic will, coherent and effective patterns of global governance have emerged. In other areas, and often in spite of considerable demand, systems of governance are inadequate, ineffectual, wanting, or non-existent.

Understanding that a coherent system is emerging is, in large part, key to appreciating the way in which global governance is currently articulated. As the remainder of this volume demonstrates, contemporary global governance is highly uneven. Some of its dimensions, particularly in the field of economic governance, are highly developed; whereas others, especially in the fields of health, environment and human rights, are underdeveloped, barely existent or wholly absent. Nevertheless, the evolving character of global governance brings with it moments of opportunity – moments in which pressure can be brought to bear on the emerging patterns of governance. In such moments, alternative possibilities have the potential to emerge, thus altering the way in which global governance is constituted. In this way, identifying the potential for alternative possibilities becomes an intrinsic part of any interrogation of global governance.

This volume aims to build on that small but significant body of literature that has begun to take global governance seriously. In doing so, we seek to contribute to the development of a more complete understanding of this emerging phenomenon. Our contribution is to explore the role of those world organisations that lie at the core of contemporary global governance. These bodies represent, as Craig Murphy has put it, 'what world government we actually have'.[3] It is these bodies that have developed, and are developing relationships with other actors to enable greater control to be exercised in given areas. And it is these bodies that have so far been called into question by the absence of coherent and plausible answers to the problems of growing inequalities. It is for these reasons that we choose to begin our examination by exploring the patterns of governance centred around the authority of particular world organisations. By concentrating on the core, we aim to better understand one piece of the wider mosaic that constitutes contemporary global governance. Our aim, then, is *not* to offer an examination of global governance in its entirety; rather, we offer a series of critical reflections on some of its most significant aspects. In doing so, we highlight the problems of the way in which global governance is currently articulated and identify areas wherein fundamental change is required. Throughout we place emphasis on understanding how patterns of governance have evolved (or not, as the case may be) in the areas of finance, commerce, development, environment, health, human security, labour and civil society. In doing so, we identify the key actors and mechanisms involved; the way in which global governance is articulated; the reasons for, and pressures behind, particular developments; and, perhaps most importantly, the most prominent oversights.

The backdrop for this book, then, is provided by an acute need to develop a better understanding of contemporary global governance; to advance a more comprehensive account of the relationship between the institutions of global governance and the areas they seek to govern; to explore the tensions thrown up by the way in which governance is exercised; to develop a better understanding of the evolution of global governance; and to explore alternative strategies and possibilities for a more inclusive and representative form of global governance. It is to these tasks that the remainder of this volume turns.

The organisation of the book

Global financial and developmental governance

The first part of the book explores recent developments in global financial and developmental governance. The two chapters comprising this section centre on the operations of the IMF and the World Bank respectively – organisations that are dealt with here specifically, but whose significance runs throughout the volume.

In the first of these chapters, Randall Germain charts what he sees as a radical change in the decision-making structures of the global economy. This change, he argues, has seen the locus of international financial decision-making move away from a system centred around the US, to one wherein a greater role can now be assumed by states not previously privy to the corridors of power. He suggests, in turn, that this movement has begun to broaden the boundaries of accountability and legitimacy to which the international financial architecture – his term for the constellation of financial decision-making bodies – is exposed. Germain argues that this movement is not the result of a conscious effort to reform the democratic credentials of the international financial architecture. Rather, he suggests, it began as a technical response to a series of financial crises in the global economy, principally, though not exclusively, associated with the Asian financial crisis of 1997–8. It has, nevertheless, begun to acquire a distinctly political dimension designed to incorporate emerging market economies into international financial governance.

Germain argues that the crises of the late twentieth century brought with them a realisation that international finance was not of secondary importance to the global economy, and that the artificial separation of the spheres of politics and economics had to be redressed. He suggests that a key part of the process of reform has required that developing countries accept primary responsibility for crisis prevention; but this ownership could only come about with concomitant changes in the decision-making structures of the international financial architecture – changes which better reflect the new role of emerging markets in financial decision-making. He argues that the creation of a new international grouping of non-G7 countries – the Group of Twenty

(G20) – has generated a potentially new and radical alteration to the way in which financial decisions are made. The newness and radicalism of this action lies in the extension, for the first time, of the international financial decision-making structure beyond the industrial core of the G7 generally, and the US more particularly.

Germain argues that this reform process has been further enhanced by the creation of the International Monetary and Financial Committee (IMFC). This new body, he contends, though unable to stop the IMF from engaging in poor policy decisions, enables all members to raise issues relating to the Fund's role in the global financial system without being hampered by the legendary asymmetries in the Organisation's voting system. Germain's examination of these developments enable him to offer an image of an emerging consensus-based international financial decision-making structure.

In spite of these more inclusive moves, the picture Germain paints is of a system of governance that remains firmly centred around the financial decision-making power of states. In the main, it is representatives of national banks and ministries of finance that populate the bodies of the financial decision-making architecture; and it is only by extending the invitation to their counterparts in emerging markets that any expansion in the representative credentials of the international financial architecture has come about. In reality, then, it remains a system of *international* financial governance, one wherein the sanctity of state sovereignty is maintained. Certainly, there is a complex system of relationships between banking institutions and national ministries that ensures private sector views filter through to the corridors of power. It is, however, the absence of a corresponding counter to private and state influence that ensures the international financial architecture remains unbalanced, albeit that its decision-making inevitably has global consequences. That said, given the history of international financial decision-making, the developments Germain details are nevertheless significant.

Paul Cammack switches the focus away from the IMF and the international financial architecture to explore the World Bank's role in global governance. Paralleling Germain, Cammack explores recent efforts by the World Bank to promote 'ownership' among its membership, particularly from developing countries. However, unlike Germain's account of inclusion through ownership, Cammack suggests instead that the Bank's efforts belie a more authoritarian approach to development. In further contradiction to Germain, Cammack argues that institutions such as the Financial Stability Forum (FSF) and the Global Corporate Governance Forum (GCGF) are essential tools through which the disciplinary dimensions of this system are exercised.

Cammack's focus is on the World Bank's Comprehensive Development Framework (CDF) and its corresponding system of governance. He argues that the World Bank has attributed the problems of development to the failure of developing countries to embody the social and structural dimensions of neoliberalism. The Bank's response has been to require that developing countries accelerate the liberalisation process by promoting a sense of ownership in global developmental governance. More than that, while states appear to be have been 'invited' to assume ownership of the CDF, they are in reality *required* to assume ownership of all the elements of the development framework.

Cammack argues that the means by which the World Bank can ensure states assume ownership of the CDF is through a matrix – a co-ordinated approach involving the international development community, governments, civil society and the private sector. The purpose of the matrix, Cammack suggests, is to enable the World Bank to move away from the micro-management of operational aspects of development programmes to an assumption of responsibility for overall strategic control. Such a movement requires that the policies of all recipient states become more transparent and accountable to the World Bank. In making his claims, Cammack takes issue with the World Bank's assertion that the matrix is not a clandestine attempt to dominate the international development arena. Moreover, and again contrary to its own denials, the World Bank is seeking to bring about strategic co-ordination across the international development community.

Cammack's vision of global governance is, then, markedly different from Germain's. Rather than the emergence of a meaningful process of reform, Cammack sees in the CDF the consolidation of a finely tuned, multifaceted system of governance that extends from the corridors of the World Bank down to the nooks and crannies of local life. In this system national governments act as important conduits, and a host of other actors assume strategic importance. They are, nonetheless, subordinate to the wishes and desires of the World Bank – something that leads Cammack to suggest that the World Bank aspires to be the 'Mother of All Governments'. Cammack's vision of developmental governance, then, is of a system co-ordinated by the World Bank that is intimate in its intrusion and acutely hierarchical in its structure.

Global environmental, cultural and health governance

The section on environmental, cultural and health governance moves away from the terrain of global economic governance. It is not, however, a wholesale departure. Economic governance is by far the most advanced and comprehensive dimension of emerging global governance, and it pervades and indeed dominates other dimensions, as we see in the next three chapters as well as in the remainder of the volume.

Lorraine Elliott begins this section with a critical examination of global environmental governance. In doing so, she argues that an apparently well populated institutional terrain masks a lack of substance in global environmental governance. She begins by examining the demand for global environmental governance, exploring something of the rate of environmental degradation as well as the tensions between sovereignty and the environment, questions of justice, and the place of the 'local' in the face of growing global inequality. The demand for global environmental governance is then contrasted with its supply. Here Elliott argues that while a global institutional framework exists, it is far from global in operation. There is an absence of substantive co-operation and democratisation; a narrow and inadequate notion of what constitutes the global; and a lack of improvement in the state of the global environment.

Elliott suggests that the real locus of power in global environmental governance lies in the Global Environment Facility (GEF) – a facility established under the joint authority of the UN Development Programme (UNDP), UN Environment Programme (UNEP), and the World Bank. But, she argues, it is the World Bank which houses and manages the GEF, albeit that the UNDP and UNEP have implementation tasks. Elliott also demonstrates that the World Bank's involvement in global environmental governance is not limited to the GEF. Rather, it has become institutionally central to the pursuit of sustainable development, as well as materially central to continued environmental decline in those countries in which it funds projects and programmes. Aspects of Cammack's assertion that the World Bank seeks to be the principal source of global power resonate loudly here.

Elliott also explores the role of the WTO in global environmental governance – an Organisation whose significance is seldom properly understood and which is explored in part in the opening pages of Wilkinson's contribution (Chapter 11). Here Elliott argues that while the WTO professes to have a monopoly on trade and environmental issues, it has brought little to the debate and contributed substantively even less to the plight of the environment. In reality, the WTO may have actually made matters worse by ruling, in certain instances, that particular national measures designed to protect the environment are discriminatory and, as a result, contravene its rules.

Stephanie Lawson expands the terrain further by exploring the tensions that exist between common understandings of culture and the contemporary human rights regime. Lawson shows how concepts have tended to objectify culture in such a way that differences between cultures are exaggerated. She argues that this has developed in such a way that cultural differences are often taken as shorthand for assuming that cultures are distinctive and, ultimately, incommensurable. Our treatment of culture as distinct 'things' has, she suggests, led to dichotic assertions of 'the West' and 'the Rest'. But Lawson also argues that underpinning this dichotomisation are some overtly political dynamics which range from postcolonial assertions of sovereign power through to justifications for economic development. The crux of Lawson's argument is that the 'problem' of culture – that is, the way in which it has been perceived – creates significant problems for the establishment of a common global human rights regime; a regime that is common to the extent that it becomes a robust dimension of a wider system of global governance.

Lawson does not, however, deny the importance of cultural differences. Instead, she suggests, culture is more appropriately understood as a process; a vehicle for change that is contingent on the moment in which it exists as well as its social, political and moral dynamism. Understood in this way,

Lawson argues, culture should not be a 'problem for human rights and global governance, but rather that which enables interaction and the transcending of difference necessary to the further development of an international human rights regime'. In stating such, Lawson is keen to reiterate that she is not suggesting that differences, whether cultural or otherwise, are neither important nor legitimate. Rather, she suggests, a human rights regime based on exaggerated notions of cultural difference must be treated with 'an acute critical awareness' of their simplicity. Moreover, an international human rights regime that eschews such simplistic approaches can work to protect culturally defined minorities.

It is this last point that is perhaps the most telling for contemporary global governance. By identifying the 'problem' of culture, and in particular our tendency to treat cultures and states synonymously, Lawson goes some considerable way towards explaining the problems of protecting the rights of minority groups. There is, then, a strong normative argument here for a re-articulated international human rights regime. That said, and echoing something of Elliott's account of the tension between environment and sovereignty, we see implicit in Lawson's discussion a recognition that the contemporary human rights regime remains firmly international. Notwithstanding the 'problem' of culture, it is the problem of sovereignty that in large part inhibits the development of a truly global human rights regime. Like Elliott, then, Lawson's implication is that the contemporary system of global governance is similarly wanting.

Richard Dodgson and Kelley Lee move the focus on further in their exploration of the development of international health governance and calls for a more global approach. They begin by plotting the development of international health governance from its beginnings in the middle of the nineteenth century. In doing so, they demonstrate that an intrinsic part of international health governance has been the growth of an organic governance framework linking intergovernmental conferences and bodies with regional health organisations, NGOs and private associations. However, they argue that despite the inclusion of non-state bodies, this system is nevertheless based upon the assumption that the responsibility for national health lies with the state – a situation perpetuated by the World Health Organisation's (WHO) almost exclusive dealings with national governments.

We also see in Dodgson and Lee's account the significance of other institutions to which we have referred earlier. In particular, they point to the role of the World Bank and the WTO, but also the Organisation for Economic Co-operation and Development (OECD), thus further underlining the significance of these organisations in the current configuration of global governance.

Dodgson and Lee argue, however, that international health governance has reached a point beyond which further development is unlikely. Questions are being raised as to the efficacy of a system of health governance centred around the principle of sovereignty, in a world characterised by widening inequalities not only in income and wealth distribution but in the human health experience. Their task, then, is to explore the potential and possibilities for a global system of health governance – one wherein the existing system of international health governance is not abandoned or made redundant, but rather remains an important part of a wider system. In doing so, Dodgson and Lee identify the essential features of global health governance as geographic, state and non-state as well as a global mindset in understanding the interrelatedness of issues such as health and trade, health and scientific endeavour and the like.

Human security and global governance

The move to Caroline Thomas' contribution – Chapter 7 – begins to tie together a number of themes teased out in the preceding chapters. Her concern is with understanding the interrelationship between the material dimensions of human security and global governance, in which she focuses on exploring the performance of various institutions in providing for the material sufficiency of the world's population.

Thomas uses as her starting point a concept of human security that has both material and non-material dimensions. In pointing to the material dimensions of human security Thomas is referring to the ability to safeguard against hunger, poverty, thirst, torture, and the like; whereas the non-material dimensions of human security encompass, among others, fair and democratic representation, dignity and human worth. For Thomas, the material and non-material dimensions of human security should be treated as an indivisible, coherent ensemble; though her concern in this chapter is with better understanding the material dimensions of human security and their relationship with global governance.

More specifically, Thomas explores the ideological contours of global governance as they are articulated in global development policy – in this, her chapter has much in common with Cammack's, albeit that the focus is somewhat different. She finds little evidence of a concerted effort to address the material dimensions of human security – a lack of evidence that calls into question the rhetoric of institutions such as the IMF and World Bank. Thomas argues that the response of these institutions at the core of contemporary global governance to widening global inequality has been to embark on a process of reform. However, in large part this process is lacking in substance, and is insufficient in its focus. Her conclusion, then, is that global governance remains wanting in its treatment of the material dimensions of human security. Thomas' implication is also that a similar pattern is evident in dealing with the non-material dimensions of human security.

Heloise Weber takes Thomas' focus on human security further by exploring the impact of microcredit and microfinance programmes in addressing material insufficiency. Weber argues that microcredit and microfinance programmes have been developed, rhetorically at least, as a means of poverty alleviation designed to nurture entrepreneurial activity. However, she suggests, the way in which these programmes have been implemented has been highly problematic. Exploring the case of the Grameen Bank in Bangladesh and the Bolivian Emergency Social Fund (ESF), Weber highlights the various problems associated with these programmes. In Bangladesh, she points to evidence which suggests that the provision of microcredit has actually increased the degree of indebtedness among local populations, locking recipients into ever-spiralling credit cycles. This is not, however, the full extent of the picture. Microcredit has clear gender dimensions. A focus by the Grameen Bank on encouraging women to take out credit has enhanced the human insecurity and material insufficiency of women. The Bolivian ESF, she argues, is similarly alarming in its lauding as a generalisable model of poverty alleviation.

Weber contends that rather than understanding microcredit and micro-finance as self-help initiatives, they are better understood as part of a global unification movement wherein the disciplinary trappings of neoliberalism are consolidated through an extension of control – that is, as a means of micro-management by the World Bank and the IMF – over events in the 'local'. This echoes much of Cammack's chapter. But it also highlights how, in certain quarters, a highly developed and intrusively intimate system of global governance has emerged, while in others this has been far from the case. Moreover, such a highly developed system has evidently concentrated the benefits in the hands of the few and, by doing so, contributed to the further widening of global inequality.

Organised labour and global governance

Part IV moves the focus on to explore the way in which global governance has developed in the field of labour – a much neglected area of study not only in international relations and international political economy, but also in industrial relations. Steve Hughes begins this part with an examination of the model of global governance put in place by the ILO. He shows how interest accommodation in the form of a tripartite system of governance – between government, business and labour – has defined ILO decision-making and guided the development of the international labour standards regime. By link-ing domestic and international interests in this way the ILO has maintained a relevance that helps explain its institutional longevity. He argues that the regime-drift experienced by the ILO during the years when the power politics of the Cold War structured its activities threatened to undermine this linkage. Regarded with a distant detachment by many of those the ILO was set up to protect, the end of the Cold War, the deepening of the multilateralist project, and the spread of market liberalisation, raised fundamental questions about the Organisation's continued relevance. However, Hughes asserts, these developments, rather than undermining the ILO, have worked to re-engage the Organisation with labour and re-energise the development of the international labour standards regime by placing the ILO at the core of demands for a reconfiguration of global governance. Moreover, he argues, the agendas advocated by successive post-Cold War Director-Generals represent a return to the root-strategies employed by their predecessors during the ILO's formative years.

In Chapter 10 Nigel Haworth builds upon Hughes' contribution by shifting the focus away from the ILO to explore the possibilities for organised labour in global governance more widely. He argues that a series of events in the global political economy in recent years have opened up the possibility of an accommodation between international organisations, transnational capital and organised labour. Such an accommodation, he suggests, results from four key factors: (1) the fall-out from the trade–labour standards debate in the WTO; (2) the increased salience of social protection in the wake of a series of economic crises; (3) processes of regional integration; and (4) the internationalisation of consumption. Haworth argues that these four movements taken together present labour with an opportunity to recover some of the influence lost at the national level during the 1970s and 1980s at the global level.

Civil society

The role of social actors is also the subject of Part V in this volume. Rorden Wilkinson begins this section with a chapter that explores the emerging relationship between the WTO and civil society (commonly taken to be NGOs). He argues that in response to public pressure the WTO has embarked on a courtship of civil society. However, it has done so in such a way that deeply constrains the development of a meaningful relationship. In part, this is the result of a framework of courtship that sets out how the WTO intends to deal with NGOs – a framework that bars any civil involvement in WTO decision-making forums. It is also, in part, the result of the way in which the WTO has chosen to engage only with those NGOs that it feels have a legitimate interest in trade issues.

Wilkinson argues that this lack of substance in the way in which the WTO has dealt with civil society stands in stark contrast to the degree to which the Organisation has nurtured substantive relations with other intergovernmental organisations such as the World Bank, IMF, and World Intellectual Property Organisation (WIPO). Moreover, he argues that the WTO administers a legal framework that significantly affects national and transnational actors, but that does not comprise a concomitant means of enabling local and regional non-governmental representation, choosing instead to lay the responsibility for issues of social concern with national governments. In this way, he sees the WTO as the centre of an emerging global system of trade regulation, but one which is distinctly limited in its approach to issues of public concern. In supporting his claims, Wilkinson explores the WTO's guidelines for dealing with NGOs. He then examines something of the way in which relations between the WTO and civil society have developed over the Organisation's first three ministerial meetings.

Wilkinson's contribution echoes much contained in previous chapters. He sees a marked imbalance wherein the needs and desires of transnational business are served through an on-going process of liberalisation, but where a corresponding acknowledgement of civil sensitivities is largely absent. In both cases the state plays an important role in global governance. It is, at one and the same time, the medium through which liberalisation is conducted, and the perceived gatekeeper of civil interests. It remains the case, however, that civil interests are inadequately represented at both state and global levels.

Lucy James takes further calls for greater representation in global governance in the final contribution to this volume. In doing so, she argues that we can learn much about the concerns of people generally, and women in particular by studying some of the organisational forms established in direct response to the perceived intrusion of global forces. To support her analysis, James explores some of the claims for representation that emerged in response to one such intrusion: that of the women-only peace camp at Greenham Common, established and maintained in the mid-1980s. She offers an insightful, nuanced and sobering account of the crowding-out of public representation at the global level.

However, James' analysis is not confined to an identification of an alternative form of governance. She further suggests that by conducting a gender-aware analysis we are better able to identify existing patterns of dominance and subordination, and are empowered to move forward with a better understanding of the various, often hidden, ways in which hierarchical relationships can be replicated. We are also better able to think about ways in which governance systems can be created that eschew an emphasis on power as the ability to control, and embrace a process of empowerment as the defining principle.

More than this, James suggests Greenham sheds light on the utility of consensus decision-making, skill-sharing and non-hierarchy as key organisational principles – principles which, she argues, can harness grassroots power and energy and, in doing so, overcome the apathy associated with much that is political. But it also offers an insight into how existing social hierarchies of race and class can find themselves replicated in an environment attempting to move away from such ordering. James does not, however, argue that a Greenham-like system ought to be replicated or forged in a like manner; merely that by reflecting upon that experience value can be derived which, in turn, can enrich debates about, and ultimately systems of, global governance.

It is this call for a more considered process of reflection that perhaps most appropriately draws this volume to a close and provides a platform for further work. Throughout the volume attention is drawn to the asymmetrical and ineffectual manner in which contemporary global governance is constituted.

Its resounding conclusion, to paraphrase Murphy, is that global governance is poorly done, and equally poorly understood.[4]

Notes

1 I am grateful to Lorraine Elliott for this term.
2 See, for instance, James N. Rosenau, *Along the Domestic–Foreign Frontier: Exploring Governance in a Turbulent World* (Cambridge: Cambridge University Press, 1997); Craig N. Murphy, *International Organization and Industrial Change: Global Governance since 1850* (Cambridge: Polity, 1994); Robert W. Cox (ed.) *The New Realism: Perspectives on Multilateralism and World Order* (London: Macmillan, 1997); Stephen Gill (ed.) *Globalization, Democratization and Multilateralism* (London: Macmillan, 1997); James P. Sewell (ed.) *Multilateralism in Multinational Perspective: Viewpoints from Different Languages and Literatures* (London: Macmillan, 2000); Michael G. Schechter (ed.) *Future Multilateralism: The Political and Social Framework* (London: Macmillan, 1999); Michael G. Schechter (ed.) *Innovation in Multilateralism* (London: Macmillan, 1999); Yoshikazu Sakamoto (ed.) *Global Transformation: Challenges to the State System* (Tokyo: United Nations University Press, 1994); and Martin Hewson and Timothy J. Sinclair (eds) *Approaches to Global Governance Theory* (Albany, NY: State University of New York Press, 1999).
3 Craig N. Murphy, 'Global Governance: poorly done and poorly understood', *International Affairs*, 76: 4 (2000), p. 789.
4 Murphy, 'Global Governance: poorly done and poorly understood'.

Part I
Global financial and developmental governance

2 Reforming the international financial architecture

The new political agenda[1]

Randall D. Germain

It is odd how just a few financial crises can make the annual meetings of the International Monetary Fund (IMF) and World Bank (together with the World Trade Organisation (WTO)) hotbeds of activism and protest. Where once these were staid affairs attended by top-level bureaucrats and finance ministers from around the world, they have recently become prime sites for protesting against the role which powerful international economic institutions play in the world today. One of the key demands voiced by demonstrators at these meetings is to make the decision-making structure of the global economy more democratic and accountable. Yet, few of these activists would probably accept just how radically one key element of this structure has changed since its formation in the closing days of the Second World War.

Back in 1945, it was assumed that the international financial architecture would be associated primarily with the IMF and International Bank for Reconstruction and Development (IBRD), as the World Bank was then known. With the inability of the IMF to assume its planned role in the early years of the post-war period, however, the onus of leadership fell to (or was seized by, depending on your point of view) the United States (US), which remained at the centre of international decision-making for the next fifty years. Over this period, despite the weakening of monetary discipline in the US and the stupendous growth of international financial markets, the history of decision-making within an increasingly globalised financial system remained firmly US-centred. Every significant architectural development, successful or unsuccessful, revolved around American efforts to shape the global context within which financial transactions occurred. As a result, the world entered the last few years of the twentieth century with an international financial architecture firmly centred on US wants and demands.[2]

It is this US-centred international financial architecture that is now being recast in terms of its decision-making structures, lines of accountability, and legitimating processes. What began in 1998 as a purely technical response to a string of financial crises with global implications – principally Mexico, East Asia, Russia and Brazil, but including others as well[3] – has acquired an unmistakable political agenda precisely in order to bring on board emerging market economies, provide a stamp of legitimacy for the often painful initiatives required to meet these crises, and deliver the complex technical improvements demanded by contemporary international financial transactions. At the same time, this agenda has re-opened long-settled questions regarding the defining principles of global financial governance.

I examine this new political agenda in three steps. First, I briefly consider the reform debate, arguing that what began as a rather technical affair has quickly evolved into a substantial political agenda that recasts significant aspects of the international financial architecture. The next section identifies the key questions which this agenda reopens, and explores how these questions relate to current developments. These questions are (1) how to attenuate the core–periphery divide which currently plagues the international financial architecture, and (2) how to recast the public/private balance within finance more generally. Finally, I close by delineating the politics of reform highlighted by this new agenda. In a nutshell, my main claim is that the measure of success for the reform effort is now indistinguishable from how well it deals with this agenda, and that the debate should move on to emphasise this development.

Shock-proof?

Given the depth of international financial turbulence in the 1990s, we should be quite impressed with the underlying strength of the international financial architecture. Designed originally for a world of relatively segmented markets and insulated national financial systems, it has adapted to the brave new world of global finance with much aplomb: the regulatory framework for currency, credit and capital markets has been regularly updated; the system of international settlements – the unseen plumbing through which most international financial transactions flow – has been made progressively more robust; mechanisms and procedures to manage individual crises on the periphery of the global financial system have been fashioned; and 'best practice' to reduce distortions and ensure an efficacious flow of capital around the globe has been developed and disseminated. As recently as 1996 these achievements led one seasoned observer to speculate that the global financial system had become 'shock-proof'.[4]

Less than a year after that conclusion, however, the onset of financial crisis in Asia sparked an important re-examination of the basic structure of the international financial architecture.[5] The largely unpredicted arrival of currency devaluations, government financial crises and systemic banking failures in a number of countries pointed to a set of common problems which, if combined, could herald disaster. These problems included currencies pegged at unsustainable exchange rates, government liquidity difficulties exacerbated by excessive short-term borrowing on international markets, and ill-supervised banking systems. In many instances these problems were compounded by massive short-term corporate and/or bank borrowing on international capital markets. Assessments of how these problems arose have evolved over time to produce a clear consensus that reform of the international financial architecture is necessary, and in which direction it should tend.

Early assessments viewed the problems largely as a result of the crisis-countries' own making. Morris Goldstein, for example, argued that the Asian countries did not manage their currency pegs astutely, given deteriorating capital accounts; their government financing was not robust enough to withstand a sudden deterioration in revenues; and, most importantly, their banking systems were inadequately supervised and ill-served their economies. The Asian crisis, from this point of view, was a much-needed wake-up call to national policy-makers and international investors alike to put right government finances, banking systems and ultimately entire developmental trajectories.[6] At this stage of the debate, the role of global finance was generally considered to be a secondary factor – amplifying national defects rather than causing them – and therefore reforming the international financial architecture meant principally augmenting the oversight powers of the IMF and providing better assistance to developing economies so that they can reform their economies along the lines of best practice.

As the spiral of financial crises continued throughout 1998 and into early 1999, however, a second wave of assessments began to acknowledge – without playing down the severe problems within crisis-countries – the crucial role played by international capital markets in the transmission of crisis from one country to another.[7] Barry Eichengreen, for example, pointed to the disastrous consequences of highly volatile short-term capital movements on crisis-countries, and on the way these forms of capital have contributed to the contagion effect.[8] He suggested encouraging the implementation of Chilean-style taxes on short-term capital inflows as a necessary third-line of defence against financial crisis for certain countries.[9] Where these authors go beyond the first wave of assessments is precisely in recognising that full capital account liberalisation, and indeed the admonition to move towards full capital mobility under all circumstances, can sometimes be unwise. Rather, they argue that we need to get right the timing and degree of liberalisation if the fruits of capital mobility are to be better distributed in the future.

These largely technical assessments provide a powerful argument for reform. Given widespread support for high levels of capital mobility, we must pay more attention to the nuts and bolts of managing the interface between national financial systems and the global financial system. Better regulation is crucial, but so too is recognising the many ways in which finance and money (understood here as the way in which exchange rates interact with capital markets) can combine to produce a volatile and explosive economic situation, as in Indonesia. Producing adequate standards and regulations and ensuring that they are adequately enforced may be a complex and highly technical process, but it is one in which the world's so-called mature financial systems have as great a stake as those in the developing world.

Over the course of 1999, this realisation produced a consensus among financial experts about the direction of reform. It centres on what might be called the 'three S's': strengthening transparency, strengthening support and strengthening regulation. Standards for data dissemination and transparency – the SDDS (Special Data Dissemination Standards) – are being improved and implemented, led by the IMF in consultation with a myriad of more specialised international bodies. These standards should enable investment decisions by market participants to be made on the best available information. Also at the IMF, a new credit facility has been approved – the Contingent Credit Lines (CCL) – designed specifically to provide funds ahead of a financial panic to support countries with sound economic fundamentals but nevertheless experiencing contagion. Finally, a new regulatory initiative – the Financial Stability Forum (FSF) – has been created to bring together key national and international regulators in an attempt to eliminate the perceived regulatory gap which enables financial contagion to spread.[10] This should bolster further economies that are basically sound yet susceptible to contagion. The bottom line here is on finding ways of strengthening the financial systems of potential crisis-countries by offering more international protection in return for changes at the national level. As one recent blue-ribbon task force has argued: 'If we are to make real headway in improving crisis prevention and management in the developing world, we must put primary responsibility back where it belongs: on emerging economies themselves and on their private creditors'.[11]

This bottom line also makes it clear why a political agenda has become a vital part of the reform effort. To make substantial progress, emerging market economies must both agree with the conclusions of the reform debate and buy into the actions which they will have to implement. 'Ownerhip' is the new buzzword in these circles. Governments of emerging market economies will have to legitimate the reform effort and be accountable to their own citizens for the economic and social pain of reform. This in turn means that the reform effort itself requires changes in the decision-making structure of the international financial architecture for it to become both more accountable and more legitimate in the eyes of the broader international community. The reality of this new political agenda is plainly visible in two important recent developments.

First, throughout 1998 a series of meetings took place, sometimes at the behest of the US or its G7 partners, and at other times occasioned by calls from outside the G7, in which a collective international response to financial crisis was developed. These meetings occurred on an *ad hoc* basis, and were known by their participants variously as the Willard Group, the G22 and G33.[12] One result of these meetings was the formation of a new international grouping of countries known as the G20. This group was formally announced at the September 1999 meeting of G7 Finance Ministers as part of the annual autumn meetings of the IMF and the World Bank, under the leadership of Paul Martin, Canada's Minister of Finance.

The G20 brings together Finance Ministers and key central bank officials from Argentina, Australia, Brazil, China, India, Indonesia, Mexico, Russia,

Saudi Arabia, South Africa, South Korea and Turkey, together with their G7 counterparts and a representative from the European Union (EU). Its agenda certainly includes technical issues such as transparency and the rest, but more fundamentally it provides a mechanism for bringing the emerging market economies into the decision-making structure of the global financial system. In this sense the G20 represents a potentially new and radical addition to the international financial architecture. For the first time the international decision-making structure has expanded beyond the G7 countries.

Second, the IMF has itself undertaken a change in its form of governance with the transformation of the long-standing 'Interim Committee' into the new 'International Monetary and Financial Committee' (IMFC). Beyond the name change is an important new principle at work in the IMFC, namely that all countries can raise – as a matter of international governance – the role which the IMF itself plays within the global financial system. Through the IMFC's constituency system, countries will be able to raise issues without in principle being hampered by their allocation of votes on the IMF's Executive Board. It is important to stress here that the IMFC will not be able to stop the IMF from engaging in bad or misguided policy – that will still depend upon the system of checks and balances contained within the IMF's Articles of Agreement and the triangular relationship between the Board of Governors, Executive Board and Fund staff. Rather, the significance of the IMFC from this perspective is that it allows the role which the IMF plays within the international financial architecture to be subject for the first time to input and negotiation on behalf of the broader international community.

Taken together, these developments indicate that a new political agenda has emerged in global finance. This agenda has centred on one question: how to enable the formerly excluded countries to acquire a genuine stake in the decision-making structure of the global financial system. The mechanisms of inclusion have centred on three specific institutional developments, in descending order of significance. First, the G20 is meant to provide more accountability to the reform efforts and to foster increased legitimacy for the kinds of initiatives that will be required to strengthen the global financial system. Second, the FSF, despite its technical origins, has acquired a politicised mandate by virtue of its efforts to develop a raft of standards that are to provide international benchmarks for regulating sound and prudential financial systems throughout the world. And finally, the IMF has inserted into its own governance structure a new mechanism of accountability to the international community, the IMFC. This new body will enable members of the IMF to debate and shape the international role of this institution beyond what was previously possible.

We are now in a position to identify with some precision the decision-making structure that is the international financial architecture. It is composed of four main pillars, each with their own supports but also buttressed by interlocking connections. One pillar is the G7, still the engine room of the global economy, but which now increasingly recognises the fundamental

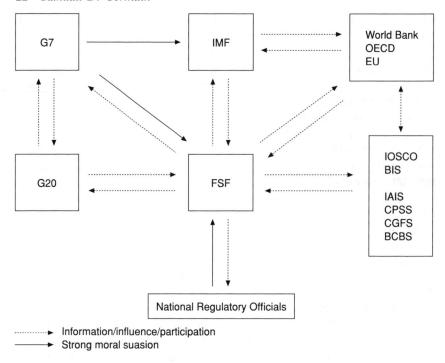

Figure 2.1 International financial architecture

dependence between its economies and the more remote bits of the global economy. Another pillar is the new G20, which is the only purpose-built institution in which the industrialised and emerging market economies can meet to discuss financial issues of mutual concern. A third pillar is the FSF, which is another new and purpose-built institution designed to meld the interests of industrialised and emerging market economies concerning regulatory issues. The final pillar is centred on the IMF but extends via information links to the entire nexus of international financial institutions (IFIs) which comprise the highest level of technical expertise regarding global financial issues: the World Bank, the Bank for International Settlements (BIS) (together with the even more specialised committees operating under its roof, such as the Basle Committee on Banking Supervision (BCBS), the International Association of Insurance Supervisors (IAIS), or the Committee on the Global Financial System (CGFS)), and the International Organisation of Securities Commissions (IOSCO). Figure 2.1 provides a schematic representation of this new international financial architecture.

This view of the architecture identifies it squarely as a structure of consensual decision-making. Why consensual? One of the remarkable attributes of the emerging international financial architecture is the absence of channels of explicit command and control. As will be discussed below, the move towards standards of behaviours and codes of best practice as the guiding strictures for global finance mean that the capacity of any one pillar to command another is muted. Rather, each pillar must use a range of carrots and sticks to entice other pillars towards their preferred mode of operation. The FSF, for example, cannot command insurance supervisors in other countries to adopt the rules and procedures which they desire; rather they have to convince these countries of the appriopriateness of doing so. Similarly, the G7 cannot command the G20 to undertake an initiative which members of the G20 feel inappropriate to their circumstances. Power, influence and moral suasion are not absent from the financial architecture, of course, but they are played out within a structure of decision-making which I would characterise as consensual rather than coercive.

In this way I would distinguish the international financial architecture from a more generalised understanding of the ensemble of rules and procedures by which international financial transactions are carried out. We may reserve such a general definition for the global financial system itself, which is the sum total of rules and arrangements through which financial transactions connect one national economy to another.[13] Rather, I find it more helpful to consider the international financial architecture as the mechanisms and structures by which these rules and arrangements get made: it is the set of institutional arrangements which determine who gets what, when and how. This view of the architecture stresses its political nature, and sees in the current reform effort a clear political agenda which is re-opening political questions that have been dormant for the past thirty years.

The new political agenda

At the heart of the new political agenda is the realisation that international politics and international economics are more tightly bound together than ever before. This is of course not a new revelation for some. There is a small but growing literature within the disciplines of international relations and international political economy that has long advocated this point of view. Confining ourselves simply to the reform debate, for example, Susan Strange maintains that it is the underlying power relations between states and markets which make possible and indeed encourage volatile financial transactions.[14] She argues that the genesis of the Asian crisis lies firmly in the increasing liberalisation of global finance, and in particular in the ill-fated attempt to liberalise the capital account before gaining full control over domestic and international financial institutions active in the crisis-country. Losing control over capital movements would not be so significant, Strange argues, if money behaved rationally and responsibly, but it has never done so. Far too many other influences determine where, on what scale and for how long capital moves, and the determination of politicians and regulators not to regain control over internationally mobile money means that Asia will by no means be the last 'crisis'. It is mad money rather than bad management that lies at the root of most financial crises.

Looking to the broader implications of the Asian crisis, Stephen Gill has recently argued that the international response reflects a fundamental tension over the particular way in which Asia will be inserted into the global economy.[15] This geopolitical tension revolves around the conflicts between America and Japan plus its protégés over developmental trajectories in Asia, on the one hand, and between the shifting strategic implications of military and economic imbalances in both China and America on the other. The result, Gill argues, is both a brutal reassertion of American power in the region and the surprising exposure of the contested basis of American power. Just how international structures of power will evolve under this condition is for him an open question.

We need not accept the entire thrust of either of these analyses in order to appreciate the centrality of a political agenda in connection with both international financial crises and the responses to them. Since my focus here is on the politics of inclusion, I want to draw attention to the way in which this political agenda has reopened two long-settled questions. First, the search for appropriate mechanisms of inclusion has once again focused attention on the question of attenuating the core-periphery divide within the global financial system. Why is this question now relevant? It is important precisely because of who is being asked to pay the costs of reform and who will receive the benefits. One of the starkest consequences of the Asian financial crisis has been the cost which the periphery has been forced to pay simply in order to weather the storm of devaluation and debt overload (much of which has been caused by the private sector).[16] Working out the costs of financial crisis is not of course a simple proposition, but on whatever grounds one chooses (commercial, economic, political, social) it is clear that the crisis-countries have borne the lion's share of the burden. To now turn around and require of them painful reforms to right their banking systems, reduce fiscal expenditure and balance budgets is in effect to ask them to pay twice for their mistakes: once for the crisis and once again to ensure it is not repeated. Paul Krugman is surely correct to assert that this is a return to the type of Depression-era economics that would be refused point blank in the industrialised economies of the world.[17]

Beyond this is the simple fact that, as a recent independent Council on Foreign Relations task force understood, it is the emerging market economies – that is, the former periphery – which are being asked to pay for the cost of reform. It is they who must join the 'Good Housekeeping Club' and meet its criteria of so-called 'best practice'.[18] But how to get at least the 'systemically significant' emerging market economies to join up? This is where the core-periphery question re-emerges after a long hiatus, because it is now recognised (1) that emerging markets are systemically significant, and (2) that they must be enticed to join the 'Good Housekeeping Club'.[19] They can no longer be written off as unimportant parts of the global financial system, suitable only for the benefit of the centre. The periphery now represents a cost to the centre, and a more equitable sharing of this cost requires a more equitable sharing of the benefits. Adapting the international financial architecture to this new equation means in principle being open to recasting the existing distribution of costs and benefits between core and periphery. Perhaps not today or even tomorrow, but certainly over the medium term.

The second question which the search for appropriate mechanisms of inclusion has reopened is striking a more acceptable balance between public responsibility and private gain. This question, which for many has been resolved over the past three decades in favour of the socialisation of the costs of meeting financial crises and the privatisation of the benefits of unfettered capital mobility, has resurfaced within the context of how to bail in the private sector to share the burden of adjustment. While these discussions have largely been carried out in highly technical terms, they connect to the question of attenuating the core-periphery divide precisely because the public/private balance is far more precarious and contested in emerging markets. Consider simply the question of regulating financial institutions. In developed, or what many now call 'mature' financial systems such as in the US and UK, regulation is in fact exercised largely through the market, by ensuring that risk management systems are robust, information provision is transparent and legal systems are independent and able to enforce contracts. In other words the imprint of the state is lightened considerably because the economic infrastructure permits the state to work through the market. Contrast this situation with that of most emerging market economies, where risk management systems are antiquated, if they exist at all, information is a private rather than a public good (and clearly not transparent and available to all in a timely and useful manner), and independent legal systems are a future objective to work towards rather than an established fact of life.[20] The state looms larger in the economic fabric of emerging markets simply because their under-developed economic infrastructure demands it.

Opening up the international financial architecture to even a more limited participation of formerly peripheral countries will inevitably reopen the debate over the appropriate balance between public responsibility and private gain. This will not, however, be a straightforward conflict, since it will occur most often within the context of highly technical issues. Nevertheless, this political agenda will slowly assert itself. Consider once again the question of regulation. Across the G7 countries, banking regulation, despite the variation in financial systems, is largely carried out with an eye to establishing sound prudential practices for the largest internationally active firms (which theoretically should encourage smaller firms to adopt these 'best practices'). In each G7 country this amounts to scrutinising at most a handful of firms which are often concentrated within one major financial centre. Compare this to Brazil, India or South Africa, where the major banks are scattered around the country. The main point here is that a public/private balance which is contested, albeit acceptable for countries at one stage of development, may be entirely inappropriate for countries at different stages of development. How this disjuncture works itself out will constitute one part of the new political agenda of reform.

We can see the new political agenda at work most clearly in the attempt to construct viable international standards to be used as benchmarks to guide international financial transactions. These standards address activities such as supervising banks, making budgets, managing public debt, and releasing public information in a timely and useful manner.[21] Most of this work is being done by international bodies in which the actual role of non-G7 countries is growing. In the FSF, for example, emerging markets like Singapore, Hong Kong and Australia are now included as formal members, and the *ad hoc* technical committees struck by the Forum for specific purposes include a broader cross-section of emerging market economies.[22] For all of these standards, in whatever forums they are being developed, the same question is being faced: how to construct standards that are appropriate for all so that all can work towards achieving them.

The growing role of international standards as part of the governance structure of the global financial system, I argue, will over time increase the salience of 'inclusion'. Standards only work if they are accepted and internalised on the part of those at which they are targeted. They are accepted to the extent to which governments can actually contribute to their construction, and they are internalised to the extent to which governments feel that they 'own' them. It is in this sense that the political agenda of inclusion will ultimately provide formerly excluded countries with a genuine stake in the governance structure of the global financial system: it is their Trojan horse. The G7 countries, which at the moment have an undeniably large influence in configuring international financial issues, have been forced to admit emerging market economies into the international financial architecture precisely because it cannot function effectively without them. From this point forward international decision-making will involve these economies; or to put it more bluntly, international decision-making will not be able to be exercised without them. This does not mean that the enormous international leverage of the G7 countries, and especially the US, will cease to operate. Rather, it is to acknowledge that the decision-making structure itself has changed. No longer is it a closed club whose rules are made only by insiders. Now it is a more open club in which the former outsiders have an actual say.

The politics of reform

The new political agenda will provide for a complex and inter-related politics of reform over the medium term. This will revolve around three axes: (1) the 'European' question; (2) the 'Malaysian' question; and (3) the 'overstretch' question. But before exploring these axes, it is worthwhile considering challenges to this argument. On one hand, it might be argued that the reform effort has been almost entirely the preserve of the US, or the G1 as it is sometimes called. The argument here is that the governance structure of global finance has not changed dramatically if at all over the past decade. It is still controlled largely by the US, whose material and ideological resources have been fully deployed to usher in a brave new world of neoliberal globalism, where the US and its corporate elite maintain their unparalleled advantage.[23] A prime example of this continuing control would be the vetting process used by the G7 to put together the membership of the G20, which some might argue was used by the US to hand-pick the members of this new institution: why Indonesia and not Malaysia, they ask, or why Turkey and not Poland?

There is of course much truth in this view of recent changes in the international financial architecture, especially if one examines closely the rather imperial views of people such as Lawrence Summers, US Secretary of the Treasury during the final years of the Clinton Administration and a long-time participant in these developments. Nevertheless, what this view underplays is the shift in the fulcrum of governance today. Even though the pendulum may still be well within a neoliberal arc, the focal point for the pendulum has shifted from a US-centred structure of governance to a wider and more genuinely international structure centred on a complex inter-meshing of states and international institutions. In short, those who are overly impressed by the ideological and material power of the US today are ignoring the way in which that power will be constrained by the emerging governance structure itself. In order to get its way the US will have to put up for negotiation the very kinds of standards it previously imposed on others by dint of it being at the epicentre of global financial governance. This is the key point to emphasise in the new architecture: it is wider and more inclusive than previously, even if at the moment American views predominate.

A second line of objection might focus on the extent of reform and argue that in its details it is more rhetoric than reality. For example, some might object to the view that the FSF is actually an inclusive institution. It has, after all, accepted only three permanent members from formerly excluded countries, one of which has been a member of the BIS for years.[24] More significantly, these critics might point to the work of the technical committees and note how similar many recommendations are to recent G10 reports. Once again, although there is a grain of truth in these charges, they too can be faulted for underplaying the significance of creating new institutions over which the initiators will have an increasingly limited sway over time. In the case of the FSF, after less than a year of operation it has already expanded its membership from the original thirty-five to thirty-nine, and it has both created and dissolved technical committees (not an insignificant achievement considering how long-lived international committees are once established: consider just how long the so-called 'Interim Committee' of the IMF lasted). The point to emphasise here is not how the power and influence of the formerly excluded countries have been restricted under an exclusive structure of governance, but rather how their place and/or role will be open to adaptation under the new structure of governance.

What then are the axes of tension within this new structure of governance? The first axis of tension involves Europe. Specifically, with the creation of the European Central Bank (ECB) and the resulting ambiguity over who speaks for Europe on global financial issues, a vacuum has developed that temporarily provides the US with a wider latitude to shape the international financial agenda. Whereas previously the Deutsche Bundesbank provided both a global counterweight to the US Federal Reserve/Treasury combination and a focal point for European views on global finance, the arrival of the ECB has emasculated this role without providing in its place an institution of similar stature. This would be less of a political problem were it not for the genuine confusion surrounding the place of the ECB within the international financial architecture.[25] Not only is there ambiguity over Europe's voice within the architecture, there is also continuing uncertainty about how this ambiguity will be resolved. The 'European' question will reverberate within the architecture for some time yet.

The second axis of tension may be labelled the 'Malaysian' problem. By this I do not mean how to contain Malaysia the country, but rather how to respond to Malaysia the example. Malaysia has taken a very different road in response to the Asian crisis, namely limiting the convertibility of its currency and severely restricting the role of international capital markets in the working of its economy.[26] In effect, Malaysia has challenged the general IMF prescription for Asia, and continues to hold out the prospect of pursuing a more 'traditional' Asian developmental trajectory. And while it is not without its darker political overtones, the example of Malaysia challenges the way in which capital account liberalisation can be held out as a panacea to financial crisis and development. To this end it has already had a positive effect, in that Malaysia's so-called 'bad' example of how to respond to financial crisis has highlighted the much 'better' example of Chile, especially now that Chile has embarked on a sustained programme of democratisation. In other words, the 'Malaysian question' has already helped to shift the consensus view on the merits of unfettered capital mobility. Read as a proxy for the ambiguous benefits of capital mobility, the 'Malaysian' question will continue to exercise the international financial architecture into the medium term.

Finally, the 'overstretch' question is a problem for the structure of governance in two respects. First, there is the amazing profusion of international committees that has emerged in response to the past decade of financial instability. Figure 2.1 gives a hint of the plethora of committees, but no more than that. Each of the institutions named on it, for example, has a further set of sub-committees which meet regularly and have their own specific mandates. Equally, this figure ignores (for the sake of simplicity) both the existence of other world organisations with an interest in financial governance, and the myriad of regional organisations also involved. The WTO, for example, has an interest in the provision of financial services, while the International Labour Organisation (ILO) has an interest in the provision of pensions. South America has a central banker's association, as does Central America and Asia. The Inter-American Development Bank has an interest, as does the European Bank for Reconstruction and Development. All of these institutions have a stake in the development of international standards, and all are consulted on some level at some point in the process. To keep this road show on the go is no mean feat.

At the same time, the actual number of people involved in all of these various committees and institutions is less than meets the eye. It is the case that at the moment this structure of governance is top-heavy with G7 participation. Yet, even with the comparatively lavish resources of the G7, the number of people involved in architectural issues from all of the finance ministries and central banks and regulatory agencies of these countries would perhaps scarcely top 200.[27] International institutions fare no better. The BIS, for example, may employ about 400 people in total, but fewer than perhaps 75 concern themselves with international matters more generally, and even fewer with architectural questions. And by international standards the BIS is awash with knowledgeable people. Such limited numbers of people is precisely how they come to know each other so well: they meet on a regular basis at different spots around the world, and as a result come to rely on each other for information, support and ultimately trust.

But this intimacy can be stretched only so far, for there are rarely more than a half dozen people in any one institution (outside of organisations like the BIS, IMF and World Bank) who are responsible for international affairs. It may seem an odd point to make, but in today's cosmopolitan and global age, most people in most governments are concerned primarily with the home front.[28] As a result, there is a serious question of overstretch and under-resourcing. Governance structures cannot run efficiently on peanuts, and the extent to which they are forced to do so means that crisis prevention and architectural strengthening will often take a back seat to other more pressing problems. And as serious as this problem is within the G7, it is far worse in the emerging market economies, which can only constrain their initial participation in the new structure of governance.

All of these questions come together when we consider the construction of international standards in light of the political agenda of 'inclusion'. Relying on international standards as benchmarks for undertaking and regulating international financial transactions is attractive precisely because it provides both a level playing field for private sector participants and guideposts for what regulators should be doing. Theoretically it should be as attractive to the US as Mexico, to Hong Kong as well as Indonesia. Practically, however, there are pitfalls. One pitfall concerns how the standards are actually put together. What is the level of input from those countries outside of the G7 which do not have as highly developed an infrastructure (social, economic, political) as the G7 countries? The reports by the three working groups struck by the G22 at their April 1998 meeting, and delivered in October 1998, are encouraging on this front.[29] Each was co-chaired by a member of the G7 and a member of what was to become the G20. Beyond that, the composition of the working groups was split roughly evenly between non-G7 membership and G7/G10 membership. This pattern was broadly replicated within the technical committees which reported recently to the FSF. This is one example of the new structure of governance at work, and a strong indication that as these standards are being constructed they will in fact be better 'owned' by emerging market economies than in the past.

At the same time, these standards must be implemented if they are to work as they are meant to, and here the widely varying levels of resources available to different governments have a bearing in terms of how far governments in emerging market economies can actually commit themselves to realising these standards. This reality also has a bearing on the amount of time and effort the individuals in these ministries, central banks and regulators can devote to convincing their political masters of the need for and legitimacy of these standards. Prudential regulation may be a plausible argument to a central banker or regulator in São Paulo, or Pretoria or New Delhi, but the implications of ensuring that banks are run along Western lines will certainly mean less money for development and other government spending in these countries. This is where the G20 must work towards legitimating a certain amount of flexibility in reaching these standards. One of the key roles of the G20 lies in providing a forum in which emerging markets can take their case for economic and social differentiation within the global financial system, or in other words for a variegated balance between public responsibility and private gain rather than a single global standard. All financial systems require benchmarks, it is true, but how these benchmarks are interpreted and achieved depends to a great extent on local or national contexts. Continued ownership of these benchmarks will be a matter of ongoing negotiation and compromise.

The final way in which the construction of international standards reflects the problems of the new political agenda of inclusion lies in the way in which progress towards achieving these standards will be judged. At the moment, judgement – such as it is – appears to lie with the IMF, which has thus far carried out a number of experimental country audits on the observance of those standards and codes which are clearly within the remit of the IMF.[30] These audits are expensive, complex and technical affairs with much scope for mishandling information and/or misinterpreting the significance of data. They are also at the moment run to a template which does not distinguish particular country circumstances, even though the IMF assessment teams rely on the countries themselves to provide much of the required information. Designed as learning exercises, they have indeed provided much food for thought to the IMF.

Nevertheless, the critical question here is who should be judging and how should this take place. It is not at all clear that the judges should come from a single international institution, although it does seem appropriate that the people carrying out these assessments should not come from national governments. And neither is it clear that penalties should be attached to non-achievement of standards, as for example was advocated recently by the independent Council on Foreign Relations task force on the international financial architecture.[31] Penalties compromise ownership, and they do so more completely if it is the centre (read here as IMF) which is in charge of imposing the penalties. It cannot be overemphasised that international standards require constant negotiation if their legitimacy is to be maintained over time, and rendering judgements is a potential flashpoint in that process.

Conclusion: the 'technical' as 'political'

Mobilising thousands of people to face a phalanx of armed police officers defending massive concrete and marble bunkers in the world's putative capital city (Washington) requires enormous levels of energy and enthusiasm coupled with a sense that something is not right in the world. No less an effort has moved those involved in reforming the international financial architecture. Over the past three years, they have addressed a complex set of inter-related issues without the benefit of a centralised authority structure and under the shadow of unpredictable financial turbulence. And in the process they have embarked on the most radical overhaul of the structure of global financial governance since 1945.

What makes this development so remarkable is that it began as a technical exercise in fine-tuning the rules of the game: strengthening international financial regulation; offering more support for international adjustment; putting in place clearer rules for the dissemination of information. Along the way, however, it became clear that technical adjustments, no matter how intrinsic to sound and prudential finance, could not carry the day. Questions of accountability, legitimacy and rule-making took their place alongside questions of transparency, standards and codes. International politics and international economics once again became visibly entwined, and indeed inseparable. The end product is a new political agenda.

In order for this new political agenda to bear fruit, however, it needs to be nourished. The best way to do this is to acknowledge more explicitly that the political dimension of reform lies at the heart of the debate. Just as with the debate over European monetary union, it is the political dynamics which will make or break the reform effort, and not the achievement of specific economic indicators or internationally recognised standards.[32] If the G20, FSF and IMFC work as envisioned and enable a genuine sense of legitimacy, accountability and due process to emerge within the international financial architecture, tremendous progress will be possible in the fight against financial crisis and instability. Achieving a genuine sense of legitimacy, accountability and process will do far more to facilitate the achievement of stability than another homily on the need for adequate information to be published in a timely and useful manner. This is not to deny the utility of transparency and any one of the hundreds of other technical details necessary to the smooth operation of the global financial system. They are important, and crucially so. But it is a reminder that we must get the big political questions right before the technical details can have their effect. We must know more about the political prerequisites of good governance before the reform debate can deliver on its promise.

Developing the political dimension of the reform debate, I believe, will make it clear just how far we have already come. Rather than seeing the capitalist or American devil lurking behind the current round of initiatives, I have argued that a significant turn has been made in our understanding of what constitutes good governance in global finance. It consists in inclusive decision-making structures which provide mechanisms not only for the creation of international standards and processes, but which also allow a certain flexibility in how those standards are interpreted so that emerging market economies can work towards them without being unduly penalised. This means most importantly recognising the different balances between public responsibility and private gain that will need to be struck across economies with different needs and developmental trajectories. It also consists in a decision-making structure which can begin to address the distributional distortions consequent upon the existing core-periphery divide within the global financial system. These distortions will not be attenuated overnight, but in order to bring emerging market economies on board there must be a sense that these issues are open to negotiation. This key insight is what makes the recent turn in the international financial architecture towards a more inclusive model of global financial governance such an important development. And only by more explicitly considering the new political agenda can we strengthen this turn and thereby help to make the global financial system safer for all.

Notes

1 This research has been supported by a grant from the Nuffield Foundation, which allowed me to undertake confidential interviews with senior officials in finance ministries, central banks and regulators across a number of G7 countries, as well as at several international financial institutions, during 1999/2000. I am grateful for the time these individuals took to participate in my research. I would also like to acknowledge the helpful comments of Andrew Walter, Michael Williams, Tony Porter, Guy Scuffham, Rorden Wilkinson and Steve Hughes, together with seminar participants at the Forum on Globalization, Bishop's University (Canada), the University of Warwick, and the 'Engaging Global Governance' workshop at Manchester University, where versions of this work were presented. Finally, I am grateful to Elaine Lowe for her help in constructing Figure 2.1. I, of course, remain entirely responsible for the views expressed below.
2 The last few years have witnessed a number of book-length accounts which highlight the political or architectural dimensions of the post-1945 global financial system. See in particular Tony Porter, *States, Markets and Regimes in Global Finance* (Basingstoke: Macmillan, 1993); Andrew Walter, *World Power and World Money* (London: Harvester Wheatsheaf, 1993); Philip Cerny (ed.) *Finance and World Politics* (Aldershot: Edward Elgar, 1993); Eric Helleiner, *States and the Reemergence of Global Finance* (Ithaca: Cornell University Press, 1994); Andrew Sobel, *Domestic Choices, International Markets* (Ann Arbor: University of Michigan Press, 1994); Barry Eichengreen, *Globalizing Capital* (Princeton: Princeton University Press, 1996); Geoffrey Underhill (ed.) *The New World*

Order and International Finance (Basingstoke: Macmillan, 1997); Louis Pauly, *Who Elected the Bankers?* (Ithaca: Cornell University Press, 1997); Randall D. Germain, *The International Organization of Credit* (Cambridge: Cambridge University Press, 1997); Benjamin Cohen, *The Geography of Money* (Ithaca: Cornell University Press, 1998); and Susan Strange, *Mad Money* (Manchester: Manchester University Press, 1998).

3 The litany of financial disasters with potentially global repercussions must also include the implosion of the European exchange rate mechanism in 1992/3, the sudden collapse both of long-established investment banks such as Barings in 1995 and new hedge funds such as Long Term Capital Management in 1998, the long simmering banking malaise in Japan, and a near-run stock market meltdown among the G7 economies in October 1998. And we should not forget that a brand new international currency was launched by the European Union in 1999, complete with a new and untried institution at its heart.

4 Ethan Kapstein, 'Shock Proof', *Foreign Affairs*, 75: 1 (1996), pp. 2–8. The bulk of Kapstein's analysis draws on his *Governing the Global Economy* (Cambridge, MA: Harvard University Press, 1994).

5 The Bretton Woods institutions themselves had already begun to be re-examined in the early 1990s as part of the general celebration of fifty years of relative monetary stability. See for example Michael Bordo and Barry Eichengreen (eds) *A Retrospective on the Bretton Woods System* (Chicago: University of Chicago Press, 1993); and Peter B. Kenen (ed.) *Managing the World Economy Fifty Years after Bretton Woods* (Washington: Institute for International Economics, 1994). This rather detached scholarly process was matched by a more focused international debate set off by the Mexican peso devaluation, and can be traced through the official communiqués of the G7 summits, beginning in Halifax in 1995 and following through to Köln in 1999. The website of the G8 Information Centre at the University of Toronto contains an extensive archive of these communiqués: http://www.G7.utoronto.ca.

6 Morris Goldstein, *The Asian Financial Crisis: causes, cures and systemic implications* (Washington: Institute of International Economics, 1998). See also Leif R. Rosenberger, 'Southeast Asia's Currency Crisis: a diagnosis and prescription', *Contemporary Southeast Asia*, 19: 3 (1997), pp. 223–51; and the various contributors to Miles Kahler (ed.) *Capital Flows and Financial Crises* (Ithaca: Cornell University Press for the Council on Foreign Relations, 1998).

7 See for example Steven Radelet and Jeffrey Sachs, 'The East Asian Financial Crisis: diagnosis, remedies, prospects', *Brookings Papers on Economic Activity 1* (1998), pp. 1–90; Jason Furman and Joseph Stiglitz, 'Economic Crises: evidence and insights from east Asia', *Brookings Papers on Economic Activity 2* (1998), pp. 1–135; Alan S. Blinder, 'Eight Steps to a New Financial Order', *Foreign Affairs*, 78: 5 (1999), pp. 50–61; and Brigitte Granville, 'Bingo or Fiasco? The global financial situation is not guaranteed', *International Affairs*, 75: 4 (1999), pp. 713–28.

8 Barry Eichengreen, *Toward a New International Financial Architecture: a practical post-Asia agenda* (Washington: Institute for International Economics, 1999), esp. ch. 4.

9 The first and second lines of defence are improved risk-management techniques for financial firms and strengthened regulation of financial firms. Eichengreen, *International Financial Architecture*, ch. 4.

10 The decision to create the FSF was taken in 1999. It was suggested by Hans Tietmeyer (then head of the Deutsche Bundesbank) in a report commissioned by the G7 to examine the appropriate response of the international community to global financial contagion. He noted that effective financial regulation depended upon adequate flows of information that spanned international borders and cut

across different financial sectors or markets, and proposed a forum within which central bankers, financial regulators and ministry of finance officials could meet to discuss issues of mutual concern. The initial report called for thirty-five members, three each from G7 countries with the remaining members drawn from committees and institutions of relevance to cross-border and cross-sectoral financial regulation, such as the IMF, Basle Committee on Banking Supervision (BCBS), International Organisation of Securities Commissions (IOSCO), and so on. The membership has since been extended to include representation from the Netherlands, Hong Kong, Australia and Singapore. Andrew Crockett, currently the General Manager of the BIS, is its initial Chairman. Both the Tietmeyer Report and the activities of the FSF can be found on its website (http://www.fsforum.org).

11 *Safeguarding Prosperity in a Global Financial System: the future international financial architecture*, Council on Foreign Relations Task Force, co-chaired by Carla Hills and Peter Peterson (Washington: Institute for International Economics, 1999), p. 3.

12 The Willard Group of finance ministers' deputies was struck after the 1997 APEC meeting in Seattle when the Prime Minister of Malaysia's call for such a group was picked up by US President Bill Clinton. Subsequent meetings of this group, initially representing about twenty countries, grew into the G22 and G33 (that is, meetings in which representatives from 22 and then 33 countries participated). They met over the course of 1998 to discuss possible reforms to the international financial architecture.

13 This is a long-standing definition that many have worked with in the past: see Benjamin Cohen, *Organizing the World's Money* (New York: Basic Books, 1977), p. 3; and Barry Eichengreen, *Elusive Stability: essays in the history of international finance* (Cambridge: Cambridge University Press, 1990), p. 271. For a critical discussion see Germain, *International Organization of Credit*, ch. 1.

14 Susan Strange, *Mad Money* (Manchester: Manchester University Press, 1998); see also her *States and Markets*, (London: Pinter, 1988) and *Casino Capitalism* (Oxford: Blackwell, 1986). In a similar vein are Stephan Haggard and Andrew MacIntyre, 'The political economy of the Asian economic crisis', *Review of International Political Economy*, 5: 3 (1998), pp. 381–92; Walden Bello, 'East Asia: on the eve of the great transformation?', *Review of International Political Economy*, 5: 3 (1998), pp. 424–44; and Louis Pauly, 'Good Governance and Bad Policy: the perils of international organization overextension', *Review of International Political Economy*, 6: 4 (1999), pp. 401–24. Other analyses which I would categorise as political in orientation but which stop short of blaming 'mad money' for the recent spate of crises include Martin Feldstein, 'Refocusing the IMF', *Foreign Affairs*, 77: 2 (1998), pp. 20–33; and Devash Kapur, 'The IMF: a cure or a curse?', *Foreign Policy*, No. 111 (Summer 1998), pp. 114–29.

15 Stephen Gill, 'The Geopolitics of the Asian Crisis', *Monthly Review*, 50: 10 (March 1999), pp. 1–10. See also Robert Wade and Frank Veneroso, 'The East Asian Crisis and the Wall Street–IMF Complex', *New Left Review*, 228 (1998), pp. 3–22; and Robert Wade and Frank Veneroso, 'The Great World Slump and the Battle Over Capital Controls', *New Left Review*, 231 (1998), pp. 13–42.

16 Blinder, 'Eight Steps to a New Financial Order', pp. 50–2; Goldstein, *The Asian Financial Crisis*, ch. 2; Wendy Dobson, 'Fallout from the Global Financial Crisis', *International Journal*, LIV: 3 (1999), p. 376; and more generally Richard Higgott and Nicola Phillips, 'Challenging Triumphalism and Convergence: the limits of global liberalization in Asia and Latin America', *Review of International Studies*, 26: 3 (2000).

17 Paul Krugman, *The Return of Depression Economics* (London: Allen Lane, 1999).

18 *Safeguarding Prosperity*, pp. 93–7.

19 The case of Thailand was crucial in prompting the acceptance of this stark fact, as no one in mid-1997 would have believed that the devaluation of the Baht could set off a chain reaction engulfing much of East Asia and drawing in the G7 countries.

20 Hong Kong, Singapore and Australia are significant exceptions to this generalisation, which helps in part to explain their resistance to the worst effects of the Asian financial crisis.

21 A compendium of these standards is now available on the FSF's website.

22 Thus far five technical committees have been struck (and subsequently disbanded) to deliver reports on various aspects of international financial stability. Membership on these committees has ranged broadly in terms of emerging market representation. These committees and their reports are all available on the FSF website.

23 For example, see the arguments advanced concerning the consequences of the Asian financial crisis by Strange, *Mad Money*, and Gill, 'The Geopolitics of the Asian Crisis'.

24 Moreover, these three members plus a fourth (the Netherlands) might be considered second class members, as they are allowed only one member each whereas G7 members have three.

25 For considerations of this problem see C. Randall Henning, 'US–EU Relations after Inception of the Monetary Union: cooperation or rivalry?', in C. Randall Henning and Pier Carlo Padoan, *Transatlantic Perspectives on the Euro* (Washington: Brookings Institution Press, 2000), and Randall D. Germain, 'The European Central Bank and the Problem of Authority', in Michael Williams and Morten Kelstrup (eds) *International Relations Theory and European Union* (London, Routledge, 2000).

26 Helen Nesadurai, 'In Defence of National Economic Autonomy? Malaysia's response to the financial crisis', *Pacific Review*, 13: 1 (2000), pp. 73–113.

27 This rough calculation is made by multiplying the average number of people involved in international issues per relevant agency by the number of G7 countries. At about five or six people per agency and three agencies per G7 country, we arrive at a total of about 125 people directly involved in these issues, plus another 60 or 70 scattered throughout associated agencies in the G7 area.

28 For example, the secretariats of both the FSF and the G20 comprise no more than a few individuals who oversee and co-ordinate the work of a thinly stretched and far-flung group of people.

29 These were the working groups on 'Transparency and Accountability', 'Strengthening Financial Systems' and 'International Financial Crises'. The reports are available from the websites of the BIS, IMF, OECD and World Bank.

30 Versions of these are available on the IMF website under the subtitle 'Standards and Codes'.

31 The taskforce argued that access to IMF resources should be tied more tightly to achieving these international standards. *Safeguarding Prosperity*, pp. 93–7.

32 For an argument along these lines, see Randall D. Germain, 'In Search of Political Economy: European monetary union', *Review of International Political Economy*, 6: 3 (1999), pp. 390–98.

3 The mother of all governments

The World Bank's matrix for global governance

Paul Cammack

It is . . . clear to all of us that ownership is essential. Countries must be in the driver's seat and set the course. They must determine goals and the phasing, timing and sequencing of programs. Where there is not adequate capacity in the government to do this, we must support and help them to establish, own, and implement the strategy. . . . The existence of the matrix is not a clandestine attempt on the part of the Bank to dominate the international development arena, or the donor dialogue in a given country. Quite the contrary. It is a tool to have greater cooperation, transparency, and partnership . . . The matrix is open to all. It is a step towards inclusion, transparency and to accountability . . . Ultimately, the matrix is a tool for the governments and people of the countries we serve. It is they who must own the programs, not us, and it is they who must set the pace.
>   (James D. Wolfensohn, 'A Proposal for a Comprehensive Development Framework', World Bank, 21 January 1999, pp. 9, 23)

Matrix. 1. The uterus or womb. **2.** A place or medium in which something is bred, produced or developed. **3.** An embedding or enclosing mass. **4.** A piece of metal, usually copper, by means of which the face of a type is cast, having the letter stamped on it in intaglio with a punch. **5.** A rectangular arrangement of quantities or symbols.
>   From *The Shorter Oxford English Dictionary on Historical Principles* (Oxford: Oxford University Press, 1977)

In January 1999 the World Bank launched its 'Comprehensive Development Framework' (CDF). At its heart was a matrix which mapped key policy issues and areas in relation to four actors: the international development community, governments, civil society, and the private sector. World Bank President James D. Wolfensohn was eager to assure his audience that the matrix was a tool for governments to own rather than a clandestine attempt by the Bank to dominate the international development arena. The argument of this chapter is that on the contrary the CDF is a vehicle for global governance managed and co-ordinated by the Bank: governments do *not* own the matrix through which it is operated, as it was devised within the Bank over a decade in accordance with its own priorities; rather, as Wolfensohn's language discloses, they are obliged to *assume* ownership of it. It is instructive, in this respect, that the definitions of 'matrix' in the *Shorter Oxford English Dictionary* move from images of birth and development to ideas of enclosure, imposition, and rigid containment. The same is true of the World Bank's matrix, which is presented as developmental, but intended and employed as a means of control.

The CDF is absolutely rigid in the set of fundamental macroeconomic disciplines it imposes. It prescribes on top of these a range of economic and social policies without parallel in their scope and in the depth and intensity of intervention they represent in the affairs of supposedly sovereign states. Presented as a vehicle for incorporating social and structural policies into an agenda previously dominated by macroeconomic policy alone, it is in fact a means of *shaping* social and structural policies so that they reinforce and extend macroeconomic discipline, and *subordinating* them to imperatives of capitalist accumulation. The launching of the CDF was accompanied by the introduction of a range of new disciplinary institutions (such as the Financial Stability Forum (FSF) and the Global Corporate Governance Forum (GCGF)), and new mechanisms designed to control policies across the board down to the smallest detail (such as Poverty Reduction Strategy Papers (PRSP), Sectoral Strategy Papers (SSP), the City Development Strategy (CDS), and a revised framework for Economic and Sector Work (ESW)). In this broader context, it is a fundamental goal of the Bank's strategy to impose 'country ownership' of the CDF both because it recognises that it lacks the means to enforce the strategy itself, and because the legitimation of its project *vis-à-vis* citizens around the world depends upon its adoption by national governments, which remain indispensable intermediaries in the project for global governance. A key aspect of the strategy, in this context, is that the CDF is presented as benevolent, facilitating and empowering. The Bank presents itself as the mother of development – but the reality is that it aspires to be the mother of all governments.

The Comprehensive Development Framework

In setting out the CDF in January 1999, Wolfensohn shared with his colleagues his conviction that the World Bank and its allies had 'contributed significantly to the betterment of mankind and to the improvement in the lives of many in poverty'.[1] He drew attention to a division of labour between the International Monetary Fund (IMF) and the World Bank (supplemented by a shared commitment to work with and support the World Trade Organisation (WTO)):

> Broadly, our sister institution [the IMF] has the responsibility for macroeconomic stabilization for our client countries and for surveillance. We have the responsibility for the structural and social aspects of development. Obviously, these are not two isolated roles and we work together

very closely on a day-to-day basis. As I have said before, the two functions are like breathing in and breathing out. An appropriate macroeconomic framework is essential for our work, but the social, structural, and human agenda, which we share with the regional banks, members of the UN system, and other partners in development, is essential for the IMF which cannot and does not prescribe in a vacuum.[2]

Wolfensohn presented development as 'a balance sheet with two sides, a coin with two sides, a duet with two parts', emphasising the need to bring the macroeconomic and the social, structural and human aspects together into an integrated framework. He identified two weaknesses in this regard – bilateral and multilateral practitioners in the development field were not working together effectively to take forward structural and social reforms alongside their macroeconomic agenda, and the governments with overall responsibility for growth and poverty alleviation did not always have 'the capacity to do so, or the resources, or sometimes even the will'. Hence the need for 'an overarching framework – an approach agreed with the government concerned – which will allow us all to work together to meet our goals for poverty alleviation and environmental sustainability'.[3]

There was nothing much wrong, in Wolfensohn's opinion, with the international architecture of the Bretton Woods system, or the macroeconomic and financial frameworks it sustained. The fault lay in the failure to integrate social and structural programmes firmly into them, and this could only be remedied by adopting a 'comprehensive, holistic framework' that would allow the Bank and its allies 'to think more strategically about the sequencing of policies, programs and projects, and the pacing of reforms'.[4] The framework Wolfensohn offered featured ten structural, human, and physical aspects, and four specific strategies (Box 3.1). Its individual elements would have been familiar to readers of the *World Development Reports* published by the World Bank from 1990 onwards.[5] In pride of place came four structural requirements: for good government, the rule of law, strong financial systems, and safety nets. The first step was to build an 'effective government framework', which entailed 'capacity building, an open legislative and transparent regulatory system, properly trained and remunerated officials and an absolute commitment to clean government'. Second, governments required 'an effective system of property, contract, labor, bankruptcy, commercial codes, personal rights laws and other elements of a comprehensive legal system that is effectively, impartially and cleanly administered by a well-functioning, impartial and honest judicial and legal system'. Third, they must

establish an internationally accepted and effective supervisory system for banks, financial institutions and capital markets to ensure a well-functioning and stable financial system. Information and transparency, adequately trained practitioners and supervisors, and internationally

Box 3.1 **The comprehensive development framework**

A. *Structural*
1 Good and clean government
2 An effective legal and justice system
3 A well-organised and supervised financial system
4 A social safety net and social programs

B. *Human*
5 Education and knowledge institutions
6 Health and population issues

C. *Physical*
7 Water and sewerage
8 Energy
9 Roads, transportation and telecommunications
10 Sustainable development, environmental and cultural issues

D. *Specific strategies – rural, urban, and private sector*
11 Rural strategy
12 Urban strategy
13 Private sector strategy
14 Special national considerations

Source: James D. Wolfensohn, 'A Proposal for a Comprehensive Development Framework', 21 January 1999.

acceptable accounting and auditing standards will be essential. Regulation and supervision must include banking, savings institutions, insurance and pension plans, leasing and investment companies. Capital markets should also be developed and strengthened as resources allow.[6]

Fourth, 'whether by informal arrangement, familial or tribal support or by government-provided programs, provision must be made for the elderly, the disadvantaged and disabled, for children, for those men and women unable to find work, and those affected by natural disasters and the aftermath of war'.[7]

With this structural framework in place, governments should provide universal primary education, aligning the needs of the market to 'progressive' social and cultural attitudes:

Construction of schools, modern curricula geared to the new technological age, and the real needs of the emerging local market, and effective teacher training and supervision all contribute to successful educational programs. Adult education, literacy and lifelong learning must be combined with the fundamental recognition that education of women and girls is central to the process of development. A government must also be careful to learn lessons of practice and history from indigenous peoples and communities, so that education is not imposed from afar but benefits from relevant local, communal experience. Finally, preschool education must be given its full weight in programs.[8]

In addition, they should bring population growth under control, and provide basic health care:

> It is obviously crucial that mothers are supported and that children get adequate health care before and during school years or they will have their capacities diminished. Governments must ensure the provision of health services for adults and elderly at communal and local levels, as well as services for family health care and family planning.[9]

Next came investment in essential infrastructure – water and sewerage, energy, and roads, transport and communications – and environmental protection, echoing the 1994 and 1992 *World Development Reports* respectively.[10] In these cases the emphasis of the Reports had been on the need for governments to secure areas where the unco-ordinated and unregulated activities of private capital either failed to produce investment in areas of infrastructure essential to industrial and agricultural enterprise, or threatened to destroy the physical environment within which entrepreneurial activity unfolded.

Against this background, the CDF demanded specific strategies towards rural and urban development, and the private sector. These comprised integrated solutions to rural development which avoided 'a return to complex comprehensive and complicated state planning', urban strategies which addressed the concentration of population in megacities, and a range of policies to promote a vibrant private sector in recognition of its character as the 'engine of growth':

> A vibrant private sector requires that crucial elements of structural policy are in place. These include trade policy, tax policies, competition and regulatory policy, and corporate governance. Conditions must be created for a climate of investor confidence – with appropriate laws, transparent regulations, and predictable taxes. Whether the issue is protection of property rights or fair and equitable labor practices, governments must give certainty to the investor about the 'rules of the game'. Provision of credit, guarantees, sources of funding for projects all play a part in the competitive search by governments for investment and for job creation. Nothing is more significant to economic growth than the private sector.[11]

Finally, comprehensive as the framework was, it left room for an element of flexibility, simply achieved by inserting 'an empty box along the top of the matrix for Special Considerations depending on the country or the region'.[12] Even here, though, it seemed that the flexibility was for the benefit of the

Bank, rather than the country itself: 'The framework should not become a straight jacket. *We need the flexibility to adjust to the varied conditions of each country.* There will be a need for setting priorities, for phasing of action based on financial and human capacity and based on necessary sequencing to get to our objectives'.[13] And in his presentation of the framework itself Wolfensohn gave as an example the case of Bolivia, where special consideration needed to be given to the 'Anti-Cocaine Production Initiative', confirming that what was at issue was not flexibility around the principal elements of the CDF, but simply identification of unique features to be taken into account in its implementation.

The twenty-eighth imperative

The most notable feature of the framework is its imperative tone – the word 'must' appears twenty-seven times, as the policies promoted by the World Bank are laid out one after another as mandatory elements of a development framework. But the exposition of the comprehensive framework is accompanied by a twenty-eighth imperative, apparently at odds with the rest:

> It is also clear to all of us that ownership is essential. Countries must be in the driver's seat and set the course. They must determine goals and the phasing, timing and sequencing of programs. Where there is not adequate capacity in the government to do this, we must support and help them to establish, own, and implement the strategy. And we must work to achieve the strategy with our colleagues in the government, in the international development community, the civil society, and the private sector.[14]

Here, then, is the contradiction at the heart of the CDF. It is defined in advance down to a level of detail, but countries are obliged to own it. And where they cannot, they must be brought to do so. In other words, the imperative that countries should 'own' and drive the strategy is not a reflection of the reality of its origins or character, or a requirement arising from the countries themselves, but an imperative for the Bank. It is simply a further instruction to the 'clients' of the Bank – 'You must own this strategy'. In this way, the twenty-eighth imperative highlights both the character and the potential fragility of the twenty-seven that accompany it, reflecting the fact that the Bank cannot succeed unless its goals are adopted, internalised and implemented by countries themselves. The instrument through which this is to be achieved is the matrix.

With the elements of the framework already identified in the *World Development Reports* and elsewhere, the CDF was actually about securing 'country ownership', rather than about identifying appropriate policies. As the quotation at the head of this chapter discloses, the Bank envisaged a co-ordinated approach involving four actors – the international development community, the government, civil society, and the private sector – and it is this co-ordinated approach that the Matrix is intended to secure. Although it is presented as an instrument for countries to use for their own benefit, it turns out to be a means of providing for the monitoring of implementation in real time. The surveillance the IMF exercised over macroeconomic policy is to be matched by an equal level of surveillance by the Bank over structural and social policy.

The matrix

The matrix was presented as a management tool to overcome the lack of co-ordination between participants in the search for development. Wolfensohn presented it (Box 3.2) as an enabling device, 'open to all' and characterised by transparency and accountability. But the accompanying detail makes clear that its logic as a management tool is to allow the Bank to step away from day-to-day control of individual programme elements and their implementation in favour of overall strategic control, and to make country policies transparent and *accountable to the Bank and its allies* in order to facilitate that control. In short, the Bank is applying to itself the principle of strategic selectivity it applies to the role of states in its overall policy guidance. Hence its reluctance to assume the role of the co-ordinator of all programmes in the matrix.

The Bank's claim that 'the existence of the matrix is not a clandestine attempt on the part of the Bank to dominate the international development arena' but 'a tool to have greater co-operation, transparency, and partnership' ignores the fact that the 'judgment of the effectiveness of programs and strategies' is to be the World Bank's judgement, and that the evaluation and accountability for which it provides a basis come down to World Bank evaluation exercised through the institutionalisation of accountability to it by country 'partners'.

Flexibility in operation of the matrix on the part of governments is limited to the *pace* at which countries wish to 'move to a comprehensive program of coordination and measurement of performance'. Its principal purpose is to allow the Bank to exercise surveillance as implementation proceeds. The matrix is a 'summary management tool', to be 'kept up to date in real time'. It is conceived as the front end of a comprehensive tracking system, encompassing all programmes behind their relevant cell, and 'kept up-to-date using modern communication and information technology, possibly with open designated websites'. First,

> the governmental structure of a country must be in charge of the process of development strategy and implementation. Government should aspire to have programs under each of the 14 headings along the top of the matrix and these will be entered into the grid. Obviously, the entries will have to be made in a form of shorthand and as I just noted, annexes

Box 3.2 **Wolfensohn on the World Bank's matrix**

'First, there is no way that the World Bank should be seen as assuming the role of the coordinator of all programs in the matrix. In some cases, under the guidance of government, we will lead the process or segments of programs. In other cases, we will follow the lead of others, and in further cases, we will not participate at all. The existence of the matrix is not a clandestine attempt on the part of the Bank to dominate the international development arena, or the donor dialogue in a given country. Quite the contrary. It is a tool to have greater cooperation, transparency, and partnership.

Second, stated more simply, the foremost objective of the matrix is to give all the players, but most especially national governments and parliamentary bodies, a framework of information which can ensure openness, a basis for coordination of effort, and for judgment of the effectiveness of programs and strategies. The matrix is open to all. It is a step towards inclusion, transparency and to accountability. Used correctly, it should stop much of the mud slinging and allow for legitimate and constructive praise and criticism – and above all, give a basis for evaluation and accountability.

Third, I recognize that the pace of coordination and of inclusion, of openness and accountability, will vary by country and by stage of political development. But in this sense, the matrix is neutral, and the government and the society it represents can alone determine the pace at which it wishes to move to a comprehensive program of coordination and measurement of performance. Ultimately, the matrix is a tool for the governments and people of the countries we serve. It is they who must own the programs, not us, and it is they who must set the pace.

Fourth, the matrix and annexes can and should be kept up to date in real time. The matrix will be a summary management tool. But behind each heading there will be annexes for each subject area, containing a substantive description and far more detailed listings of short and long-term goals, programs, their present status, timing, cost and progress. These annexes can, and should, be kept up-to-date using modern communication and information technology, possibly with open designated websites.'

Source: 'A Proposal for a Comprehensive Development Framework', pp. 22–4.

behind each subject heading will give fuller details. For example, an annex on Justice Systems, an annex on education, giving far more detail on each subject. Government should include not only national programs, but provincial and state, city and municipal to the extent that they are relevant.[15]

Second, despite its denials, the Bank *is* seeking to bring about strategic co-ordination across the international development community. After listing the IMF, UN agencies and programmes, the WTO, the European Union (EU), regional development banks, bilateral agencies and international organisations as those multilateral and bilateral participants 'involved in the programmatic thrusts', Wolfensohn comments that:

> All of these participants, as well as the World Bank Group, are involved in projects and programs for development. At a time of lessening resources for overseas development assistance and budgetary restraints on agencies which reduce available human resources, each of us needs to know what the other is doing so that we can cooperate and avoid duplication of effort.[16]

Third, civil society is to be *engaged in* programmes and projects defined from outside, in order to maximise their prospects for acceptance:

> Depending on local political circumstances, civil society has a greater or lesser voice, but our experience is that by engaging civil society in projects and programs, better results are achieved both with design and implementation and usually greater effectiveness, including more local ownership. I think we all recognize more and more that local ownership is the key to success and project effectiveness.[17]

In sum, Wolfensohn concludes, 'The Matrix will allow us to see quickly what is going on in a country from the point of view of structural and social development, and will also show us what is not going on'. For this goal to be secured, however:

> The annexes to the matrix will play a crucial role. They might start with a general overview of the objectives of the government over the long term in each subject area. It will be crucial in each annex to set forth where the country stands in terms of achievement and where they want to go. The matrix should be read in terms of the stipulated and agreed goals. There would follow a strategy for implementation with a timeline. Thereafter, one could imagine a more detailed listing of projects achieved, projects underway, and projects planned, together with a listing of those institutions providing assistance and a detailed description of the projects planned and undertaken with their results. The format of the annexes should be set according to the subject and to those participating in preparing and managing it.[18]

The matrix, then, is unequivocally a management tool through which the Bank and other agencies can monitor government policy across the board and in detail, against objectives and programmes agreed with the Bank. It was proposed as the principal instrument in a strategy of comprehensive global governance spear-headed by the Bank in close liaison with the IMF, to be co-ordinated with other relevant multilateral and bilateral actors in the area of international development. It remained to be seen, however, whether the Bank could even begin to turn its dream of global governance into reality.

Towards a Global Architecture of Governance

Since January 1999 the World Bank has indeed been systematically putting into place the elements of a Global Architecture of Governance (GAG). It has developed an operational tool through which commitment to the CDF and use of the matrix can be secured and monitored – the Poverty Reduction Strategy Paper (PRSP) – and it has surrounded the CDF and the Poverty Reduction Strategy Papers with a range of complementary disciplinary instruments which give it increasing scope for an unprecedented level of intervention in the domestic affairs of states. As we shall see, the PRSP is structured and employed to ensure direct IMF intervention in dictating the broad framework of macroeconomic policy, while the World Bank takes the lead in ensuring that social and structural policies are systematically subordinated to it, and will induce the institutional and behavioural changes that will lock it in place. In the period since the CDF and the PRSP were proposed, the CDF itself has been trialled and evaluated; a large number of interim PRSPs and a smaller number of final PRSPs have been agreed; a number of countries have accepted the matrix as an operational tool along the lines prescribed by the Bank; a method has been devised to extend the system beyond the heavily indebted and impoverished countries who are most easily persuaded of the need to obey the joint dictates of the Bank and the Fund and assume ownership of the CDF; and an effort has been made to co-ordinate the elements of a larger overarching framework within which the CDF and the PRSP can take their place. The Bank has also launched a process of systematic internal reform intended to transform its ability to play the strategic role of global leadership it sees as essential if the system is to work. These developments testify to the seriousness with which the Bank has launched itself on a process of creating a Global Architecture of Governance, and of transforming itself as an institution in the process.

Poverty Reduction Strategy Papers

The PRSP is a key mechanism in the World Bank's Global Architecture of Governance. It was introduced as an instrument for operationalising the CDF in a paper on the HIPC (Heavily Indebted Poor Countries) Initiative by the Joint IMF/World Bank Development Committee (officially the *Joint Ministerial Committee of the Board of Governors of the Bank and the Fund on the Transfer of Real Resources to the Developing Countries*) on 17 September 1999.[19] The paper reported an elaborate process of consultation with NGOs focused on the virtues of outcome-oriented poverty reduction programmes as prerequisites for debt relief, then proposed, in the form of a requirement for prior agreement of PRSPs, a mechanism which used the language and

Box 3.3 **The proposed Poverty Reduction Strategy Paper (PRSP)**

Content

To support the government's effort to formulate and implement a poverty reduction strategy, we propose a new vehicle – a Poverty Reduction Strategy Paper (PRSP) – that would have the following essential characteristics:

*   It must ensure consistency between a country's macroeconomic, structural and social policies and the goals of poverty reduction and social development.
*   It should serve as the basis for designing Bank and Fund lending operations, and as a framework with which all ESAF (Enhanced Structural Adjustment Facility) – and Bank-supported programs should be consistent.
*   It must be produced in a way that includes transparency and broad-based participation in the choice of goals, the formulation of policies and the monitoring of implementation – with ultimate ownership by the government.

The first two of the key characteristics noted above imply minimum requirements for the content of the PRSP, namely:

*   Medium- and long-term goals for poverty reduction and social development, with a range of relevant outcome-related indicators for monitoring progress in areas key to poverty reduction (which will include but not be limited to the social sectors).
*   A macroeconomic framework consistent with the poverty reduction and social goals (over a minimum three-year horizon).
*   The structural reforms and priorities and sectoral strategies (a three-year agenda) and associated funding needs (domestic and external) necessary to deliver the growth and poverty reduction objectives.
*   Anti-poverty and other social policies, linked to an analysis of the social impact of macro and structural policies, and associated funding needs (domestic and external).
*   Overall external financing needs (including technical assistance needs and expected providers) for each year of the program.

Process

Governments would be expected to take the lead both in drawing up a PRSP and in conducting consultations with civil society and other stakeholders. The consultative process could, however, be facilitated by the Bank, with the involvement of the Fund on macroeconomic policies and in relevant structural areas, and others where appropriate. Governments may also need to seek extensive technical assistance – including from the Bank and Fund – on the elaboration of policies within the PRSP.

A full-fledged reworking of the PRSP might take place, say, every three years. Annual reviews and updates would be necessary in the interim, however, if the framework were to remain sufficiently current to be a basis for Bank and Fund lending operations. The extent of these updates would depend in part on the comprehensiveness of earlier PRSPs and on the results of a review of selected outcome indicators.

The PRSP would be sent to the Executive Boards of the Bank and the Fund, both of which would take formal decisions endorsing the PRSP as the framework for each institution's lending operations. The final version of the PRSP would be published at this point (although drafts would likely have been made publicly available during the consultative process).

Source: 'Heavily Indebted Poor Countries (HIPC) Initiative: Strengthening the Link between Debt Relief and Poverty Reduction', World Bank/IMF Development Committee, DC/99–24, 17 September 1999, Box 8, p. 31.

ideas of some NGO contributors to the consultation to impose and validate precisely the set of policies and priorities developed by the IMF and the World Bank in advance – a classic case of the manipulation of 'participation' as part of a strategy of securing hegemony. The PRSP was to be a 'tripartite document endorsed by the government, the Bank and the Fund'.[20] As the summary of its content in Box 3.3 reveals, the strategy was to tie social and structural policies directly to IMF-approved macroeconomic frameworks; it was to be 'owned' by the government, but on the basis of content agreed and where necessary provided by the Bank and the Fund; and it was to be monitored and updated annually, and reworked completely at three-year intervals. In other words, the Bank and the Fund claimed the right to monitor and amend economic, social and structural policies across the board in heavily indebted countries; and with the CDF and its matrix supplemented by the PSRP, they were in a position to exercise it.

Implementing the CDF and the PRSP

By September 2000 there were twelve pilot CDFs in place, and in ten of the twelve cases a matrix was being developed or about to be adopted.[21] A learning-group of CDF pilot-country directors chaired by Mr Wolfensohn was meeting regularly, and a quarterly tracking procedure had been set up. It was acknowledged at the same time that progress on implementing the matrix had been slower than expected. The Bank therefore proposed to 'more systematically align its instruments, processes and way of working with the CDF approach', and in particular to align its Country Assistance Strategies (CAS) and Country Policy and Institutional Assessments (CPIA) more closely with the CDF, and in turn to align Social and Structural Reviews (SSR) with the CAS and the CPIA. At the same time the Bank would reform its own organisational environment with a view to 'making the matrix approach excel', and seek to 'create a community of CDF change agents who support one another in nurturing the CDF approach'.[22]

By the same point in time thirteen Interim Poverty Reduction Strategy Papers (Albania, Benin, Bolivia, Chad, Ghana, Honduras, Kenya, Mali, Mozambique, São Tomé and Principe, Senegal, Tanzania, and Zambia) and two full Poverty Reduction Strategy Papers (Burkina Faso and Uganda) had been considered as part of the HIPC Initiative. However, the Managing

Director of the IMF and the President of the World Bank reported problems arising from poor country-level data and limited institutional and analytical capacity to prepare full PRSPs, and foresaw difficulties in costing inputs and outcomes, tracking poverty-related public expenditure, and integrating poverty reduction strategies into a consistent macroeconomic framework.[23] These concerns arose from

> tensions that were inherent in the approach we all adopted a year ago: first, the tension between accelerating debt relief and maintaining the pace of IDA [International Development Association] and IMF concessional assistance, while at the same time ensuring that HIPC resources and concessional financing are linked to country-owned strategies for sustainable poverty reduction; and second, the tension between country ownership and the requirement on the part of IDA and the IMF to assess whether the content of country strategies provides an adequate basis for the institutions' concessional lending and debt relief.[24]

The statement captured the fundamental change in the character of debt relief as a result of its incorporation into a framework intended to secure a comprehensive set of policies defined by the IMF and the World Bank, yet simultaneously to be 'owned' by and embedded in countries as a result of local processes of participation and deliberation. It recognised that progress in releasing money would be slowed by the need to await the development of adequate 'poverty reduction' strategies which would ensure that funds were directed to appropriate ends; and it admitted that 'the more assurances sought (in terms of strategy, content and process, and implementation and monitoring), the greater the difficulty of early delivery and of securing country ownership'. However, the bottom line was clear: the pace of progress would still depend on the speed with which country 'clients' could adapt themselves to requirements defined in advance by the Fund and the Bank: 'Ultimately the pace at which our institutions can move in the directions we all desire reflects the nature of the approach endorsed by the international community and the pace at which countries themselves can work in accordance with this approach'.[25]

The Chief Executives of the Bank and the Fund were well aware of the fictitious nature of 'country ownership':

> Ownership versus 'assessment' is a particularly difficult issue. The process envisaged a year ago properly emphasized the need for country ownership of strategies; the concept that there could be no single blueprint for such strategies; and that home-grown approaches to poverty reduction, based on countries' own unique circumstances, experience and capacities, were to be encouraged. The staffs (in Joint Staff Assessments) and the Executive Boards of IDA and the IMF (in discussions of country documents and staff assessments), however, were expected to take a view

about the appropriateness of a country's PRSP as a basis for debt relief and IDA and IMF concessional assistance. In addition the fiduciary framework underpinning concessional assistance considered desirable by the international community (including our own institutions) has tended to become stronger. Both countries and development partners have drawn attention to the implicit conflict between these two concepts.[26]

In short, they noted, 'there has been a tendency on the part of development partners, including members of the NGO community, simultaneously to express concern (which we share) about ensuring genuine country ownership, but also to propose specific areas of policy that country strategies should cover'.[27] The proposed response was to offer 'guidance that does not breach the principle of ownership in the context of joint missions to discuss strategy formulation with governments', to develop a 'PRSP Sourcebook' offering guidance on best practice, and to organise 'outreach and learning events'. In other words, the principle of country ownership would be secured by telling countries what to do when they asked. In the end, 'country ownership' came down to two things. First, the Bank and the Fund must not write the documents for them; and second, the countries themselves, rather than the Bank and the Fund, were responsible for organising support for the policy package through local consultation and participation.

Conclusion: the CDF as a comprehensive dependency framework

The CDF has been presented by the World Bank as a means of incorporating structural and social issues into development, but on closer inspection it has turned out to be a means of tying them to a rigid IMF-prescribed macroeconomic framework and a disciplinary agenda devised and promoted by the Bank. In summary, IMF surveillance of macroeconomic policy is to be matched by Bank surveillance of social and structural policy. With this goal in mind, the Bank is now actively engaged upon extending the scope of its CDF–PSRP framework and drawing its 'development partners' into the process. Four full PRSPs and thirty-two Interim PRSPs were in place by March 2001.[28] The Bank was moving (with a target date of 1 July 2002) to a point where all Country Assistance Strategies (CAS) presented by the International Development Association (IDA) to the Boards of the IMF and the World Bank would be underpinned by sector-by-sector SSPs (Sectoral Strategy Papers) and by an agreed PRSP, with the intention that 'all Bank lending and nonlending activities in IDA countries will be organized under a CAS business plan responding to the PRSP'.[29] The models here were Burkina Faso and Uganda, for whom the Bank Board discussed Country Assistance Strategies based on PSRPs in November 2000.

Finally, the CAS–CDF–PSRP framework was to be extended beyond the small group of low-income countries covered by the HIPC Initiative to the much larger group of World Bank-classified 'Middle-Income Countries', with the intention of generalising the disciplinary framework developed in the CDF and the PRSP to all countries eligible for International Bank for Reconstruction and Development (IBRD) lending (Box 3.4). Middle-income countries are to be asked to present a 'vision of development' in the form of a 'Letter of Development Strategy', incorporating a systematic and comprehensive diagnosis of its priorities. The matching CAS will identify a programme of Economic and Sector Work (ESW), so that all the Bank's 'lending products' can be aligned to support medium-term reform programmes in turn underpinned by enhanced public expenditure management capacity. This comprehensive framework will in turn allow strengthened collaboration with the IMF, and a clear division of labour between the Bank itself, the Fund and the multilateral development banks.[30]

The CDF–PRSP framework, with its supporting matrix, has not been developed purely as a means of addressing debt relief and poverty reduction in a small number of low-income countries heavily dependent on World Bank and IMF support: it has been trialled with the most heavily indebted countries, prior to being extended to the remaining clients of the Bank and the Fund as a generalised means of intervention in economic and social policy and political governance. In other words, it constitutes a Global Architecture of Governance which takes a giant step beyond the International Financial Architecture already under construction. A key element of this Global Architecture of Governance is that countries should assume 'ownership' of the essential disciplinary elements through which it is exercised – the CDF and its matrix, and the PRSP through which it is operationalised. As we have seen, the Chief Executives of the IMF and the World Bank have proved themselves to be aware both of the need for 'country ownership', and of the reality that the set of policies they are invited to 'own' have been defined in advance by the Bank and the Fund. The way to square the circle, they propose, is for the Bank and the Fund to provide technical assistance to strengthen strategy formulation and participation, and to offer, as some countries were realistic enough to request, 'extra guidance on the expected core content of PRSPs and the participatory processes to be used in preparing them'.[31] The Bank now proposes to supplement the CDF, the matrix and the PRSP with the provision of 'sound diagnostic analysis and advice' through its enhanced Economic and Sector Work, and to focus its strategic efforts on two integrative diagnostic analyses or 'core integrative assessments', a '*fiduciary assessment* . . . to analyze the country's public financial accountability arrangements, including its systems for public expenditure, procurement, and financial management', and a *development policy review* – 'a concise cross-cutting assessment of policy reform and institutional development priorities for growth and poverty reduction'. The additional analytic products developed for each country through ESW will then 'provide building blocks for the core integrative instruments described above and would aim to help countries build capacity'.[32] The Bank does indeed aspire to be 'the mother of all governments'.

Box 3.4 World Bank task force proposals for middle-income countries

Strengthen the Country Assistance Strategy as the key vehicle for agreeing on a focused program of World Bank Group lending and nonlending support, based on the country's development vision and priorities, a systematic and comprehensive diagnosis, and an informed view of support that is or can be provided by others.

Invite countries to present their vision of development as a basis for support from all development partners and the starting point for the Bank's CAS. Invite countries to set out this vision in the form of a Letter of Development Strategy.

Rebuild and systematize the Bank's economic and sector work. This is needed if the Bank is to be more effective in helping countries identify and implement development priorities and build capacity. The CAS should set out a program of ESW, including development policy reviews, fiduciary assessments, and other diagnostic ESW, carried out wherever possible with clients and other development partners.

Develop lending products that match the needs of middle-income countries. Investment lending can be a powerful vehicle for transferring knowledge, testing new approaches, and supporting in-depth programs when hands-on Bank expertise is needed. Programmatic adjustment lending can effectively support medium-term reform programs, particularly when synchronized with national budget and policy cycles, and its use is likely to expand where there is sufficiently strong country performance and fiduciary and public expenditure management capacity. A new deferred drawdown option is proposed for use with policy-based loans. This would meet the needs of countries that are currently able to borrow from the market, but are concerned both to remain continuously engaged with the Bank and to enhance their debt management flexibility. It would also help countries that wish to remain engaged with the Bank but for the time being do not need to borrow from the Bank, although they are at a stage of development when experience suggests they may need support again in the future.

Use these enhancements and improved processes to reduce the cost of doing business with the Bank and as a basis for greater country and institutional selectivity. The improved and more systematic policy dialogue will help countries focus on key policy priorities, and, combined with a streamlining of Bank internal processes, will help reduce the cost of doing business with the Bank. It will also allow the Bank to cooperate more effectively with other multilateral development banks (MDBs) and other development partners (and better exploit synergies within the Bank Group), exercising greater selectivity at the country level about which of the priorities for each country the Bank itself should support. Other areas for enhanced institutional cooperation with other MDBs should also be explored, starting with fiduciary assessments, where there are shared institutional needs.

Strengthen collaboration with the IMF. The improved processes and strengthened analytic and diagnostic work will help the Bank to better advise countries on social, structural, and sectoral policies and institutions, paralleling and complementing the work of the IMF on macroeconomic policies and related institutions. They should foster more structured and streamlined Bank–Fund cooperation in the policy dialogue with and support for middle-income countries, along the lines of the enhanced framework being developed for low-income countries.

Source: Development Committee, 'Supporting Country Development: Strengthening the World Bank Group's Support for Middle Income Countries', DC 2001–005, 10 April 2001, Box 1, p. 3.

Notes

1 James D. Wolfensohn, 'A Proposal for a Comprehensive Development Framework', Memo to the Board, Management and Staff of the World Bank Group, 21 January 1999, p. 1.
2 'Proposal for a CDF', p. 3.
3 'Proposal for a CDF', pp. 5–6.
4 'Proposal for a CDF', p. 8.
5 The comprehensive framework was rehearsed in the 1997 World Development Report, *The State in a Changing World*, but this largely summarised policies outlined in previous reports. For an overview of their content, and the argument that they constitute an explicit programme for the creation of an easily exploitable global proletariat, see Paul Cammack, 'Attacking the Poor', *New Left Review*, 2: 13 (January–February 2002), pp. 125–34.
6 'Proposal for a CDF', pp. 10–11. Compare *From Plan to Market* (World Bank, 1996), especially chapters 5–7.
7 'Proposal for a CDF', pp. 11–12.
8 'Proposal for a CDF', pp. 13–14. Compare *Poverty* (World Bank, 1990).
9 'Proposal for a CDF', p. 14. Compare *Investing in Health* (World Bank, 1993).
10 'Proposal for a CDF', pp. 15–18. Compare *Development and the Environment* (World Bank, 1992), and *Infrastructure for Development* (World Bank, 1994).
11 'Proposal for a CDF', pp. 19–20.
12 'Proposal for a CDF', p. 20.
13 'Proposal for a CDF', p. 8, emphasis mine.
14 'Proposal for a CDF', p. 9.
15 'Proposal for a CDF', p. 24.
16 'Proposal for a CDF', p. 25. This is an old theme, highlighted in the 1990 World Development Report. After setting out the elements of what would mature into the comprehensive development framework there, the Report commented that 'These principles . . . should be regarded as applicable to the aid community as a whole. If the aid strategy outlined here were adopted and followed consistently by bilateral donors, nongovernmental organizations, and multinational agencies, its effectiveness would be greatly increased'; and at the end of the Report it urged other institutions to follow the lead of the World Bank, denying aid to countries that were not 'serious about reducing poverty' – or in other words, unwilling to restructure their economies and societies comprehensively along the lines required by the Bank. See *Poverty* (World Bank, 1990), pp. 4, 137.
17 'Proposal for a CDF', p. 26.
18 'Proposal for a CDF', p. 28.

19 Development Committee, 'Heavily Indebted Poor Countries (HIPC) Initiative: Strengthening the Link between Debt Relief and Poverty Reduction', DC/99–24, 17 September 1999.
20 'HIPC Initiative', p. 30, paragraph 74.
21 Development Committee, 'Comprehensive Development Framework: Progress Report', DC/2000–17, 7 September 2000. The twelve pilots were in Bolivia, Côte d'Ivoire, Dominican Republic, Eritrea, Ethiopia, Ghana, Kyrgyz Republic, Morocco, Romania, Uganda, Vietnam, and the West Bank/Gaza.
22 'CDF Progress Report', pp. 13–14.
23 'A Joint Memorandum from the Managing Director of the IMF and the President of the World Bank', 7 September 2000, in Development Committee, 'Heavily Indebted Poor Countries (HIPC) Initiative and Poverty Reduction Strategy Papers (PRSP): A Joint Memorandum from the Managing Director of the IMF and the President of the World Bank and Reports on Progress in Implementation', DC/2000–18, 8 September 2000.
24 'Joint Memorandum', p. 5.
25 'Joint Memorandum', p. 5.
26 'Joint Memorandum', p. 6.
27 In fact they went much further: 'NGOs have stated that IMF macro-conditionality for these countries remains stringent; that recent PRGFs are not different from previous ESAFs (for example in Tanzania and Honduras); that there are no references to changes in the macroeconomic framework with respect to integrating poverty reduction concerns; and that it remains unclear how full PRSPs will integrate a fully costed poverty reduction strategy into a consistent macroeconomic framework . . . Some also question what would happen if a country-owned PRSP or I-PRSP were to propose a strategy that differed from Bank–Fund thinking, and wonder under what circumstances, if any, the Bank and/or Fund might reject a country strategy', International Monetary Fund and International Development Association, 'Poverty Reduction Strategy Papers – Progress in Implementation', paragraph 25, pp. 13–14, in 'HIPC Initiative and PRSP', at pp. 63–4.
28 IBRD/IDA, 'Strategic Directions for FY02–FY04: Implementing the World Bank's Strategic Framework', 28 March 2001, p. 2.
29 'PRSP – Progress in Implementation', paragraph 45, p. 21.
30 Development Committee, 'Supporting Country Development: Strengthening the World Bank Group's Support for Middle Income Countries', DC 2001–005, 10 April 2001.
31 'Joint Memorandum', p. 6.
32 'Supporting Country Development', p. 7.

Part II

Global environmental, cultural and health governance

4 Global environmental governance

Lorraine Elliott

Introduction

Calls for new forms of governance are a response to the political, economic and social challenges of globalisation and the increasing complexity of the international agenda. Global *environmental* governance has become a leitmotif of contemporary environmental politics, something to be theorised as an idea and to be realised in material form. It is constructed and contested, a political artefact which inscribes a parabola of normative and material possibilities on the axes of world politics – states and markets, the local and the global.[1] A precise definition remains elusive. It is variously presented as a desideratum; as a useful shorthand to describe changes in contemporary international political practice; as a metaphor for 'world collective life'; and as a Trojan horse for neoliberalism and green corporatism. These images of global environmental governance co-exist at the same time as they are in contest. The consequences have been theoretical confusion and institutional uncertainty.

The debates about global environmental governance are something more than those over 'demand' – that is, why do we need it – and 'supply' – that is, where do we find it and in what form. In liberal-institutionalist terms it is generally perceived as a more effective form of multilateral management which is essential if the international community is to meet the goals of mitigating and where possible reversing the impacts of global environmental change. The assumption is, as Sand puts it, that 'we know better' and 'we can do better'.[2] Law locates such governance in a 'revamped liberal multilateralism'.[3] Wapner identifies it as 'world collective life'.[4] Young tends to reduce it to the familiar pattern of regimes and the 'establishment and operation of social institutions' to 'resolve social conflicts, promote sustained cooperation . . . [and] alleviate collective action problems'.[5] Vig defines it as the 'coordination of action [which] can occur through many different institutions including private social and economic ones'.[6] For Soroos it is the 'existence of laws and policies that regulate behaviour as well as the institutions that facilitate the adoption and implementation of them'.[7] A range of institutions now contribute to and help define the practices of global environmental governance.

Yet, as this chapter argues, the congested institutional terrain still provides more of an appearance than a reality of comprehensive global governance. Global environmental governance is more than 'doing better' or expanding the network of institutions and decision-makers. It is a political practice which simultaneously reflects, constitutes *and masks* global relations of power and powerlessness. It is neither normatively neutral nor materially benign. In practice, it has come to legitimise a neoliberal ecopolitics, characterised by a rehabilitation of the state, liberal-individual notions of justice, and a technocratic emphasis on managerialism, standard setting and rules-based behaviour. This is nowhere more evident than in the involvement of the World Bank and the World Trade Organisation (WTO) in environmental politics and the contests over transparency, democracy and accountability which have accompanied it. In defining the global as (and confining it to) the international, this particularistic and centralised form of environmental governance has marginalised local voices. In response, local voices are demanding to be heard and are constituting alternative, albeit often not clearly articulated, forms of resistance to globalism.

This chapter examines these contested faultlines of global environmental governance. It begins by assessing demands for a global governance for the environment before turning to an analysis of the contours of contemporary environmental governance. I conclude here that environmental governance is neither global nor successful.

'Globalising' environmental governance: demands

The environmental agenda is extensive and there are few environmental problems which are now not subject to some kind of international debate and agreement, either because they affect the global commons or shared resources, because they generate 'transboundary externalities',[8] or because they are so widespread as to qualify as problems of common concern. The challenges are exacerbated because scientific evidence confirms that environmental degradation is happening at a magnitude and rate higher than at any time in human history as a result not of cataclysmic events but the everyday practices of human economy and society. Emissions of greenhouse gases have continued to rise, increasing concentrations to levels significantly higher than at the beginning of the Industrial Revolution.[9] The second full assessment report released by the Intergovernmental Panel on Climate Change (IPCC) argues that on the 'balance of evidence' there is a 'discernible human influence on global climate'.[10] The consequences are no longer in the realm of futurology: the average rate of warming could be greater than at any time in the last 10,000 years. The loss of species and genetic diversity is estimated at up to 100 to 10,000 times higher than the pre-human rate.[11] Deforestation in both tropical and temperate forests continues at an annual rate of about 12 million hectares: up to 40 per cent of the world's rainforest has disappeared in the last three decades. Desertification affects between 25 and 35 per cent of the earth's land surface and between one-sixth and one-quarter of the world's population. Many of the world's fisheries (accounting for about 16 per cent of the world's protein source) are either over-fished or close to exhaustion. Up to 34 per cent of all fish species could be at risk from human activity.[12] The per capita availability of water continues to decline and over eighty of the world's countries, primarily the poorer ones, are now facing severe water stress – and this number is expected to rise. Extensive and excessive resource use, energy inefficient lifestyles, industrialisation and the pursuit of economic growth are inextricably linked to environmental degradation, within and across state borders. Global energy use has increased by almost 70 per cent since 1971.[13] The social and economic impacts are extensive: increased poverty, malnutrition and food insecurity, increases in human, plant and animal disease, dislocation of peoples from home and habitat.

The environmental agenda has thus become more complicated as well as more urgent. It no longer focuses only on narrowly defined 'environmental' problems and the search for solutions through scientific knowledge and the adoption and implementation of environmental standards. As well as problems such as climate change, ozone depletion, deforestation, loss of biodiversity, desertification, oceans pollution, toxic waste and species protection (among others) the politics of the global environment now embraces issues as diverse as intellectual property rights, trade, tourism, emissions trading, green taxes, foreign direct investment, telecommunications, urbanisation, consumption and production. Environmental degradation is therefore now a global issue – ecologically, politically and economically – with a concomitant sense of urgency reflected in international forums. The UN General Assembly has identified the environment as 'one of the main global problems facing the world today'.[14] Even before the end of the Cold War, the G7 called (in 1989) for 'decisive action to understand and protect the earth's ecological balance'[15] although they have done little to heed the imperatives of their own demands. It is this sense of magnitude and urgency which has given rise to demands for 'global environmental governance'. Two debates are at the heart of these demands. The first is the sovereignty–environment nexus, caught up in disputes over the extent of globalisation and the nature of the state. The second is the question of justice and the place of the local in the face of growing and globalised inequities within and between countries.

Sovereignty, the state and the environment[16]

Demands for global environmental governance are embedded in anxieties about the adequacy and capacity of state-centric institutions, practices and ideologies in the face of environmental challenges which render borders porous and expose the continued fragility of assumptions about discrete boundaries between 'inside' and 'outside'. The interdependencies of the global ecosystem are incongruent with the geopolitics of the international state system. It is not simply that self-regarding states, in the Realist iconography, cannot meet the challenges of global environmental change through orthodox self-help modalities. It is that the state itself – its autonomy, its capacity and its legitimacy – is being eroded by the very nature of environmental problems which do not respect territorial borders. As the Brundtland Report put it, 'the Earth is one but the world is not'.[17] The existence of transboundary and global environmental degradation is taken as a 'symptom of the diminishing authority of the nation-state'.[18] Sovereignty is thus an ecopolitical contradiction: an 'immutable . . . principle of international relations'[19] *and* a 'persistent and resilient myth' which is 'antithetical to the prerequisites for global ecological security'.[20]

Existing institutions and conventional patterns of world politics, embedded in state-centrism and a commitment to the state as the 'sole legitimate source of public policy',[21] are therefore perceived to be increasingly poorly placed to manage the challenges of global environmental change. To meet those challenges, international environmental agreements must be precautionary rather than reactive. They must respond to changing scientific knowledge, establish environmental standards and identify modalities by which those standards can be met and monitored. The decentralised and fragmented nature of the international state system is cast as a barrier to more effective co-operation in pursuit of such agreement. International diplomacy, international law and international institutions – understood by many as the major components of governance – are chastised as too immature, as ill-suited to global environmental problems and as incapable of keeping pace with the interdependencies of the global environment.[22]

The liberal institutionalist response has been to pursue reform, to make international institutions more effective and efficient and to ensure that environmental agreements and the procedures by which they are negotiated are, at minimum, co-operative, collective and democratic. They are required to be co-operative and collective because independent or unilateral action by states or governments is *ineffective* in the face of transboundary and global environmental problems and *inefficient* in the face of shared or common environmental concerns. They are required to be democratic and participatory to take account of the competing interests of a variety of stakeholders ranging from business and corporate actors through local governments and scientific associations to indigenous peoples' organisations and environmental NGOs. The democratic efficiency argument assumes that environmental agreements will work better if all those who are affected by the environmental problem under consideration or who have legitimate interests in the search for a solution are included in negotiations. This includes local voices and local concerns, territorially embedded within states but often silenced or marginalised in the interests of *globally* embedded economic elites.

Justice, equity and the environment

The pursuit of more effective environmental governance resonates (or at least it should) with democracy not just as an end, but a means to ensuring that the inequities which are a defining characteristic of global ecopolitics are acknowledged, addressed and overcome. Those who are most immediately and disproportionately hit by the ecological, economic and social consequences of environmental decline and the scarcity of environmental services are those who are already economically and politically marginalised – the poor, indigenous peoples, and women, especially but not exclusively in developing countries. They are, as David Law observes, 'least able to buy their way out of environmental difficulties'.[23] The poor – peoples and countries – have also contributed least to global environmental degradation. The international political economy of the environment is characterised by the shadow ecologies of the industrialised world in which the invisible causes of environmental decline are embedded. The contemporary challenges of global environmental change are those of displacement across time and space.[24] They are, therefore, intimately bound up with questions of justice and equity. The problems are complicated further because, as Redclift and Sage remind us, 'common property resources throughout the globe are being privatised at an alarming rate'.[25] They are, in effect, being taken out of the hands of the poor and communities for whom communual ownership and management provides environmental sustainability and a subsistence livelihood.

If there are environmental 'free-riders', they are not found among the poor. The richest 20 per cent of the world's population (mainly but not exclusively in the industrialised world) account for 86 per cent of total private consumption expenditure, consume 58 per cent of the world's total energy, own 87 per cent of the world's vehicles, and emit 53 per cent of the world's carbon dioxide emissions.[26] Global environmental governance must, therefore, overcome the environmental problems of affluence as much as it seeks to overcome the poverty which is often a proximate but not systemic cause of environmental degradation.

'Globalising' environmental governance: supply

Many claims are made for an already-existing global environmental governance that is co-operative, participatory and democratic, and innovative (albeit still piecemeal and *ad hoc*). It offers, according to Young, 'promising new approaches'[27] to the demands of global environmental change. These claims are worthy of further investigation.

Since the early 1970s, the terrain of environmental governance has become congested with multilateral environmental agreements (MEAs) and with formal and informal institutional structures dedicated to environmental negotiation, standard-setting and the management of transboundary and global environmental change.[28] The public face of this international activity has been the UN summits – the 1972 UN Conference on the Human Environment in Stockholm, the 1992 UN Conference on Environment and Development in Rio (also called the Earth Summit) and, although much less well known, the 1997 UN General Assembly Special Session to Review Agenda

21 (the plan of action adopted at the Rio Summit). Global environmental summitry has authored and been supplemented by a raft of declarations, plans of action and functionally specific conventions, and by interminable working groups (*ad hoc*; open-ended; expert), intersessional meetings, commissions, preparatory committees, international negotiating committees, subsidiary bodies, conferences of parties, intergovernmental panels and forums, and several formally constituted secretariats.

At the same time environmental diplomacy has been at least partially democratised. Indeed, Agenda 21 made great play of the principles of 'democracy and transparency' which were to guide the 'global partnership for sustainable development'.[29] The Agenda devotes several chapters to what are there called the 'major groups' or the 'independent sector', acknowledging their role as partners in the pursuit of sustainable development, requiring governments to involve them in decision-making and implementation, and stressing the importance of access to information and knowledge about environmental policies and problems. An increasing number of non-governmental organisations are accredited to international environmental conferences and negotiations. At the United Nations General Assembly Special Session (UNGASS), for the first time, NGOs were able to deliver speeches to the plenary session and have access to ministerial level consultations.

Global environmental governance is also marked by an increasingly sophisticated web of environmental principles.[30] Some, such as the precautionary principle, where the polluter pays principle and common but differentiated responsibilities, are intended primarily to elaborate more specific rights and obligations for states and to enact normative guidelines for regulatory mechanisms. Others, such as intergenerational equity, the common heritage of (hu)mankind and environmental rights, have the potential to widen the scope of those to whom obligations are owed in international law beyond states and beyond present generations. In theory, this incorporates a deeper ethic of justice in international law and articulates an ethic of stewardship rather than management for jurisdictions both within and beyond the borders of states. Sustainable development has been confirmed as *the* guiding principle of international environmental negotiation and best practice. Defined in the 1987 report of the World Commission on Environment and Development as 'development that meets the needs of the present without compromising the ability of future generations to meet their own needs',[31] sustainable development has been an attempt to manage the links between the imperatives of environmental protection and economic growth.

The United Nations (UN) remains the public face of global environmental governance, despite concerns about its capacity and the 'obvious inadequacy of [environmental] initiatives' taken under its auspices.[32] Many of the UN's specialised agencies have some kind of environment-related responsibilities written into or inferred from their mandates. Over thirty UN specialised agencies and programmes are now involved in the implementation of Agenda

21 and the pursuit of sustainable development.[33] These include the Food and Agriculture Organisation (FAO), the International Maritime Organisation (IMO), the World Meteorological Organisation (WMO) and the United Nations Development Programme (UNDP). Two UN bodies have dedicated environmental tasks – the United Nations Environment Programme (UNEP, established after the 1972 Stockholm Conference) and the Commission on Sustainable Development (CSD, established after the 1992 Rio Summit to demonstrate that something really had been 'achieved'). UNEP has a vague mandate to monitor, co-ordinate and catalyse. Despite the parsimony of financial support from UN member states, UNEP has taken an active lead role in co-ordinating international negotiations (on ozone depletion, biodiversity and desertification, for example) and providing secretariat support for a number of environmental conventions. Its other successes have included the regional seas programme and the highly successful Global Environmental Monitoring System (GEMS). The CSD has no executive, compliance or sanction powers. Its primary role is to monitor and examine progress on the agreements adopted at the UN Conference on Environment and Development (UNCED), a task it has pursued through annual sessions (and less formal inter-sessional meetings) in conjunction with voluntary reporting from member states on their implementation of Agenda 21, and through what it calls 'multi-stakeholder dialogues'.

In all, there *is* a pattern of increasing negotiation, co-operation, participation and institutional development. Whether this can be justifiably called *global* environmental governance is another matter. Indeed, I suggest here that it cannot, on three related grounds. First, the tests of co-operation and democratisation have been met more rhetorically than substantively. Second, the 'global' is particularistic rather than universal, normatively embedded in state-centrism and ultimately blind to local voices and the demands of justice and equity. Finally, environmental governance, whether defined as global or international, has not improved the state of the global environment.

Reassessing co-operation?

Liberal optimists derive comfort from the expanding web of agreements and institutions as attempts to 'generate global responsibility from within the state system'.[34] As noted above, states have agreed to work together guided by the principles of democracy and transparency according to Agenda 21. Each decade sees an increase in the number of agreements negotiated, adopted and implemented. The years immediately following the Rio Summit were characterised by a bout of frenzied negotiating activity which seemed to suggest that states and governments were energised by the Summit and were prepared to move quickly to give effect to the principles and agreements they had either negotiated or signed there. The two UN treaties opened for signature at Rio – the Framework Convention on Climate Change (FCCC) and the Convention on Biological Diversity (CBD) – were given speedy international legal effect within two years of the conference and a number of other environmental agreements were adopted in the glare of post-Rio international attention.[35]

Despite this, co-operation has been primarily evidenced in a willingness to negotiate rather than in substantive outcomes. The 'unprecedentedly high degree of international co-operation and *mutual understanding*'[36] that is a minimum requirement for global environmental governance is not forthcoming. Environmental treaties and institutions are less than effective at meeting the environmental challenges before us. The exigencies of consensus diplomacy give rise to lowest common denominator agreements or, as Underdal puts it, the 'law of the least ambitious programme'.[37] Treaties are cautious agreements with permissive sanctions and inadequate targets. Institutions often lack formal competence and real powers. They are often poorly funded and have little political clout. The mechanisms of environmental governance do not 'institutionalise global responsibility' (despite claims to the contrary).[38]

Both UNEP and CSD have achieved more than they could have been expected to (although the record of CSD is weaker in this regard) but less than they need to. Neither has executive powers. Both have been constrained by political factors from the outset and by a continuing lack of political and financial commitment from member states, despite declaratory flourishes to the contrary. At the 1972 Stockholm Conference, developed countries were reluctant to authorise another specialised agency which would require their financial support. Developing countries – often newly independent – were opposed to any new UN body which might have an effective mandate (or even an ineffective one) to place restrictions on development and economic growth on environmental grounds. Existing UN agencies already dealing with some aspect of the environmental agenda were intent on guarding their turf (although, according to Soroos, none of them wanted to take responsibility for implementing the Stockholm Action Plan[39]). As noted above, UNEP is thus authorised only to catalyse, co-ordinate and monitor. The CSD has remained primarily a talking shop and has faced considerable difficulties in proving its worth.[40]

Real authoritative and executive institutional power in global environmental governance is located outside the UN, or at least for the most part outside its effective formal control. The Global Environment Facility (GEF), established in 1991 under the joint authority of UNEP, the UNDP and the World Bank, has become the primary funding mechanism for the 'global environment'. Its mandate is to fund the incremental costs to developing countries of their attempts to limit the global impacts in four key environmental areas: oceans pollution, climate change, loss of biodiversity and ozone depletion. All three agencies have implementation tasks, but it is the World Bank which houses and manages the GEF Secretariat and the GEF Trust Fund. This central and authoritative role played by the World Bank has kept the GEF under critical scrutiny even though it was restructured in 1994 to make it both more democratic (at least in terms of developing country representation) and more transparent.

The World Bank's contribution to global environmental governance is not confined to the GEF. It has become institutionally central to the pursuit of sustainable development, as well as materially central to continued environmental decline in those countries in which it funds projects and programmes.[41] Since the early 1990s the World Bank's environmental profile has increased with the expansion of the Environment Department, the appointment of a Vice-President for Environmentally and Socially Sustainable Development Network and the commissioning of various internal and external reports on environmental assessment requirements and the Bank's overall environmental strategy. The Bank's environmental profile has also increased, or at least been made more public, with relentless attention from NGOs and grassroots organisations to the environmental impact of Bank-funded projects, the continued dislocation of local communities in the face of Bank-supported infrastructure projects, including large dams and highways, and the environmental inconsistencies in the continued funding, for example, of fossil-fuel based energy generation plants. As Soroos notes, 'despite . . . efforts to improve its environmental image, questions persist about whether the World Bank has actually enacted sufficient reforms'.[42]

The most recent, least transparent and perhaps most powerful addition to the institutional and ideational structures of global environmental governance is the WTO. The WTO's interest in the environment supposedly harks back to the 1970s with the establishment under the General Agreement on Tariffs and Trade (GATT) – in 1972 – of an environmental working group which did not in fact meet until 1992 as the GATT Group on Environmental Measures in International Trade (EMIT). The new WTO's Committee on Trade and the Environment (CTE) is a product of the Marrakech Agreement, mandated to discuss a range of environment and trade related issues including the use of trade restrictive measures in MEAs. Its report to the December 1996 Singapore WTO Ministerial Conference, in which it recommended more discussions, is generally dismissed as having added little to the debate.

Greatest attention has focused on two aspects of the WTO's involvement in environmental governance. The first is its lack of transparency. CTE meetings are dominated by trade experts and have been closed to environmental and civil society organisations. The second is the impact of WTO rulings and agreements on attempts by governments to implement domestic environmental protection legislation through restricting the import of products which do not conform to certain environmental standards. GATT and WTO dispute panels have generally ruled that such actions are incompatible with provisions which prohibit trade discrimination on the basis of production methods.[43] Thus, environmental protection is regarded with some distaste by liberal trade economists as a cover for economic protectionism.

Tensions between developed and developing countries over environmental degradation and sustainable development remain. There has been little real commitment to the important cross-sectoral concerns about providing new and additional financial and technology resources, debt, inequitable trading relations or poverty alleviation, all of which featured in the Brundtland Report as crucial to the global pursuit of sustainable development. Global funding for sustainable development remains unacceptably low, despite a reaffirmation at Rio of the UN's 0.7 per cent ODA/GNP target. Many industrialised countries have been keen to depoliticise the international environmental agenda, directing attention away from controversial issues of funding to the technical (and allegedly non-political) tasks of establishing modalities and implementing standards.

The retreat from the optimism and apparent commitment of Rio was most evident in Earth Summit II – the (19th) UNGASS Review of the Implementation of Agenda 21. Only five years after the Summit whose motto was 'last chance to save the Earth', governments attending UNGASS were unable to reach consensus on a political statement and, despite adopting a Programme for Further Implementation, could find little of real substance to agree upon except that 'the planet's health is generally worse than ever'.[44] At best, this modified governance is 'too slow [and] too laborious'.[45] At worst, it represents a 'total disconnection' with reality.[46]

Defining the 'global': whose common future?

The sense of the 'global' has been captured in metaphors intended to reflect our shared vulnerability to and responsibility for global insecurities – 'our common future',[47] a 'global partnership',[48] and 'our global neighbourhood'.[49] Despite this emphasis, the global has been defined in a way that serves to advantage the privileged interests of the few rather than the collective interests of the many. Indeed, it has been exacerbated by the growing involvement of the World Bank and particularly the WTO in global environmental governance. In their critique of the 'rigid neo-liberal ideas' of the Bretton Woods institutions, Redclift and Sage identify a deep integration of the 'global economy which has enabled the majority of the population in the North to greatly expand its capacity for consuming the resources of the Southern hemisphere'.[50] The hegemony of globalism is not one of equitable burden sharing. Shiva argues that the global, as presently constructed, represents a 'particular local and parochial interest which has been globalised through the scope of its reach'[51] where that parochial interest reflects the concerns of the most powerful industrialised countries and the world's economic and multinational corporate elites.

The local is most often written out of the liberal optimistic version of global environmental governance. There has been growing unrest among NGOs and grassroots organisations that the much lauded democratisation of environmental governance has done little to democratise or make equitable the outcomes, with the poor, indigenous communities and women (especially in developing countries) disproportionately affected by the impact of environmental degradation while contributing little, globally, to their causes. As Woods suggests, there is 'little evidence of any widespread consensus or acceptance of a moral case for alleviating inequalities . . . or for reforming the international system in the name of justice'.[52] The emphasis on effective and efficient institutions takes little real account of the relations of power and powerlessness which characterise the global politics of the environment. Problems of ecology and politics are recast as solutions to be found in technology, modernisation and the benefits of economic liberalism. Yet environmental degradation is not simply the result of past ignorance, weak policies or the wrong policy choices. It is, as Paul Wapner observes, also 'an expression of privilege and power'.[53] Thus the poor are demonised as perpetrators of environmental decline and as a barrier to sustainable development, rather than attention being paid to the ways in which poverty and insecurity are, as Redclift and Sage note, socially transmitted.[54] At the same time multinational corporations, globally responsible for extensive environmental degradation and resource depletion, are cast as corporate environmentalists upon whom we can rely for the solutions to sustainable development.

In this particularistic version of the global, environmental concerns which do not meet the privileged criteria of the global are excluded from the arena of responsibility of the world community of states, narrowing rather than expanding the agenda of commitment. Thus climate change and ozone depletion are 'global', requiring commitment from all countries regardless of their contribution to the problem and neatly avoiding the fact that these 'global' and 'common' problems are created very much by the activities of a few. Desertification is not 'global' and therefore, despite the extent to which the causes of desertification are often caught up in the globalised and shadow economies associated with land degradation, deforestation and industrialised agriculture, there is much less commitment to the principles of burden sharing.[55]

Environmental challenges such as loss of biodiversity and deforestation contribute further to suspicions about how the global is defined and in whose interests. It is primarily Northern-based corporations which have benefited and will continue to benefit from the exploitation of genetic diversity – 'gene robbery', as Shiva calls it[56] – particularly in the field of pharmaceuticals and agriculture. Tropical deforestation constitutes an ecological 'double assault' on climate change in particular as well as biodiversity and deforestation. While the 'global' benefits are disproportionately accumulated by industrialised countries, developing countries are expected to bear the main economic costs of mitigating biodiversity and tropical forest loss in the interests of the 'global'. Further, the difference between local environmental problems and what we understand as global concerns is often a matter only of degree. As Lipschutz and Conca point out, 'phenomena such as soil erosion and land degradation that are depicted as "local" – and thus relegated to a lesser sense of urgency – are . . . [nevertheless] linked by economic, political and social institutions of much broader, and often global, extent'.[57]

The 'global' also remains firmly embedded in state-centrism. The patterns of environmental governance which dominate global ecopolitics do not represent a morphing of state-centrism into some kind of post-Westphalian order whose normative and institutional co-ordinates are different albeit uncertain. The state is central to international environmental public policy and the sovereignty principle is alive and well, everywhere affirmed in multi-lateral environmental agreements. The principle that states have the sovereign right to exploit their own resources is a standard invocation. Governments pursue 'national' interests rather than global ones, despite the countervailing principle that states should not cause damage to the environment of other states or areas beyond national jurisdiction. 'Global' environmental govern-ance does not encourage or require states to act as the local agents of the common good.[58]

The role of the state is not, however, fixed in the arena of global ecopolitics, particularly in light of the contest and uncertain relationship between globalisation and the sovereign state. While the state as interested self-maximiser or agent of elite economic interests is perceived as 'enemy' of the environment, it is also seen as the vehicle by which those corporate interests can be challenged. The role of the state in the face of the environmental challenges of globalisation can thus be strengthened because it has the resources to enforce the implementation of environmental agreements even as those international environmental agreements themselves are seen to limit sovereign choice and actions.[59] This ambivalence towards the state and sovereignty is perhaps most evident in intellectual critiques of and public opposition to the WTO as a proto-supranational organisation with the authority to overthrow sovereign attempts to protect the environment, as noted above.

The increasingly ambiguous and indeed ambivalent role of the state in world ecopolitics is also bound up in uncertainties about the nature of political community and the reconfiguration of identity. Both globalisation and environmental change are, in some highly contested way, deterritorialising identity and unbundling it from the state. The social bond based on the state is weakening.[60] In the face of the state's increasing inability to fulfil the social contract to provide security, including security from environmental degradation and its social and economic consequences, its normative appeal and its legitimacy are, if not in decline, certainly under scrutiny.[61] The con-sequences are equally contested. There is much emphasis on a Kaplanesque fragmented and violent identity politics or a Huntingtonian transformation into civilisational identities, the former at least tied closely to assumptions about conflict over scarce resources and environmental decline. A more optimistic scenario raises the possibility of a 'widespread environmental awareness' which provides the basis for 'a real world-wide community'.[62] Thus communitarian and particularist nationalism gives way to cosmopolitan identities based on mutual obligation and commitment beyond the borders of the state.

The examination of new sites of political and normative activity are also bound up in critical understandings of environmental governance as a *transformative* experience rather than an institutional practice. Resistance to the neoliberal 'global' has been most strongly manifest in a re-localisation of world politics against what Falk calls the 'predatory dimensions of globalization'.[63] Non-state activity is not new to environmental politics. It is now conventional to accept the existence of 'global civil society' or 'world civic politics'[64] or 'world domestic politics'.[65] Contemporary environmental civil activism is, however, more than a quantitative development – more NGOs engaged in a wider range of activities, reflecting the addition of new actors to the global politics of the environment. It is, in its most radical form, qualitatively different: transnational, vigilant, resistant. It is perceived as an 'expression of the globalization of democratic sentiments'.[66] Civil society thus exists, in theory at least and sometimes in practice, as the voice of the 'local' in a mutually constitutive 'tug-of-war' with the state. In the contours of global environmental politics, civil society is variously presented as evidence of the commitment of states and institutions to a more democratic pluralist form of environmental governance and as evidence of the incapacity of states and the inadequacies of state-centric ideologies in which states are being pushed beyond their own sovereign purposes. Cox identifies this rather more radically as a 'new dialectical surge of countervailing forces'.[67] Nevertheless, it is becoming increasingly important to distinguish between civil society as resistance globalism, and civil society as professionalised non-state activism. Chatterjee and Finger, for example, are intensely critical of the NGOs who have become environmental managerialists and insiders to the multilateralism of environmental governance.[68] Participatory rights run the risk of becoming most meaningful for those NGOs which are 'well-organised, well-financed and well-informed'.[69]

Protecting the environment: continued decline

Young suggests that the ultimate test of an effective governance system is that it must 'channel behaviour in such a way as to eliminate or substantially ameliorate the problem that led to its creation'.[70] As suggested earlier in this chapter, this has not happened. The blunt conclusion of UNEP's first *Global Environmental Outlook*, published just prior to UNGASS, was that 'from a global perspective, the environment has continued to degrade ... [and] progress towards a sustainable future is just too slow'.[71] The Secretary-General's report *Global Change and Sustainable Development: Critical Trends*, published at the same time, also drew attention to continued dangers associated with patterns of unsustainable development while also holding out the possibility of positive and effective policy interventions.[72] UNEP's second *Global Environmental Outlook* simply reinforced the view that not enough has been done or achieved, observing that 'the global system of environmental management is moving ... much too slowly'.[73]

Recently negotiated agreements will do little to reverse this trend.[74] The CBD has done little to halt continued species extinction: much of the recent negotiation under the CBD has focused on intellectual property rights, biosafety and the commodification of genetic information. Land degradation continues despite the Convention to Combat Desertification. The Kyoto Protocol which sets greenhouse reduction targets for industrialised countries will do little to come close to stabilising atmospheric concentrations of greenhouse gases – that would require cuts in CO_2 emissions of up to 60 per cent – and even stabilised concentrations will not reverse the impacts of global warming. Deforestation has not been slowed in most of the countries in which it has been identified as an issue for concern – and there is still no legally binding agreement on deforestation or even agreement on what constitutes a sustainably managed forest. Where deforestation has been halted, often by government decree as in Thailand or China, it is simply displaced elsewhere. Forests in temperate, usually industrialised countries continue to be decimated by disease and pollution. Projections for water capacity suggest that within three decades up to two-thirds of the world's population could be facing moderate to high water stress. Indeed, the difficulties surrounding the sixth Conference of Parties (COP 6) in 2000 and 2001 brought into question the very future of the Kyoto Protocol and the commitment of the greenhouse profligate industrialised countries to make the deep cuts needed to address climate change.

Conclusion

There is no doubt that there have been changes in the international governance of the environment and the management of environmental change. The contemporary suite of environmental organisations, agreements and principles is much more extensive and comprehensive than that of the early 1970s when transboundary environmental concerns began to attract serious international attention. There have even been some successes. Implementation of the Montreal Protocol has resulted in the likely repair of a depleted ozone layer by about 2050. Under the Basel Convention, the transboundary dumping of toxic waste has been slowly reduced, although production of such waste seems to have been little affected. As argued in this chapter, this increase in multilateralism, rules-based co-operation and recognition of stakeholders – while welcome – does not qualify as *global* governance. Most international environmental agreements go nowhere near encoding the kinds of behaviours and targets that are required to mitigate let alone halt or reverse the negative impacts of environmental change. The negotiation of such agreements is characterised by national interest contests and a general unwillingness to commit the kind of funding that is required to achieve sustainable development at either a national or global level. The ecological footprint of the richer countries continues to dominate and distort the world economy and those who are disproportionately disadvantaged by the social and economic consequences of environmental change remain on the margins of environmental governance.

The problems lie in more than 'shortcomings in institutions, political will and resources'.[75] Environmental multilateralism does little to acknowledge or address the *structural* causes (and consequences) of environmental degradation. The challenge is therefore more than adopting better environmental policy and management practices.[76] The most appropriate strategies for achieving a genuinely global form of environmental governance remain uncertain and contested. The broad contours of global environmental governance are more clear. At its base is a genuine commitment to common and shared interests, ecological values and an emphasis on human rather than state security. Such a commitment mandates the empowerment of the 'local' and those most directly affected by environmental degradation as a way to hold accountable public and private power and authority. It requires greater transparency, less centralisation, and a more equal and equitable sharing of wealth and technology. It requires, in effect, new forms of political community and a new pattern of politics that is truly global rather than simply internationalism with a kinder face.

Notes

1 For more on how the global politics of the environment is located along these axes, see Lorraine Elliott 'The Global Politics of the Environment: the hegemony of neo-liberalism', in Stephanie Lawson (ed.) *The New Agenda for International Relations: from polarization to globalization in world politics* (London: Polity Press, 2001).

2 Peter H. Sand, *Lessons Learned in Global Environmental Governance* (Washington, DC: World Resources Institute, 1990) p. 1.

3 David Law, 'Global Environmental Issues and the World Bank', in Stephen Gill (ed.) *Globalization, Democratization and Multilateralism* (London/Tokyo: Macmillan/United Nations University Press, 1997), p. 171.

4 Paul Wapner, 'Governance in Global Civil Society', in Oran R. Young (ed.) *Global Governance: drawing insights from the environmental experience* (Cambridge, MA: MIT Press, 1997), p. 65.

5 Oran R. Young, 'Rights, Rules and Resources in World Affairs', in Oran R. Young (ed.) *Global Governance: drawing insights from the environmental experience*, p. 4.

6 Norman J. Vig, 'Introduction: Governing the International Environment', in Norman J. Vig and Regina S. Axelrod (eds), *The Global Environment: institutions, law and policy* (Washington, DC: CQ Press, 1999), p. 5.

7 Marvin S. Soroos, 'From Stockholm to Rio: the evolution of global environmental governance', in Norman J. Vig and Michael E. Kraft (eds), *Environmental Policy in the 1990s: toward a new agenda* (Washington: CQ Press, 1994), p. 301.

8 See Young, 'Rights, Rules and Resources'.

9 Intergovernmental Panel on Climate Change, *IPCC Second Assessment: climate change 1995* (Geneva: UNEP/WMO, 1995), p. 4.

10 IPCC, *Second Assessment*, p. 5.

11 World Resources Institute, *Sustainable Development Information Service: global trends* (Washington, DC: WRI, 2000) [http://www.wri.org/trends/index.html; accessed 26 June 2000].

12 See WRI, *Global trends.*
13 See WRI, *Global trends.*
14 United Nations General Assembly, 'International cooperation in the monitoring, assessment and anticipation of environmental threats and in assistance in cases of environmental emergency', A/RES/44/224, 85th Plenary Meeting, 22 December 1989.
15 Cited in A. J. Fairclough, 'Global Environmental and Natural Resource Problems – their Economic, Political and Security Implications', *The Washington Quarterly*, 14: 1 (Winter 1991), p. 96.
16 For an extended treatment of these issues, see Andrew Hurrell, 'A Crisis of Ecological Viability? Global environmental change and the nation state', *Political Studies*, XLII (1994), pp. 146–65; Karen T. Litfin, 'Sovereignty in World Eco-politics', *Mershon International Studies Review*, 41: 2 (November 1997), pp. 167–204; Paul Wapner 'Reorienting State Sovereignty: rights and responsibilities in the environmental age', in Karen T. Litfin (ed.) *The Greening of Sovereignty in World Politics*, (Cambridge, MA: MIT Press, 1998). I acknowledge here the intellectual dangers that arise from working within the 'Westphalian shadowland' which continues to privilege the state as the starting point for interrogation, even those which proceed from a critical standpoint. See Richard Falk 'Global Civil Society: perspectives, initiatives, movements', *Oxford Development Studies*, 26: 1 (February 1998), p. 100.
17 World Commission on Environment and Development, *Our Common Future* (Oxford: Oxford University Press, 1997), p. 27.
18 Tony Brenton, *The Greening of Machiavelli: the evolution of international environmental politics* (London: Royal Institute of International Affairs/Earthscan, 1994), p. 7.
19 Maurice Strong, 'ECO '92: critical challenges and global solutions', *Journal of International Affairs*, 44: 2 (Winter 1991), p. 297.
20 Patricia Mische, 'Ecological Security and the Need to Reconceptualise Sovereignty', *Alternatives*, XIV (1989), pp. 394–5.
21 Marc A. Levy, Peter M. Haas and Robert O. Keohane 'Institutions for the Earth: promoting international environmental protection', *Environment*, 34: 4 (1992), p. 36.
22 See Lorraine Elliott, *The Global Politics of the Environment* (London: Macmillan Press, 1998), p. 97.
23 Law, 'Global Environmental Issues', p. 177.
24 See Paul Wapner, 'Environmental Ethics and Global Governance: engaging the international liberal tradition', *Global Governance*, 3: 2 (May–August 1997), pp. 213–31.
25 Michael Redclift and Colin Sage, 'Global Environmental Change and Global Inequality: North/South perspectives', *International Sociology*, 13: 4 (December 1998), p. 512.
26 See United Nations Development Programme, *Human Development Report 1998* (New York: Oxford University Press, 1998).
27 Young, 'Rights, Rules and Resources', p. 1.
28 Krueger counts almost 200 multilateral environmental agreements. See Jonathan Krueger, *International Trade and the Basel Convention* (London: Royal Institute of International Affairs/Earthscan, 1999). Weiss suggests that there are over 900 international legal instruments with 'one or more important provisions concerned with the environment'. See Edith Brown Weiss, 'The Emerging Structure of International Law' in Vig and Axelrod, *The Global Environment*, p. 111.
29 United Nations Conference on Environment and Development, *Report of the United Nations Conference on Environment and Development: Annex II, Agenda 21*, A/CONF.151/26 (vol. I–III), 12 August 1992, paragraph 38.2.

30 For more on these key principles, see, *inter alia*, Elliott, *The Global Politics of the Environment*, pp. 100–5; 214–15; Edith Brown Weiss, *In Fairness to Future Generations: international law, common patrimony and intergenerational equity* (Dobbs Ferry, NY: Transnational Publishers, 1988).

31 WCED, *Our Common Future*, p. 43.

32 Oran Young, 'Global Governance: toward a theory of decentralized world order', in Young (ed.) *Global Governance: drawing insights from the environmental experience*, p. 274.

33 See Jared Blumenfeld, 'Institutions: the United Nations Commission on Sustainable Development', *Environment*, 36: 10 (1994), p. 3.

34 Wapner, 'Reorienting State Sovereignty', p. 283.

35 These included the 1994 UN Convention to Combat Desertification (to use its short title); the 1995 UN Agreement on Straddling and Highly Migratory Fish Stocks; the convening of a global summit on the sustainable development of small island states in 1994; the adoption of the 1997 Kyoto Protocol to the Framework Convention on Climate Change; the 1998 convention on Prior Informed Consent; the negotiation and adoption of a Protocol on Biosafety in 2000, and negotiations for a convention on Persistent Organic Pollutants.

36 Fairclough, 'Global Environmental and Natural Resource Problems', p. 83; emphasis added.

37 Cited in Sand, *Lessons Learned*, p. 6.

38 See, for example, Wapner, 'Reorienting State Sovereignty', p. 230.

39 Marvin S. Soroos, 'Global Institutions and the Environment: an evolutionary perspective' in Vig and Axelrod (eds), *The Global Environment*.

40 See Lorraine Elliott, 'Tries Hard, Could do Better: the United Nations and global environmental governance', paper presented to American Political Science Association Annual Meeting, Atlanta, 2–5 September 1999.

41 For a *very* lengthy and detailed history of the environment in the World Bank, see Robert Wade, 'Greening the Bank: the struggle over the environment, 1970–1995', in Kapur Devesh, John P. Lewis and Richard Webb (eds), *The World Bank: its first half century – Vol 2. Perspectives* (Washington, DC: Brookings Institution, 1997).

42 Soroos, 'Global Institutions and the Environment', p. 46.

43 The most famous of these rulings (both involving United States legislation) are the tuna–dolphin ruling of 1991 and the shrimp–turtle ruling of 1998. Other trade and process and production methods related debates include those over eco-labelling and sustainable timber.

44 United Nations Department of Public Information (UN DPI), 'Earth Summit Review Ends with few Commitments', *Round-up Press Release*, DPI/1916/SD, July 1997 [http://www.un.org/ecosocdev/geninfo/sustdev/es5final.htm; accessed 4 March 1998].

45 Razali cited in UNDPI, 'Earth Summit Review'.

46 Bramble cited in UNDPI, 'Earth Summit Review'.

47 WCED, *Our Common Future*.

48 UNCED, *Report*.

49 Commission on Global Governance, *Our Global Neighborhood* (Oxford: Oxford University Press, 1995).

50 Redclift and Sage, 'Global Environmental Change', p. 507.

51 Vandana Shiva, 'The Greening of the Global Reach', in Wolfgang Sachs (ed.), *Global Ecology: a new arena of political conflict* (London: Zed Books, 1993) p. 150.

52 Ngaire Woods, 'Order, Globalization and Inequality in World Politics', in Andrew Hurrell and Ngaire Woods (eds) *Inequality, Globalization and World Politics* (Oxford: Oxford University Press, 1999) p. 12.

53 Wapner, 'Environmental Ethics', p. 216.

54 Redclift and Sage, 'Global Environmental Change', p. 500.
55 The EC and the US were strongly opposed to having desertification described as a 'global' problem during the negotiations for the Convention to Combat Desertification, even though over one-third of the world's land surface is affected or threatened by this extensive form of land degradation.
56 Vandana Shiva, 'Biodiversity, Biotechnology and Profit: the need for a people's plan to protect biodiversity', *The Ecologist*, 20: 2 (March/April 1990), pp. 44–7.
57 Ronnie D. Lipschutz and Ken Conca, 'The Implications of Global Ecological Interdependence', in Ronnie D. Lipschutz and Ken Conca (eds), *The State and Social Power in Global Environmental Politics* (New York: Columbia University Press, 1993), p. 331.
58 The phrase is Hedley Bull's; see Andrew Linklater, 'The Evolving Spheres of International Justice', *International Affairs*, 75: 3 (1999), p. 478.
59 Of course the counter argument is that acceding to an international agreement is an act of, rather than a diminution of sovereignty.
60 See Richard Devetak and Richard Higgott, 'Justice Unbound? Globalization, states and the transformation of the social bond', *International Affairs*, 75: 3 (July 1999), pp. 483–98.
61 See, for example, Hurrell, 'A Crisis of Ecological Viability'; Litfin, 'Sovereignty in World Ecopolitics'.
62 Daniel Deudney, 'Global Environmental Rescue and the Emergence of World Domestic Politics', in Ronnie D. Lipschutz and Ken Conca (eds), *The State and Social Power in Global Environmental Politics* (New York: Columbia University Press, 1993), pp. 289–90.
63 Richard Falk, 'Global Civil Society', p. 104.
64 Paul Wapner, *Environmental Activism and World Civil Politics* (Albany, NY: State University of New York Press, 1996).
65 Deudney, 'Global Environmental Rescue'.
66 Litfin, 'Sovereignty in World Ecopolitics', p. 192.
67 Cited in Richard Falk, 'Environmental Protection in an Era of Globalization', *Yearbook of International Environmental Law*, 6 (1995), p. 22.
68 Pratap Chatterjee and Matthias Finger, *The Earth Brokers* (London: Routledge, 1994).
69 Anon., 'International Environmental Law', *Harvard Law Review*, 104: 7 (May 1991), p. 1589.
70 Oran R. Young, *International Governance: protecting the environment in a stateless society* (Ithaca: Cornell University Press, 1994), p. 30.
71 United Nations Environment Program, *Global Environmental Outlook: executive summary* (Nairobi: UNEP, 1997) [http://www.unep.org/unep/eia/geo1/exsum/ex2.htm; accessed 10 March 1998].
72 United Nations Secretary-General, *Global Change and Sustainable Development: critical trends*, Report of the Secretary-General, Commission on Sustainable Development, Fifth Session, 1997 [http://www.un.org/dpcsd/dsd/trends.htm; accessed 5 March 1998].
73 UNEP, *Global Environmental Outlook 2000: GEO-2000 UNEP's millennium report on the environment* (London: Earthscan, 1999), p. xxiii.
74 One of the few MEAs which has had some success is the Montreal Protocol on substances that deplete the ozone layer. Even if the reversal of ozone depletion is not yet achieved, the social and economic costs will continue for some decades to come, and parties to the Protocol are now facing the challenges of illegal trade in ozone depleting substances (ODS).
75 Peter S. Thacher, 'Multilateral cooperation and global change', *Journal of International Affairs*, 44: 2 (Winter 1991), p. 435.
76 For a reformist summary of global governance for sustainable development, see WCED, *Our Common Future*, p. 65.

5 Global governance, human rights and the 'problem' of culture[1]

Stephanie Lawson

Introduction

The 'cultural turn' in the social sciences generally, and in the discipline of International Relations (IR) in particular, has had a significant impact on normative theory over the last decade or so. In many political debates, 'culture' certainly seems to have replaced 'ideology' (as generally understood in right/ left terms) as a key normative focus. The reasons for this are various, but in IR it is at least partly related to the end of the Cold War. As one leading human rights commentator has said, the post-Cold War period has seen a significant renewal of interest in the merits of universal versus relative value systems and the role of culture in their detection and interpretation.[2]

The culture concept is clearly central to the debates revolving around cosmopolitan and communitarian approaches to moral issues in world politics. At the heart of these debates lie a range of theoretical and practical issues to do with human rights. And of course human rights are central issues for global governance in the post-Cold War era and are implicated in a range of specific global policy concerns from aid and development to sanctions and humanitarian intervention.

The contemporary international human rights regime – an integral part of contemporary global governance – consists of an ensemble of formal and informal institutions and practices, including the United Nations and a plethora of regional bodies and non-government organisations (NGOs). The development of these institutions and the practices generated by them has been an on-going process since the United Nations Commission on Human Rights was established in 1946, and the foundational document, the Universal Declaration of Human Rights, was formally passed by the General Assembly in 1948.

The two major covenants that followed – that is, the covenant on civil and political rights and the covenant on economic, social and cultural rights – have subsequently formed the basis of an assumed cultural, even civilisational, division between 'the West' and 'the Rest', even though lip-service is frequently paid to the indivisibility of these two clusters of rights. This was clearly apparent in the 'Bangkok Declaration' issued by the leaders of a number of

Asian countries preceding the Vienna Convention in 1993. The cluster of civil and political rights is seen to reflect an historically and culturally specific 'Western' concern with individual rights. Indeed, the whole package of ideas surrounding the notion of 'the individual' is seen to be uniquely and irredeemably 'Western'.

On the other hand, the ideas and principles underscoring the cluster of economic, social and cultural rights are seen to reflect not individual rights, but collective rights. And, in turn, the notion of collective rights is seen as reflecting the cultural milieu of most 'non-Western' people/s. Thus a very neat, and very simplistic, cultural/moral dichotomy has been produced between the individualistic West and the collectivist non-West. Arguably, this is simply another bipolar disorder that has afflicted political and social theory far too much in recent times. And it has also created difficulties for the legitimacy of an international human rights regime.

The 'problem' of culture for human rights and global governance lies essentially in the relativistic notion that because these issues are deeply value-laden, they cannot be anything other than 'culture-specific'. This, in turn, is based on an assumption that the entire value-system that an individual, or a community, possesses is more or less determined by their 'cultural patrimony'. This term is very closely aligned with a concept of tradition. 'Cultural patrimony' has been defined as denoting 'a world of shared, public meanings, which are inherited from the past, developed and contested in the present, and transmitted across the generations to the future'.[3] While this definition clearly emphasises the idea of continuity between the past, present and future of a distinct community, it also includes a more specifically dynamic element, and that is, that cultural patrimony is open to contestation in the present and therefore to change.

The idea of culture as a medium of change is something that we shall return to later in this chapter. First, however, it is important to look at aspects of the culture concept and how it has developed in the social sciences. Of particular interest is the way in which the concept was developed in the discipline of anthropology and how this has fed into the social sciences more generally, and IR in particular. One point to be noted from the start is that anthropological theories of cultural relativism were developed at a particular time, under particular circumstances, and for particular purposes. Moreover, while the early doctrine of cultural relavism did have some quite radical political implications at the time it was formulated, in more recent times it has been deployed to support some profoundly conservative and authoritarian political projects. In turn, these are clearly important for contemporary issues of human rights and global governance.

Culture and the social sciences

The concept of culture almost defies definition, but that has rarely prevented academics and other intellectuals from attempting the task. Indeed, such a

complex, ambiguous and shifting concept is often regarded as a challenge –
as is well illustrated by the enormous number of books and articles that
have been generated as a result.[4] I shall take a recent work by Chris Jenks as
a starting point, for he has conveniently identified four major strands of
thinking about culture that help to provide an initial contemporary focus.
These are:

1   Culture as a cerebral category which embodies the idea of human intel-
    lectual, literary and artistic achievement as reflected in the evaluative
    approach of Matthew Arnold.
2   Culture as a more embodied and collective category which includes a
    notion of intellectual and moral development and which was initially
    informed by the evolutionary theorists who pioneered anthropology.
3   Culture as a descriptive and concrete body of material arts as well as
    intellectual work, carrying with it notions of elitism.
4   Culture as a social category which encompasses the whole way of life of
    a people.[5]

The first and third categories are less relevant (although not entirely
irrelevant) to the main issues that I want to deal with in this chapter. The
second and fourth categories, however, capture some of the key elements of
an anthropological approach. In relation to this, another recent work on
cultural politics by Glenn Jordan and Chris Weedon[6] has also provided
four categories of culture, two of which coincide to some extent with the
approaches to be dealt with here. These are:

1   Culture as 'a particular way of life, whether of a people, a period or a
    group' and which is therefore informed by a 'common spirit'.
2   Culture as 'the signifying system through which necessarily (though among
    other means) a social order is communicated, reproduced, experienced
    and explored'.

The key point of the first category is that culture cannot be reduced to
any particular individual, but exists only as the property of a particular group.
Insofar as this denotes the existence of cultures in the plural, it envisages a
world made up of individual cultural entities. These are usually 'named'
cultures such as 'Aboriginal culture', 'Japanese culture', 'classical Greek
culture', 'Aztec culture', and so on. This category accords with the most
common anthropological applications of the concept.

The second category implies a concept of culture as immanent, that is, as
a dimension of virtually all economic, social and political institutions, and
which resides in, what Jordan and Weedon call 'a set of *material* practices
which constitute meanings, values and subjectivities'. They argue that this
conception of culture comes out of cultural studies, and takes two main forms:
'In its weaker dialectical form, it suggests that as human beings create culture,

so culture creates them. In its strong version, a version which comes out of structuralist and poststructuralist theory, culture determines subjectivity'.[7]

There are numerous problems and issues raised by these definitions or categories. The first that I shall mention briefly here is the notion that culture encompasses 'the whole way of life of *a* people' and therefore exists as the property of a particular, identifiable group that can be marked off from other groups. This leads to the idea that one can identify and isolate an entity as *a* culture – a singular, unique totality. And if one subscribes to the view that moral values are specific to these entities, the next logical step is to assign these entities the status of free-standing, self-contained moral systems in their own right. If cultural specificity is also to be equated with moral specificity then this in turn gives rise to the notion of moral incommensurability as a fact of life, if not a feature of the natural world. This is clearly a problem for the idea of an international human rights regime that is founded on or depends on a notion of the universality of human rights. And it is also a problem for the very idea of global governance.

The 'problem' of culture and moral incommensurability in the theory and practice of international relations has conventionally been resolved in what seems to be a very neat way. I have noted already the tendency evident in some important approaches to culture to envisage the world as consisting of individual cultural entities which may then become 'named cultures'. While anthropologists and others interested in small-scale societies have usually spoken of very localised groups such as 'the Tiwi',[8] political scientists and international relations scholars have usually focused on 'the state'. States, of course, also have names. The point that I am getting to here is that in so much ordinary discourse the names of states and the names of cultures are very often conflated. And very few have problems in taking the name of a geo-political entity such as Japan or Sweden or China, and then talking about 'Japanese culture' or 'Swedish culture' or 'Chinese culture'. The practice is so commonplace and so much a part of our ordinary vocabulary that it becomes simply part of the world as we know it.

The most important point, however, is that conventional IR theory has generally accepted the conflation of culture and state. This is so even though it is recognised that states may contain any number of different cultural groups or minorities. As long as they were termed 'sub-state' then it seems that they could be safely ignored from an IR point of view. This suited the classic realist approach to issues of morality in the international sphere too. If morality was, in the final analysis, a product of culture, and culture was contained within the state, then there was clearly no need to include issues of morality, such as human rights, in the sphere of international relations. This also clearly supports a cultural relativist perspective on international morality.

Nationalist views on culture as well as some versions of communitarianism are similar. With respect to nationalism, the state of course is based on the concept of the nation which is itself usually defined in cultural terms. As I have already suggested, however, most would agree that it is unrealistic to assume that states are completely homogeneous and that cultural differences within states do not exist. In fact, with few exceptions, cultural heterogeneity is probably the most pervasive feature of virtually all modern states. This is despite many 'nation-building' efforts to promote national unifying ideologies and assimilate minorities to a dominant culture. Nonetheless, the ideal at the heart of nationalist theory is a state for each nation, and a single nation for each state.

At another level, if cultures are to be equated with nations and subsumed within states, then it also follows that the cultural differences that count in international relations are those *between* states. I have mentioned already the relativist implications of this position. It also needs to be noted that this position feeds into such issues as sovereignty, independence and non-intervention, not to mention the efficacy of an international human rights regime.

In summary, if it is accepted that morality can only be understood as a product of a particular culture, it follows that what constitutes a 'human right' can only be understood in the context of any particular culture. And if culture is regarded as contained within a sovereign independent state, then clearly intervention by another state or group of states constitutes an unwarranted attack on the right of that state to determine its own moral standards. Culture is then subject to a statist resolution and human rights effectively become subordinate to state rights.

Not surprisingly, this kind of logic has been promoted most strongly by leaders of authoritarian states with poor human rights records. I shall come back to this shortly. In the meantime, more needs to be said about the development of the culture concept in anthropology. Clearly there is not the space to set this out in too much detail, but the critical point I want to make concerns the historical and cultural specificity *of* the theories of historical and cultural specificity themselves that not only underscore the doctrine of cultural relativism, but which have come to pervade so much of the contemporary discourse on human rights and related issues in international ethics.

To provide a proper account of the rise and development of the culture concept and its impact on moral theory would take us on a journey starting at least as far back as Herodotus, through the debates of the pre-Socratics and their concerns with *physis* and *nomos*, to the rise of the modern state and early theories of nationalism, and to a number of significant German thinkers including Herder and Fichte, and then through to the present day. By so doing, incidentally, we would find something of a trans-historical concern with questions of cultural specificity and their implications for moral theory, epistemology, theories of history and so on – a finding which in itself has some interesting implications for theories of historical contextualism.[9]

For obvious reasons of time/space, this account will have to start more than a century ago. It is generally accepted that the modern technical or anthropological meaning of culture became established in English usage in

1871 when Edward B. Tylor, a prominent British social anthropologist, put forward what is still one of the most commonly cited definitions in English: 'Culture or Civilization, taken in its widest ethnographic sense, is that complex whole which includes knowledge, belief, art, morals, custom, and any other capabilities and habits acquired by man as a member of society.'[10] English usages had of course been subject to the influences of other European connotations. Prominent among these was the German concept of *Kultur* (which had itself been adapted from the French) and which had been used more or less as a synonym for civilization.[11]

German Romantic writers in general, and Johann Herder in particular, have been cited as major influences in the development of social scientific thought about culture in the modern period. Herder's ideas certainly seem to have had a profound influence on the emerging discipline of anthropology in the British academy and, later, the development in the US of cultural anthropology. Williams reports, for example, that Tylor was influenced very strongly by Herder, especially to the extent that the latter had spoken of 'cultures' in the plural, thereby denoting the existence of particular and variable cultures evident across different nations and periods of time.[12] Tylor and other anthropologists, following Herder and subsequent Romantic writers, attached themselves firmly to the idea that humanity was sorted into different, unique 'cultural groups' and that these constituted the essential units of human existence.

These ideas provided an important stimulus to the twentieth century anthropological doctrine of cultural relativism which was first developed in an explicit form by the German-American anthropologist, Franz Boas and his followers (most notably Alfred L. Kroeber and Robert H. Lowie). But whereas Tylor had developed his ideas largely within the evolutionary schema which dominated during his time – and which was based implicitly on a hierarchy of 'lower' and 'higher' cultures, Boas and his followers did something quite different, and which is of continuing importance to the way in which culture has been conceptualised in social scientific thought ever since.

While Tylor's work did dispense with some explicit biological links to culture, it was nonetheless characterised by an evolutionary mode of thought which implicitly placed cultural groups in a hierarchy from 'primitive' to 'advanced'. What the Boasian school sought to do was rupture completely the link between culture and biology. The Boasian school aimed very specifically to counter some of the racist assumptions of eugenics and racial anthropology that were prevalent at the time, and this required dispensing with any idea of hierarchy and invoking instead a notion of relativism. But in excluding all biological elements of human behaviour, culture came to be viewed as a bounded realm of phenomena in which virtually all human action was fully determined by social factors.[13]

The point I am making here is that the theory of cultural relativism, *and* the specific notion of culture on which it was based, and on which much subsequent moral theory has been built, emerged in a particular time and place and had a particular task to perform. It was certainly no more 'value-neutral' in itself than the racist theories to which it was opposed, and which it sought to *de*pose.

On the question of values, theories of cultural relativism of course had a great deal to say. In their monumental work of 1952, Kroeber and Kluckhohn came to the conclusion that the properties of culture that seemed most distinctive of it, and most important in its analysis, were values. They said: 'In fact values provide the only basis for the fully intelligible comprehension of culture, because the actual organization of all cultures is primarily in terms of their values.' Moreover these were always 'variable and relative, not predetermined and eternal'.[14] Clearly, the conceptualisation of culture in this way could scarcely avoid having a significant impact on moral theory.

Political science was also strongly influenced by these developments. The period before the Second World War saw the rise of studies under the banner of 'national character' which clearly rested on particularistic notions of culture. Some of these adopted a 'natural history' perspective which drew on nineteenth-century organic models of society. In these, the spirit or soul of the nation, revealed through 'its' culture, emerged as the product of such a long growth process that they were considered to be virtually permanent and unchangeable.[15]

The effective conflation of culture with *a* society was strengthened further in comparative politics in the post-war period through the 'political culture' school. Through the identification of cultural characteristics at the national political level, it was invested with a very strong statist element – thereby privileging, among other things, the role of national political elites. This occurred within some anthropological studies as well, and to the extent that these identified 'cultures' were operating at a national (state) level, their findings were not very different from those of the comparative political scientists.[16]

Although the political culture school was not strictly deterministic in its assumptions, its perspectives were nonetheless marshalled in the construction of political theories of causal determinism. This allowed issues such as political development to be understood as 'rooted' in distinctive national histories and the socialisation of individuals within a particular cultural framework.[17] In turn, this fed back into, and reinforced, theories of moral relativism based on cultural differences. Such differences, however, were assumed to have moral significance largely at the level of the state while sub-state cultural differences received only marginal acknowledgement at best – an approach which also accords with the classical realist assumptions in IR theory mentioned earlier.

Another point to note is that the separation of culture from biology effected by the theory of cultural relativism is often seen as effecting a rigid separation of culture from nature *per se*.[18] But this is arguable. While it is certainly the case that the theory of cultural relativism sought to repudiate *one particular view* of nature associated with biology – and in the process contributed to the demise of 'scientific racism' and other theories based on biological premises – the idea of 'nature' was smuggled back in via other means.

To put it simply, the notion of *a* culture as an 'integrally organised totality' lends itself very readily to the assumption that it is the *natural* vessel within which humans thrive. What then becomes contingent is not the the unit as such, but the particular differences between cultural units. Indeed, 'difference' itself may be objectified in such a way that it becomes a 'natural' dividing line between human communities. The effect is to eliminate contingency as an element in the construction of separate social, political, and moral spaces in the form of 'one culture, one nation, one state'.

To summarise this section, the strenuous assertion of cultural difference, and of the idea that separate cultural entities are more or less equivalent to incommensurable value systems, has been a long-standing feature of the discipline of anthropology. It has also fed into some important areas of political science. Taken together these strands of social and political theory have tended, at least implicitly, to reproduce or reinforce nationalist – and naturalistic – categories of human separation either in existing statist containers or in the case of ethnonationalist secessionist movements, in a possible future state.

This cluster of ideas also tends to support the idea of a state which is legitimised and authenticated through the sovereignty of its cultural essence. This means that both the authentic membership of the community, and the unique moral code it is assumed to possess, is largely determined by this essence. Ideas of this kind have implications not only for practices of exclusion, but also for the way in which 'members' of the community are treated. For example, it has been suggested that one of the ways in which the 'science of culture' has in fact corrupted the 'ethics of culture', especially in its deterministic assumptions, has been to bind each individual person far too tightly into the strait-jacket of his or her social origins.[19] This is apart from the observation that communities do not always treat their own members kindly.[20]

Another issue raised by the deployment of culture in defining the nation, and in turn the state, is the actual choice of definitive cultural elements, *and* who gets to do the choosing. Culture, among other things, functions as a means of social and political control. And as John Clammer has noted, it is two-faced: 'it is both the necessary vehicle for personal and collective identity [but] it can also oppress and distort'.[21] Moreover, political inequality within a group is frequently legitimated by reference to 'the culture' itself. In other words, elite defences of privileged roles are often founded on the self-referential moral structure of 'the culture'. And this is portrayed, more often than not, as embedded deeply in the historical traditions of the entire group.

This also means that the radical nationalism purveyed by some political elites as part of a postcolonial project may go hand-in-hand with a profound cultural conservatism which may not entail a project of emancipation for the ordinary people concerned, but rather a continuation of elite privilege.[22]

In addition, it has been noted that nationalist attempts by political elites to base a state on a cultural group inevitably involves the establishment of 'a decisive hierarchy of cultural allegiances' and its imposition on every person within the assumed cultural group.[23] This has often given rise to heavy-handed exercises in forced cultural homogenisation within the boundaries of states. This was common throughout the modern period in Europe. It has been a feature of many postcolonial regimes around the world as well. And it has obviously led to numerous human rights abuses ranging from acts of repression to ethnic cleansing and wholesale genocide.

To illustrate some of these points, the next section of the chapter will look more closely at some aspects of the contemporary debates about culture and human rights in the Asia-Pacific region. Here, culturalist discourses have produced not only statist categories of culture, but regionalist ones as well. The latter, in particular, are deeply implicated in the broader idea of 'the West' versus 'the Rest'. I shall focus the discussion principally on what, for convenience, I shall call 'Asianism' and its implications for contemporary human rights issues.

Asianism

I mentioned at the beginning that the two UN covenants on human rights – that is, the covenant on civil and political rights and the covenant on economic, social and cultural rights – have been used as a basis for dividing the world between 'the West' and 'the Rest'. This kind of exercise has been especially evident in the so-called 'Asian values' debate which I have else-where described as giving rise to a form of Occidentalism.[24] As far as human rights are concerned, the debate has revolved around a number of issues ranging from political repression, the treatment of minorities, the status of women and labour standards to broader postcolonial concerns to do with cultural and economic imperialism.

At a general level, the cluster of economic, social and cultural rights have been embraced by political leaders in a number of countries in the region – especially China, Singapore, Indonesia and Malaysia – as constituting the essential starting point for approaches to the whole array of human rights. While official rhetoric has tended to give broad endorsement to the universality, indivisibility and inalienability of all categories of human rights, there has been a heavy emphasis on the economic, social and cultural cluster of rights, together with the relegation of civil and political rights to a lower order of priority. Indeed, the former cluster of rights is very often presented as superior to civil and political rights as well as reflecting authentic Asian values.

The most common justification for this approach may be summarised briefly as follows. First, basic subsistence rights must be secured firmly, for it is obvious that sustaining life itself is a prerequisite to the enjoyment of other rights. And in order to secure basic subsistence rights, a certain level of economic development must be attained which, in turn, requires a certain degree of political stability. Political stability, and hence economic development, may be jeopardised if too many political and civil freedoms are permitted. So it is incumbent on state authorities to ensure that political and civil rights do not compromise development objectives. Once a certain level of development is achieved then, and only then, should further political liberalisation be considered. This line of reasoning reflects a pragmatic prioritisation of the categories of rights encapsulated in the idea of 'rice before freedom'.

A second dimension of the argument concerns the question of cultural values. Apart from the practical developmental imperatives, the prioritising of economic, social and cultural rights is also seen as reflecting an inherently 'Asian' approach to human rights generally, especially in the sense that they reflect a concern for the community as a whole rather than individuals. At the same time, political and civil rights, with their focus on the individual person as the bearer of rights – and little apparent emphasis on the duties and obligations that the individual has to the community – are seen as essentially 'Western'. In other words, the latter set of rights are seen as anchored firmly in the broad cultural milieu of the West while the former are viewed as rights which reflect the essential, authentic and legitimate values of 'Asian' societies. This perspective, incidentally, implies more than just the deferment of political and civil rights until such time as a sufficient level of economic, social and political development has been achieved. It suggests that the very nature of these rights is essentially incompatible with Asian culture *per se*.

This further implies that such rights should not be allowed full expression in Asian contexts at all – and that it is incumbent on responsible governments in the region to contain any such tendencies within tolerable limits. An alternative approach is to simply *revise* the basic understanding of political and civil rights, and the democratic institutions and practices of government which enshrine them, so that they reflect more closely the assumed values of Asian societies. This would also prevent the contamination of these societies with undesirable Western practices and values.[25]

A revisionist exercise of precisely this kind has been carried out by the ruling elite in Singapore. Here, a very high level of economic development has already been achieved and so it is scarcely possible to cite development imperatives as a reason for the continuing deferral of full political and civil rights. In 1984, Deputy Prime Minister Goh Chok Tong released a statement which outlined the goal of surpassing Switzerland's standard of living as measured by gross domestic product by the end of the millennium: by the mid-1990s Singapore was well ahead of target.[26] The continuing curtailment of civil and political rights must therefore be justified by reference to other imperatives, and the 'cultural values' argument provides the most convenient of all possible bases for justification. It not only seems to be self-sustaining in terms of contextual authenticity – there is also no use-by date for 'culture' as there is for development targets which are often set in terms of achieving certain quantifiable goals by a specified time.

But in most parts of South East Asia, economic development still has a long way to go in terms of providing a comfortable level of subsistence for many of the people, not to mention educational and other important social and cultural objectives. In contemporary human rights debates, economic development continues to be promoted as the most pressing task of government. One country in the region that has pursued developmental imperatives relentlessly is Malaysia, especially since Dr Mahathir bin Mohamad came to power in 1981. And in terms of standard economic indicators, it has achieved considerable success, the financial crisis of the late 1990s notwithstanding. At the end of his first decade as Prime Minister, Mahathir had set out an ambitious development plan called 'Vision 2020' aimed at making Malaysia a fully developed country (as measured in comparison with the industrialised West) in the course of the next three decades.[27]

More interesting in the Malaysian case, however, is the paradoxical nature of unremitting developmentalism in the direction of Western-style industrial/economic modernisation together with an almost obsessive concern with promoting traditional cultural values. Such apparently contradictory objectives are not all that uncommon. Singapore under Lee Kuan Yew and Goh Chok Tong has been very much the same. And in Japan, rapid industrial and social modernisation has been pursued relentlessly, resulting in a certain fixation on the (alleged) uniqueness of Japanese culture and identity.

Turning now to the historical and geographical specificity of the 'Asian values' debate itself, the first thing to be noted is the particular postcolonial context in which it has emerged. The principal colonisers in the South East/East Asian area, where the debate has been especially vigorous, were of course from Western Europe. The Japanese are an integral part of the region's colonial history as well, but to the extent that the 'Asia' that is imagined in the Asian values debate is constructed largely against an image of 'the West', the history of Japanese colonialism does not figure in the kind of postcolonialism that provides much of the ideological atmosphere surrounding the debate. And it is notions about the collective rights of 'peoples' to self-determination in the context of freedom from Western imperialism (rather than Japanese or other more local forms of colonialism) that have helped constitute important aspects of the broad postcolonial context.

As mentioned earlier, there are also the socially oriented notions of human rights which stress the importance of economic, social and cultural rights. One point I want to make here is that although it is commonly claimed in contemporary discourses that this particular cluster of rights is inherently 'Asian' in a cultural sense (while individual rights are not), and that it is even definitive of 'Asian values', it is quite clear to anyone possessing even the briefest acquaintance with socialist ideology that these rights also have a significant history in Western political thought. This raises the issue of whether that rhetorical claims about the intrinsic 'Asianess' of economic, social and cultural rights have a much more significant political dimension as distinct from a cultural dimension.

The political dimension is evident enough in the Bangkok Declaration and other official speeches by political representatives from some Asian countries issued in the run-up to the Vienna World Conference on Human Rights in 1993. There were many references to the need for a proper 'balance' between individual and collective rights, for historical cultural particularities to be fully recognised as having a special legitimacy. But above all, the document's paramount claim centred on the *political* 'right' of sovereign states to attend to their own domestic affairs. This was evident in three major points made in the declaration:

- the discouragement of any attempt to use human rights as conditionality for extending development assistance;
- an emphasis to be maintained on the principles of respect for national sovereignty and territorial integrity as well as non-interference in the internal affairs of states, and the non-use of human rights as an instrument of political pressure;
- the reiteration of the principle that all countries, large and small, have the right to determine their political systems, control and freely utilise their resources, and freely pursue their own economic, social and cultural development objectives.[28]

In summary, acknowledgement of the equal importance of all categories of rights was qualified considerably by the unremitting stress on economic and developmental factors. Related to this was the emphasis on the idea that the level of support for individual civil and political rights in many Western countries could not, or should not, be emulated in Asian countries where a range of economic, cultural or social factors dictated other priorities. While there were statements in support of the universality of human rights, these were vaguely formulated, ambiguous or contradictory when read in conjunction with the equally strong references *to cultural and historical particularities.*[29]

Conclusion

One of the general themes that I return to, by way of conclusion, concerns the conceptualisation of 'culture' in the social sciences and some of its general implications for human rights and global governance. I have been concerned to demonstrate that discussions about culture and morality, especially where these involve the values underpinning human rights, have usually been based on a particular conception of culture developed in the social sciences, especially in the discipline of anthropology. Anthropology has also tended to divide the world into two distinct realms – the 'West' and the 'Rest'. Although at a general level its very name proposes that its focus is the 'study of Man', it has in fact been very much concerned with the study of non-industrialised societies – or non-Western societies. Moreover, the major contrasts that have been drawn between human societies have very often been between non-Western societies and Western ones.

Anthropology is certainly not the only discipline to have done this, but because it is the one which has been most intimately concerned with the culture concept, and has had such a profound influence on the way in which culture has been conceptualised in other social sciences, it is hard to escape the conclusion that the discipline is deeply implicated in the bipolar disorder that I mentioned earlier and which has had a significant influence on contemporary political and social theorising as well as on so many practical discussions of human rights in recent years. This disorder, as I said, is based on a very simplistic cultural/moral dichotomy between the 'individualistic West' and the 'collectivist non-West'.

In the introductory section of this chapter, I also mentioned the idea of culture as a medium of change – that while there is something to the idea of culture as social inheritance, it is also important to incorporate a recognition of the contestability and changeability of culture. This is implicit in a dynamic notion of culture as a process rather than a thing: a notion that contrasts quite sharply with the idea of culture as a thing which a community possesses – or which possesses a community – and which is used principally to define difference between communities.

What I am arguing is that the objectification of culture as a thing is based on a conservative and static notion of culture that largely ignores – or at least glosses over – its contingent nature as well as its social, political and moral dynamism. And it is in terms of this dynamism that an adequate understanding of culture, and the role that it plays in human life and interaction – including moral interaction – is best developed. Understood in this way, culture should not be a 'problem' for human rights and global governance, but rather that which enables interaction and the transcending of difference necessary to the further development of an international human rights regime. None of this should be taken to imply that differences (cultural or otherwise) are not important or legitimate. And indeed, an international human rights regime can work in a very positive way to protect culturally defined minorities within states.[30] My point is that arguments against the possibility or efficacy of an international human rights regime that are based on exaggerated notions of cultural difference must be treated with an acute critical awareness of the normative problems of simplistic culturalist approaches.

Finally, something needs to be said about the tenor of some of the recent discourses in normative IR theorising that so often invoke notions of geographical, historical and cultural specificity. When we talk about these kinds of specificities in relation to communities, countries or regions, and accept these specificities as given, then we are really not getting any further away from how classical realism viewed international morality. After all, classical realism was profoundly anti-universalistic in its take on normative issues and very much inclined to endorse ideas about cultural and moral specificity as contained within states. In addition, when the language of specificity is applied to categories such as 'the West' and 'non-West', as Samuel Huntington has done in his non-statist (but nonetheless realist) framework of understanding,[31] it mires itself deeply in a polarised Orientalist/Occidentalist framework of interpretation.

Enclosing groups of humans defined on the basis of some kind of cultural/historical specificity within impenetrable sovereign boundaries is also precisely what authoritarian leaders around the world have so often done. And it is from behind these boundaries that criticism of such matters as human rights abuses have been fobbed off, and resistance to the development of international law to deal with these abuses has been mounted. Let me hasten to add here that although the discussion has singled out some countries in the Asian region for criticism, other 'Western' countries like the US and Australia, which have often been at the forefront of rhetorical campaigns stressing the importance of international human rights standards, have also been less than willing to tolerate international scrutiny and criticism of their own practices.[32]

Without some notion of cosmopolitan morality – that is, of a morality that can operate in the sphere *between* groups (however they may be defined) and not just *within* them, we can make no sense of things such as 'crimes against humanity', let alone mount any effective practical action to deal with them. Human rights abusers may justify their misdeeds as having been necessary in meeting the needs of a specific time, place and situation. But how can this justify practices such as ethnic cleansing or genocide, in any place, at any time, or in any situation? The events in Germany in the 1940s, Cambodia in the 1970s, and the genocides in Rwanda and East Timor, can scarcely be taken as the 'local', 'specific' concern of those involved. A moral theory which privileges particularism over universalism has great difficulty in dealing with such issues.

At the same time, it is clearly no easy matter to delineate just what the proper concerns of an international community or a cosmopolitan morality are. And there are undoubtedly as many problems with rigid or absolute forms of universalism. But the idea that there are such things as culturally or historically specific bounded communities which are entitled to do their 'own thing' – often to women, children and other more or less powerless sectors – is unacceptable. Claims about geographical, historical or cultural specificity have become too much of a cliché in contemporary normative theory. While recognising the importance of pluralism and difference, these claims should not be invested automatically with some kind of intrinsic moral worth of their own. Rather, claims to specificity must be recognised as sometimes having instrumental political value to elites who are often a great deal less interested in culture *per se* than in preserving their own positions of power. And *this* point is itself part of the specificity of the contemporary discourse about 'specificity' itself. Being alert to this, while at the same time guarding against the kind of unwarranted moral imperialism long denounced by both relativists and pluralists, is difficult. But in the final analysis it is the only tenable way to deal with the 'problem' of culture and the human rights aspects of global governance in the twenty-first century.

Notes

1 This chapter draws from a number of other papers and articles I have written in recent years which deal with culture and normative international theory. These include: 'Democracy and the Problem of Cultural Relativism: Normative Issues for International Politics', *Global Society*, 12: 2 (1998), pp. 251–70; 'Dogmas of Difference: Culture and Nationalism in Theories of International Politics', *Critical Review of International Social and Political Philosophy*, 1: 4 (1998), pp. 62–92; 'Perspectives on the Study of Culture and International Politics: From the *Nihonjinron* to the New Asianism', *Asia-Pacific Review*, 16: 2 (November 1999), pp. 24–41; 'Conceptualizing "Culture" in Cultural Politics: Issues, Theories and Methods in International Relations', paper presented to a conference on 'Cultural Politics: Issues, Theories and Methods', University of East Anglia, 22 January 1999; 'Anyone for Golf? Cultural Values, Human Rights and Developmentalism in Contemporary Malaysia', paper presented to the Annual Convention of the International Studies Association, Los Angeles, 14–18 March 2000.
2 Philip Alston, 'The Best Interests Principle: Towards a Reconciliation of Culture and Human Rights', in Philip Alston (ed.) *The Best Interests of the Child: Reconciling Culture and Human Rights* (Oxford: Clarendon Press, 1994), pp. 5–6.
3 Timothy O'Hagan, 'The Idea of Cultural Patrimony', *Critical Review of International Social and Political Philosophy*, 1: 3 (Autumn 1998), p. 152.
4 One of the best-known is a very wide-ranging survey of definitions of culture undertaken by the anthropologists Kroeber and Kluckhohn almost fifty years ago in which hundreds of definitions from both anthropological and non-anthropological sources in English, French and German were systematically assembled and analysed. See A. L. Kroeber and Clyde Kluckhohn, *Culture: A Critical Review of Concepts and Definitions* (New York: Vintage Books, 1963).
5 Chris Jenks, *Culture* (London, Routledge, 1993), p. 10.
6 Glenn Jordan and Chris Weedon, *Cultural Politics: Class, Gender, Race and the Postmodern World* (Oxford, Blackwell, 1995).
7 Jordan and Weedon, *Cultural Politics*, p. 8. Note that this category is derived from the later (1981) work of Raymond Williams.
8 The Tiwi are a group of aboriginal people who occupy a remote island off the coast of northern Australia. In a standard sociology/anthropology textbook published in the 1980s, a two-page story about them is introduced in the following terms: 'This account of their norms of sexual behaviour, courtship and marriage points to the extraordinary contrast between our own family norms and those of pre-industrial people'. Note that the explicit purpose of the text is to highlight cultural difference, especially as between 'industrial' and 'pre-industrial' (read Western and non-Western) people.
9 The theory of historical contextualism is in some ways another version of relativism and one from which contemporary opponents of universalism have derived much of the language of historical and/or cultural and/or geographical specificity.
10 Kroeber and Kluckhohn, *Culture*, p. 11.
11 Raymond Williams, *Keywords: A Vocabulary of Culture and Society* (London, Fontana/Croom Helm, 1976), pp. 77–8.
12 Williams, *Keywords*, p. 79. According to Williams, Herder also identified the variability of social and economic groups within a nation. For another account

of Tylor's debt to German historical ethnology, see John H. Honigman, *The Development of Anthropological Ideas* (Homewood IL: Dorsey Press, 1976), esp. p. 32. For a recent and very thorough account of these developments, see also Adam Kuper, *Culture: The Anthropologists' Account* (Cambridge, MA: Harvard University Press), 1999.

13 Horigan, *Nature and Culture*, p. 18.

14 Cited in Kuper, *Culture*, p. 58.

15 See Maarten Brands, 'Political Culture: Pendulum Swing of a Paradigm? The Deceiving Perspective of Change', in Maurice Cranston and Lea Campos Boralevi, *Culture and Politics* (Berlin: Walter de Gruyter, 1988), p. 131.

16 Marco Verweij, 'Cultural Theory and the Study of International Relations', *Millennium*, 24: 1 (Spring 1995), p. 96. This author cites Margaret Mead (on America) and Ruth Benedict (on Japan) as following this line.

17 See Larry Diamond, 'Introduction: Political Culture and Democracy', in Larry Diamond (ed.) *Political Culture and Democracy in Developing Countries* (Boulder, CO: Lynne Reinner, 1994), pp. 8–9.

18 This is certainly the view put forward by Horigan.

19 Fleischacker, *Ethics of Culture*, p. 144.

20 Mary Douglas quoted in Alan Scott (ed.) 'Introduction: Globalization: Social Process or Political Rhetoric', in Alan Scott (ed.) *The Limits of Globalization: Cases and Arguments* (London: Routledge, 1997), p. 2.

21 John Clammer, *Values and Development in Southeast Asia* (Petaling Jaya: Pelanduk Publications, 1996), pp. 4–5.

22 For extended discussion on this point see Stephanie Lawson, *Tradition Versus Democracy in the South Pacific: Fiji, Tonga and Western Samoa* (Cambridge: Cambridge University Press, 1996). In this context, it is also worth noting Amaturo's point that the culture concept needs to be thoroughly investigated in order to understand more fully its role in the production of power relations. But whereas Amaturo proposes that a political system is culturally defined, my argument suggests that a cultural system may be politically defined. See Winifred L. Amaturo, 'Literature and International Relations: The Question of Culture in the Production of International Power', *Millennium*, 24: 1 (Spring 1995), pp. 2–3, 24.

23 Fleischacker, *Ethics of Culture*, p. 132.

24 Occidentalism has been a theme in a number of chapters or articles. See, for example, Stephanie Lawson, 'Cultural Relativism and Democracy: Political Myths About "Asia" and the "West"', in Richard Robison (ed.) *Pathways to Asia: The Politics of Engagement* (St Leonard's: Allen and Unwin, 1996), pp. 108–28.

25 This, incidentally, would be very similar to the revisionist exercise that has been carried out in relation to an 'Asian' model of democracy. The most interesting attempt at reconceptualising democracy in this way was carried out in Singapore where traditional Confucian values were purportedly incorporated in a new model of democracy called 'consencracy' by one of its proponents. Note that the 'demos' is absent from this neologism.

26 Garry Rodan, 'Class Transformations and Political Tensions in Singapore's Development', in Richard Robison and David S. G. Goodman (eds) *The New Rich in Asia: Mobile Phones, McDonald's and Middle-Class Revolution* (London: Routledge, 1996), p. 22.

27 See Khoo Boo Tek, *Paradoxes of Mahathirism: An Intellectual Biography of Mahathir Mohamad* (Kuala Lumpur: Oxford University Press, 1995), p. 329.

28 The Declaration adopted by the Ministers and Representatives of Asian States, who met in Bangkok from 29 March to 2 April 1993, pursuant to General Assembly Resolution 46/116 of 17 December 1991 in the context of preparations for the World Conference on Human Rights reproduced in James T. H. Tang

(ed.) *Human Rights and International Relations in the Asia-Pacific Region* (London, Pinter: 1995) as Appendix I, pp. 204–7.

29 Tang (ed.) *Human Rights and International Relations in the Asia-Pacific Region*, Appendix I, pp. 204–7.

30 For a specific study specifically concerned with this point see Michael Jacobsen and Stephanie Lawson, 'Between Globalization and Localization: A Case Study of Human Rights Versus State Sovereignty', *Global Governance*, 5: 2 (1999), pp. 203–19.

31 Samuel P. Huntington, 'The Clash of Civilizations?' *Foreign Affairs*, 72: 3 (1993).

32 For a pertinent commentary on the US case, see Martin Kettle, 'Judge, Jury and Executioner on Human Rights, But Never in the Dock', *Guardian Weekly*, 22–8 June 2000, p. 6. On Australia, there was a furore in early 2000 over the implications of mandatory sentencing laws in the Northern Territory and Western Australia for aboriginal people. The conservative Australian government under John Howard reacted very defensively over international criticism of its human rights record in this respect.

6   Global health governance

A conceptual review

Richard Dodgson and Kelley Lee

> The solution lies not in turning one's back on globalization, but in learning how to manage it. In other words, there is a crying need for better global governance . . .
>
> (UN Deputy Secretary-General Louise Frechette, 'What do we mean by global governance?', Address by the UN Deputy Secretary-General, *Global Governance Autumn Meetings Series*, *Global Governance and the UN Beyond Track 2*, Overseas Development Institute, London, 8 December 1998)

> global governance cannot replace the need for good governance in national societies; in fact, in the absence of quality local governance, global and regional arrangements are bound to fail or will have only limited effectiveness. In a way, governance has to be built from the ground up and then linked back to the local conditions.
>
> (Raimo Vayrynen, 'Preface', in Raimo Vayrynen (ed.) *Globalization and Global Governance* (Oxford: Rowman and Littlefield, 1999), p. xi)

Introduction

In today's world of increased health risks to all populations there are a growing number of national health policy outcomes that can no longer be assured through domestic action alone. The need for collective action by governments, business and civil society to better manage these risks is leading us to look for new rules and stronger institutions and better practices at the local, national and global levels. Part of the increasing health risk and the lack of an adequate local, national and global response is caused by factors outside the health sector – trade and investment policies; debt burden and international development assistance. There is an acute need for public health interests to be placed higher on these agendas to protect and promote people's health. The current system of international health governance (IHG) does not meet these needs, indeed, it has been shown to include a number of gaps and shortcomings. In light of these shortcomings and the need for collective, rule-based actions, rather than un-sanctioned unilateralism, the idea of global health governance (GHG) has become a keen topic of interest and debate in the field of international health.

This chapter contributes to this emerging debate by reviewing the conceptual meaning and defining features of GHG. The chapter begins with a brief discussion of why GHG has become an important subject of debate. The particular impacts that globalisation may be having on individuals and societies, and the fundamental challenges that this poses for promoting and protecting health, are explained. This is followed by a review of the history of IHG and, in particular, the central role of the World Health Organisation (WHO). The purpose of this section is to draw out the distinction between international and global health governance, and the degree to which there is presently, and should be, a shift to the latter. This leads to an identification of key challenges faced by the health community in bringing about such a system in future. The chapter concludes with suggestions on how the key types of actors and their respective roles in GHG might be defined further.

Health governance

Governance can be defined as the actions and means adopted by a society to promote collective action and deliver collective solutions in pursuit of common goals. Defined as such, governance must be seen as a broad term, that encompasses the many ways in which human beings, as individuals and groups, organise themselves to achieve agreed goals. Organisation of this nature requires agreement on a range of matters including membership within the co-operative relationship, obligations and responsibilities of members, the making of decisions, means of communication, resource mobilisation and distribution, dispute settlement, and formal or informal rules and procedures concerning all of these. Defined in this way, governance pertains to highly varied sorts of collective behaviour ranging from local community groups to transnational corporations, from labour unions to the UN Security Council. Governance thus relates to both the public and private sphere of human activity, and sometimes a combination of the two.

Importantly, governance is distinct from government. As Rosenau writes:

> Governance is not synonymous with government. Both refer to purposive behaviour, to goal oriented activities, to systems of rule; but government suggests activities that are backed by formal authority ... whereas governance refers to activities backed by shared goals that may or may not derive from legal and formally prescribed responsibilities and that do not necessarily rely on police powers to overcome defiance and attain compliance.[1]

Government, in other words, is a particular and highly formalised form of governance. Where governance is institutionalised within an agreed set of rules and procedures, regular or irregular meetings of relevant parties, or a permanent organisational structure with appropriate decision-making and implementing bodies, we can describe these as the means or mechanisms of governance, of which government is one form.[2] In other cases, however, governance may rely on informal mechanisms (for example, custom, common law, cultural norms and values) that are not legally formalised.

Health governance concerns the actions and means adopted by a society to organise itself in the promotion and protection of the health of its population. The rules defining such organisation, and its functioning, can again be formal (Public Health Act, International Health Regulations) or informal (Hippocratic Oath) to prescribe and proscribe behaviour. The governance mechanism, in turn, can be situated at the local/subnational (district health authority), national (Ministry of Health), regional (Pan-American Health Organisation), international (World Health Organisation) and the global level. Furthermore, health governance can be public (national health service), private (International Federation of Pharmaceutical Manufacturers Association), or a combination of the two (Malaria for Medicines Venture).

International health governance

Historically, the locus of health governance has been at the national level as governments have assumed primary responsibility for the health of their domestic populations. Where the determinants of health have spilled over national borders to become international (transborder) health issues (such as infectious diseases), two or more governments have sought to co-operate together on agreed collective actions. Health governance of this nature spans many centuries, with the adoption of quarantine practices amidst flourishing trade relations and the creation of regional health organisations.[3] The process of systematically building institutional structures and mechanisms to protect and promote human health across national borders, however, began more concertedly in the nineteenth century. Following the conclusion of the Napoleonic Wars, European states formed a number of international institutions to promote peace, industrial development and address collective concerns including the spread of infectious disease. This process of institutionalisation of IHG, according to Fidler, was a consequence of the intensified globalisation of health during this period. Notably, these initiatives enjoyed the support of political and economic elites across European societies who believed that the cross-border spread of disease would hamper industrialisation and the expansion of international trade.[4]

The first institution to be created during this period was the International Sanitary Conference, with the inaugural conference held in 1851. The achievements of this meeting, and the ten conferences subsequently held over the following four decades, were limited. Importantly, however, the conferences formalised a basic principle that has defined subsequent efforts to build IHG, namely the recognition that acting in co-operation with each other

---

Box 6.1 **World and European Conferences on Health, 1851–1913**

1851 First Sanitary Conference, Paris
1859 Second Sanitary Conference, Paris
1866 Third Sanitary Conference, Istanbul
1874 Fourth Sanitary Conference, Vienna
1881 Fifth Sanitary Conference, Washington
1885 Sixth Sanitary Conference, Rome
1887 Liquor on the North Sea, venue unrecorded
1892 Seventh Sanitary Conference, Venice
1893 Eighth Sanitary Conference, Dresden
1894 Ninth Sanitary Conference, Paris
1897 Tenth Sanitary Conference, Venice
1899 Liquor Traffic in Africa, Brussels
1903 Eleventh Sanitary Conference, Paris
1906 Liquor Traffic in Africa, Brussels
1909 Opium, Shanghai
1911 Twelfth Sanitary Conference, Paris
1911 Opium, The Hague
1913 Opium, The Hague

Source: Craig N. Murphy, *International Organisation and Industrial Change: Global Governance since 1850* (Cambridge: Polity Press, 1994), p. 59.

---

through agreed procedures and mechanisms would enable national governments to better protect their domestic populations from those health risks that cross their borders. As such, the institutions adopted were envisioned as an extension of participating governments' responsibilities in the health field to the international (inter-governmental) level.

Along with this emerging sense of an international health community constructed of co-operating states, was a growing body of scientific knowledge that was beginning to be shared in a more organised fashion.[5] Scientific meetings on health-related themes reflected substantial advances during this period in understanding the causes of a number of diseases, such as cholera and tuberculosis. In addition, international meetings were held on social issues that impacted on public health, notably the trafficking of liquor and opium (Box 6.1). Twelve health-related international institutions had been established by 1914,[6] the most prominent of which were the International Sanitary Bureau (later the Pan American Sanitary Bureau) in 1902 and Office International d'Hygiene Publique (OIHP) created in Paris in 1907. The OIHP was a milestone in IHG in that it provided a standing (rather than periodic) forum for countries to exchange ideas and information on public health.[7] This was followed in 1920 with the formation of the Health Organisation of the League of Nations.

From the mid-nineteenth century, the non-governmental sector also began to grow and contribute to IHG, essentially filling gaps or supplementing government action. For example, religious missions and The Rockefeller Foundation's International Health Division (established in 1913) led the way in supporting health services and disease control programmes in the poorest or worst affected parts of the developing world. The International Committee of the Red Cross (established in 1863) succeeded in establishing the Geneva Convention, a precursor of future international health regimes in setting out norms of behaviour and moral values for treating casualties of war. By the 1920s, these non-governmental health organisations had joined with inter-governmental health organisations to shape a vision of IHG that was increasingly defined by humanitarianism, rather than primarily economic and trade principles. Together, they supported the belief that international health co-operation should seek to provide health to as many people as possible (for instance, social medicine or public health). To achieve this required a strong emphasis on universality as a guiding principal, attained through the inclusion of as many countries as possible in any system of health governance that was formed.

International health governance post-1945

This vision appeared a step closer with the establishment of the World Health Organisation in 1948. The ideal of universality was, and remains, central to its mandate and activities of this post-war inter-governmental health organisation. As stated by the Constitution of the WHO (1946), the overall goal of the organisation is 'the attainment by all peoples of the highest possible level of health'. Even in the face of scepticism at the attainability of such a mandate, and challenges to the appropriateness of social medicine,[8] the WHO was founded with a strong commitment to addressing the health needs of all people. The universalism of the WHO has been reaffirmed on a number of occasions since 1948.[9]

The WHO's pledge to universality, however, has been strongly defined by the sovereignty of its member states. As the central pillar of post-war IHG, the working assumption of the Organisation has been that *health for all* can be achieved by working primarily, if not exclusively, through the governmental institutions of sovereign states, notably ministries of health. Universality, in this sense, is measured by the number of member states and their attendance in the World Health Assembly (WHA). Where a large number of countries participate, such as in the WHA, it is assumed that the health needs of all peoples are being represented. The role of WHO, in turn, is to support the efforts of governments in their efforts to promote the health of their populations.

Since its early years as an institution, a notable feature of the WHO has been its principle of recognising NGOs as important contributors to achieving the goals of the organisation. In practice, however, this actual role has been limited – that is, until perhaps the late 1990s. A recent study, for example, found that the Organisation engaged little with NGOs in twelve lower-income countries unlike the trend by many bilateral aid agencies and other UN organisations such as UNDP and UNICEF.[10] At headquarters and regional levels, NGOs may observe, but not participate in, proceedings of the WHA or meetings of the regional committees, and have little access to the many programme-related meetings dealing with more specific health issues. The WHO has continued to focus strongly on member states and, in particular, ministries of health, despite a growth in the diversity of actors involved in international health.

Of the multiplicity of actors that operate alongside the WHO in the health field, the World Bank is the most prominent because of its unrivalled financial resources, but there remain questions over the representativeness, transparency and accountability of its governance. Even more problematic are the Organisation for Economic Co-operation and Development (OECD) and World Trade Organisation (WTO) which approach health foremost from an economic and trade perspective. The WTO, in particular, has been widely criticised for its lack of transparency despite the potential of its policies to fundamentally influence broad spheres of international relations. NGOs and other actors from within civil society are also becoming more numerous and influential in their contributions to international health. However, important issues of governance, in particular legitimacy and accountability, again surround the actions and influence of these actors.[11] The emergence and growing influence of a multiplicity of actors has led Zacher to describe IHG in the 1990s as an 'organisational patchwork quilt'.[12] The WHO has embarked upon a process of reform, to change some of its traditional governance features, notably its strong focus on ministries of health, by engaging other public and private sector actors, and creating new consultation mechanisms. At the same time, it has reiterated its commitment to universality as the defining principle of its activities. How to define, let alone achieve health for all, remains an enduring challenge.

In summary, IHG has evolved with the intensification of trans-border human interaction over a number of centuries, becoming more institutionalised from the mid-nineteenth century with the establishment of inter-governmental mechanisms to promote health co-operation. During the twentieth century, this institutional framework has grown and spread, encompassing both rich and poor countries in all regions of the world. The defining feature of this system of IHG has been its focus on the state. By the late twentieth century, however, the globalisation process has challenged this state-centric system of health governance. It is within this context that discussions and debates about global health governance have emerged.

Globalisation and international health governance

Many argue that globalisation is reducing the capacity of states to provide for the health of their domestic populations and, by extension, inter-governmental health co-operation is also limited. This chapter sees globalisation as a historical process that is characterised by the changes in the nature of human interaction across a range of spheres including the economic, political, technological, socio-cultural and environmental. These changes are globalising in the sense that boundaries hitherto separating us from each other are being undermined and transformed. These boundaries – spatial, temporal and cognitive – can be described as the dimensions of globalisation. Briefly, the spatial dimension concerns changes to how we perceive and experience physical space or geographical territory. The temporal dimension concerns changes to how we perceive and experience time. The cognitive dimension concerns changes to how we think about ourselves and the world around us.[13]

Globalisation has impacted upon the existing mechanisms and structures of IHG in the following ways. First, globalisation has introduced or intensified trans-border health risks defined as risks to human health that transcend national borders in their origin or impact. Such risks include emerging and re-emerging infectious diseases, various non-communicable diseases (such as lung cancer, obesity, hypertension) and environmental change (for instance, global climate change). The growth in the geographical scope and speed in which trans-border health risks present themselves, directly challenge the existing system of IHG that is defined by national borders. The mechanisms of IHG, in other words, may be constrained by its own state-centric nature in effectively tackling global health.[14]

Second, as described above, globalisation is characterised by a growth in the number and degree of influence of non-state actors in the governance of health issues. Many argue that the relative authority and capacity of states to protect and promote the health of domestic populations has declined in the face of globalising forces that affect the basic determinants of health from beyond national borders, and that erode national resources for addressing their consequences.[15] Non-state actors have gained relatively greater power and influence both formally and informally. The emerging picture is becoming more complex, with the distinct roles of state and non-state actors in governance activities such as agenda setting, resource mobilisation and allocation, and dispute settlement becoming less clear. New combinations of both state and non-state actors are forming, as reflected in a myriad of terms such as partnerships, alliances, coalitions, networks and ventures. This apparent *hybridisation* of governance mechanisms around certain health issues is a reflection of the search for more effective ways of organising societies to promote global health. At the same time, however, it throws up new challenges for creating appropriate and recognised institutional mechanisms for, *inter alia*, ensuring appropriate representation, participation, accountability and transparency.

Third, current forms of globalisation appear to be problematic for sustaining, and even worsening existing socio-economic, political and environmental problems. The UNDP, for example, reports that neoliberal-driven forms of globalisation have been accompanied by widening inequalities between rich and poor within and across countries.[16] In a special issue of *Development*, authors cite experiences of worsening poverty, marginalisation and health inequity as a consequence of globalisation. In some respects, these problems can be seen as 'externalities' or 'global public bads' that are arising as a result of globalising processes that are insufficiently managed by effective health governance.[17] As Fidler writes, these deeply rooted problems 'feed off' the negative consequences of the globalisation of health, creating a reciprocal relationship between health and the determinants of health. Although many of these problems are most acute in the developing world, they are of concern to all countries given their trans-border nature.[18]

Fourth, globalisation has contributed to a decline in both the political and practical capacity of the state, acting alone or in co-operation with other states, to deal with global health challenges. While the globalisation process is one occurring gradually over several centuries, its acceleration and intensification from the late twentieth century has brought attention to the fact that states alone cannot address many of the health challenges that arise. Infectious diseases are perhaps the most prominent example of this diminishing capacity, but equally significant are the impacts on non-communicable diseases (such as tobacco-related cancers), food and nutrition, lifestyles and environmental conditions.[19] This decapacitating of the state has been reinforced by initiatives to further liberalise the global trade of goods and services. The possible health consequences of more open global markets have only begun to be discussed within trade negotiations and remain unaddressed by proposed governance mechanisms for the emerging global economy.

The fourth of the above points is perhaps the most significant because it raises the possibility of the need for a change in the fundamental nature of health governance. As mentioned above, IHG is based upon the belief that the state is primarily responsible for the health of its people and able, in co-operation with other states, to protect its population from health risks. The globalisation of health, however, means that the state may be increasingly undermined in its capacity to fulfil this role alone; that IHG is necessary but insufficient; and that additional or new forms of health governance may be needed. Some scholars and practitioners believe that this new system of health governance needs to be global in scope, so that it can deal effectively with problems caused by the globalisation of health.[20]

Towards a system of global health governance?

Essential elements of global health governance

The term global health governance is still a new addition to the health lexicon. However, from discussions on the form that it does and should take, it is possible to discern elements that are essential to GHG. The first is the need to 'deterritorialise' health, in a sense, by going beyond the primary focus on the state. GHG is representative of all relevant stakeholders in membership, participation and responsibility, both state and non-state. As described above, IHG has been firmly defined by its state-centric nature. The fact that virtually all countries are member states of the WHO, has been seen as fulfilling the criteria of universality. In contrast, the World Bank is deemed less representative, because of its limited state membership. Other health-related UN funds and programmes, such as UNICEF and the United Nations Fund for Population Activities (UNFPA), are governed by a selected number of donor and recipient countries. Regional health organisations, by their nature, offer membership to states within specific regions.

Globalisation, however, brings into question the definition, and hence representation, of interests by states alone. GHG suggests the need to recognise and give meaningful participation of a greater plurality of interests to capture both the territorial and supraterritorial features of global health issues. Of course, as described above, non-state actors have long played an important role in health governance. The difference here lies in the degree, and nature, of that involvement. As is described below, there are examples of health governance emerging that incorporate non-state actors more intimately and numerously within processes of decision-making.

Importantly, this does not mean that the state or structures of IHG will disappear or become redundant, but rather that they will need to become part of a wider system of GHG. The WHO and other institutions of IHG will continue to play a significant role in GHG, and states continue to be one of the governed within GHG.[21] But states and state-defined governance alone is not enough. As described by the Commission on Global Governance, '[global governance] must . . . be understood as also involving NGOs, citizens' movements, multinational corporations, and the global capital market', as well as a 'global mass media of dramatically enlarged influence'.[22] Thus, the concept of global health emphasises the need for governance that incorporates participation by a more broadly defined global public, engaged in collective actions, and managed by a range of formal and informal mechanisms and rules.

The challenges of achieving effective forms of health governance that incorporate both state and non-state actors are considerable. More democratic forms of health governance face the task of defining and then achieving the appropriate balance and combination of state and non-state actors, with mechanisms for enabling representation and participation. Moreover, there is need for greater clarity in what particular contributions different actors should make to GHG, and how governance mechanisms can be created to ensure that these roles are fulfilled. State and non-state actors require systems of accountability to each other, and to the constituencies that they represent. Conflicts of interest are also likely to emerge, and there is a need for ways of resolving such conflicts in a transparent way. Overall, the principle of closer state/non-state co-operation is an increasingly accepted one, but the 'nitty gritty' of what this should look like in practice and for what purposes, is only beginning to be explored within the health sector.

The issue of meaningful participation and responsibility also remains problematic. For example, the WHA is attended by all member states of WHO but there are considerable inequities in their capacity to follow proceedings and contribute to decision-making. Indeed, despite the ongoing process of strengthening the decision-making capacity of the least developed countries within the WHO, it may be argued that real decision-making within the organisation is taken outside of the WHA by the Executive Board (limited and rotating membership), Director-General or individual programmes. The capacity to influence such decisions are weighted in favour of a small group of financially influential donor countries who, as Vaughan *et al.* argue, do not distort priorities but encourage vertical management systems and increase problems of co-ordination by earmarking extra-budgetary funds (EBFs).[23] The key challenge posed for greater geographical globalism, therefore, is how to give all states an equitable voice and opportunities to participate within a system of GHG.

Second, GHG must be built on a conceptualisation of health that is more multi-sectoral and multidisciplinary. The centrality of biomedical approaches to health has been apparent in IHG in the form of disease-focused research and policy programmes, the skills mix of international health officials, and the primacy given to ministries of health and health professionals. Globalisation, however, brings into question how we define the determinants of health and how they can be addressed. For example, globalisation has emphasised even more poignantly the need for greater attention to the basic determinants of health including so-called non-health issue areas. Chen *et al.* argue that globalisation is eroding the boundary between the determinants of public (collective) and private (individual) health.[24] For example, susceptibility to tobacco-related diseases, once strongly linked to, and blamed on, the lifestyle choices of individuals, is increasingly seen as attributable to the world-wide marketing practices of tobacco companies. In recognition of these changes, a global system of health governance would draw on a greater diversity of skills and experience to include the biomedical/health and social sciences. It would centre on ministries of health, and health-related institutions, but be open to contributions from other sectors such as trade, education, environment, agriculture, and other relevant sectors.

The main challenge to achieving greater sectoral and disciplinary globalism lies in the danger of casting the health 'net' too openly, so that everything becomes subsumed within the global health umbrella at the expense of feasibility. Opening up GHG too indiscriminately can dilute policy focus and impact. Keeping the focus too narrow can risk overlooking key determinants of global health. Defining the scope of GHG, therefore, remains a balance between recognising the interconnectedness of health and a multitude of globalising forces, as well as the need to define clear boundaries of knowledge and action.

Mapping global health governance

To begin the task of designing and building a system of GHG, both as it appears to be currently evolving and more prospectively, requires identification

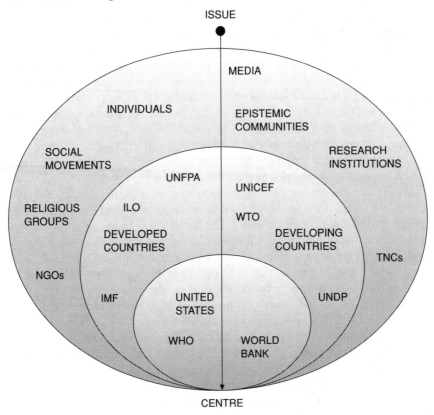

Figure 6.1 Global health governance mapped

of the key actors and their contributions to such a system. This mapping exercise must first recognise the diversity and dynamic nature of global health that, in turn, produces governance mechanisms that may vary with the nature of the health issue, and the political and economic priorities at any given time. Figure 6.1 offers an attempt to identify the key actors concerned with GHG and their potential position at a given point in time. WHO and the World Bank are shown as central because they represent the main sources of health expertise and development financing respectively. They are accompanied by a cluster of other institutions, states and non-state actors, that fan outwards including, but not restricted to, the International Monetary Fund (IMF), WTO, UNICEF, International Labour Organisation (ILO), UNDP and UNFPA. Specific institutions of the US government, such as USAID, are included as politically and economically influential.

Relations between these different actors are relatively good, although there has been a growing confusion of mandates among the UN organisations that have substantial involvement in the health sector. In large part, this has been the result of efforts to develop multi-sectoral approaches to both health and development, as well as key areas (such as, reproductive health, environmental health) that bring together the activities of two or more organisations.[25] Globalisation invites a further widening of the net of relevant organisations, requiring engagement with actors that have little or no formal mandate in the health field. Notable have been efforts to establish greater dialogue between WHO and the WTO. While historically trade has intimately defined and in many ways confined international health co-operation, officially the two spheres have been addressed by separate institutions. Nonetheless, the direct linkages between trade and health are increasingly well-appreciated,[26] underscored by high-level meetings between the two organisations since the late 1990s. At present, WHO holds official observer status on the Council of the WTO and committees relating to Sanitary and Phytosanitary Measures (SPS) and Technical Barriers to Trade (TBT) agreements. However, the capacity to articulate public health concerns regarding, for example, the agreement on Trade-Related Intellectual Property rights (TRIPs), has been hampered by the framing of health among trade officials as a 'non-trade issue', and as such the reluctance of certain countries to discuss health within the context of trade negotiations. Moreover, the ability of the WHO to influence the WTO has been hampered by the fact that states (many of which are members of both organisations) have accorded a higher priority to trade issues, rather than those relating to human health. As such, there remain considerable barriers to incorporating health as a legitimate and worthy concern on the global trade agenda, a point that cannot be ignored as we consider the development of GHG.

The states and institutions of GHG are surrounded by the wide variety of actors, that together make-up civil society. Civil society is defined as 'a sphere of social interaction between economy and state, composed above all of the intimate sphere (especially family), the sphere of associations (especially voluntary associations) and forms of public communication'.[27] Thus, prominent actors within civil society include NGOs, social movements, epistemic communities, business and the media. Depending on the definition, the important sphere of private for-profit business may or may not be included in civil society, but clearly forms an important type of actor in GHG.

Importantly, the specific position of different actors, and types of actors, in GHG is expected to vary with the health issue and over time. As such, they will move closer or farther from the centre of the map. The following examples demonstrate this and, in doing so, highlight pointers for the future development of GHG. First, relations among the diverse NGO community are constantly changing depending on the issue. On certain issues, they may be willing to form strategic networks or alliances with other NGOs, thus representing an important governance mechanism within GHG. Such a mechanism was formed around the global campaign against the marketing of breast milk substitutes which led to the formation of the International Baby Food Action Network. Co-operation between the International Baby Food Action Network, UNICEF, the WHO and selected governments led to the launch of the International Code of Marketing on Breast-Milk Substitutes in 1981. Like-minded NGOs also came together to form a more permanent, but still highly fluid, global social movement around the issues of the environment and women's health. Individually, these movements opposed each other at the UN Conference on the Environment and Development (1992), yet worked together to propose an alternative view of development at the World Summit for Social Development in 1995. Close relations between the women's health movement, states and the UNFPA was a defining feature of the International Conference on Population and Development (ICPD) (1994). Relations between the women's health movement and some states, in particular the US, were also so close that members of the women's health movement were part of the official government delegations that attended the Cairo conference. The majority of the parties involved in the conference believed that such close relations played a central role in shaping the ICPD's commitment to reproductive health.[28]

Closer relations among state and non-state actors is also characterising WHO's global strategy on tobacco control. In September 1999, the first meeting of the Working Group on the Framework Convention on Tobacco Control (FCTC) was attended by 114 states and 31 NGOs. The Tobacco Free Initiative (TFI) holds that participation by NGOs is central to the overall success of the FCTC, and has sought to construct a global NGO network to support the FCTC. Links have also been formed with representatives of the women's movement to ensure that the issue of tobacco and women's health is discussed as part of the Beijing Plus 5 process. At the same time, TFI has developed links with the business community, in particular, pharmaceutical firms, to discuss how nicotine replacement treatments can be made more widely available. Other co-ordination efforts have been focused on bringing together different UN organisations through the formation of a UN Ad Hoc Inter-Agency Task Force on tobacco control.

The efforts to build formal and informal links with such a diverse range of stakeholders on tobacco control is indeed unprecedented, and an example of emerging forms of GHG. The goal of adopting a legally binding treaty and associated protocols is also a new development in institutionalising global governance in the health sector. Moreover, in ensuring that states will act collectively on both a global and national level, the FCTC is an example of how 'behind-the-border' convergence could be promoted in the future. This is significant as it represents an important stage in the development of WHO and the solution of global health problems.

The FCTC is based upon the example of international regimes that have emerged to promote collective action on global environmental problems. These international regimes can be defined as 'sets of implicit or explicit principles, norms, rules and decision-making procedures around which actors' expectations converge in a given area of international relations'.[29] In addition to the FCTC, other examples of international regimes in the field of health are the International Code for the Marketing of Breast Milk Substitutes and the

Codex Alimentarius. These examples of trans-border health regimes demonstrate that regimes have played a significant role in IHG. The current organisational form and remit of the FCTC indicate that regimes will be a feature of GHG in the future.

This chapter, among others, supports this view. However, this support is tempered by a number of issues relating to the regimes and the FCTC in particular. First, regimes should not be seen as a simony for or alternative to governance.[30] Rosenau comments that governance,

> is not confined to a single sphere of endeavor. It refers to the arrangements that prevail in the lacunae between regimes and, perhaps more importantly, to the principles, norms, rules and procedures that come into play when two or more regimes overlap, conflict, or otherwise require arrangements that facilitate accommodation among the competing interests.[31]

Second, international regimes suffer from a failure to incorporate effective mechanisms of enforcement into their make-up. This aspect of the FCTC is still to be negotiated; however, the adoption of an effective and meaningful enforcement mechanism will be a strong indication of the willingness of states to 'pool' their sovereignty and act collectively to construct mechanisms of GHG. Third, the extent to which the FCTC serves as a model for future GHG depends on the successful achievement of meaningful involvement of relevant stakeholders in governance. As discussed above, it is already clear that NGOs and other non-state actors are involved in the process of developing the FCTC. However, an in-depth evaluation of how these actors have perceived the negotiation process and how they have contributed would be important. Critical reflection on how workable and effective the mechanisms for participation and representation have been would also be essential. Finally, in the context of the development of GHG, the main concern is whether the FCTC model can be replicated in other areas. The global consensus on the need to control tobacco is so significant because the field of global health is normally split on political, economic and medical/scientific issues. For the FCTC model to be replicated, a consensus on the nature of other health problems and, most importantly, how they should be solved needs to develop. Thus, building consensus should be of prime concern for those seeking to build an integrated system of GHG.

A third notable example of emerging GHG is global public–private partnerships (GPPPs) defined as 'a collaborative relationship which transcends national boundaries and brings together at least three parties, among them a corporation (and/or industry association) and inter-governmental organisations, so as to achieve a shared health-creating goal on the basis of a mutually agreed division of labour'.[32] Defined as such, a number of GPPPs can be identified, some of the most prominent of which are the Albendazole Donation Programme, the Medicines for Malaria Venture and the International AIDS Vaccine Initiative. The idea of building partnerships with business is at the centre of UN-wide views on the governance of globalisation. For this reason, and the fact that GPPPs bring much needed resources to high profile health programmes, the number of public–private partnerships are likely to grow in the future.

Like the FCTC negotiation process, GPPPs require a period of reflection on a range of governance issues. Buse and Walt, for example, query the accountability and long-term durability of GPPPs. They raise the question of who benefits from GPPPs, the people they seek to treat or the pharmaceutical companies who gain good press by supplying the drugs.[33] The governments of some lower-income countries, a number of NGOs and UN institutions have questioned the viability of building links between actors that have fundamentally differing objectives and interests. Indeed, the Executive Director of UNICEF recently commented that 'it is dangerous to assume that the goals of the private sector are somehow synonymous with those of the United Nations, because they most emphatically are not'.[34]

The future development of GHG will depend, in short, on the creation of appropriate and agreed governance mechanisms that capture the essential criteria. Indeed, all the different approaches to global governance discussed above highlight the need for global governance to be based upon the consent and participation of the governed. In particular, scholars believe that the participation of civil society and other actors in GHG can contribute towards building a consensus on the need for collective action.[35] Kaul *et al.* also argue that closure of the 'participation gap' in GHG will hasten the delivery of health as a global good. These same scholars comment that, 'by expanding the role of civil society and the private sector in international negotiations, governments can enhance their leverage over policy outcomes while promoting pluralism and diversity in the process'.[36]

The FCTC stands as an example of how a wide range of institutions, states, NGOs and other actors can participate in the formation of GHG. However, the issue of how to increase the participation of 'the governed' in GHG remains problematic for such reasons as the unwillingness of some NGOs to work with states for fear that they are co-opted. Moreover, the policy-making structure of many of the institutions in GHG is not designed for the involvement of a large number of non-state actors. At the same time, other institutions, in particular the WTO, are still not willing to allow the participation of civil society in decision-making (see Chapter 11). Many member states, especially those that are new to democracy or do not have experience of working with civil society, have doubts about increasing the participation of non-state actors in the development of GHG. Despite these issues, an increase in the participation of non-state actors must occur if the move from IHG to GHG is to continue and be completed.

How the participation of civil society in global governance can be increased is currently open to debate. For example, supporters of a liberal form of global governance believe that this objective would be best met by reforming existing institutions. However, other scholars have advocated the establishment of institutions whose membership is drawn exclusively from civil society. These views are not exclusive; indeed, some mix of the two will most likely characterise the institutional structure of GHG in the future. What is most important is that any new or reformed institutions of GHG is based upon the participation of a wide number of different actors and the principles of accountability and transparency. The inclusion of these principles is central to securing the longevity and legitimacy of GHG. Moreover, the inclusion of these principles will ensure that the mechanisms and structures of GHG will remain responsive to the needs of the people it seeks to help.

Conclusion

The purpose of this chapter has been to review GHG and, in turn, to highlight the challenges faced in moving towards such a system. This has led to the identification of essential features of GHG – geographical, state and non-state, and disciplinary and sectoral globality – that can be seen as either an enhancement or break from the system of IHG that emerged in the nineteenth century. The transition from IHG to GHG faces a number of fundamental challenges both analytically and practically. Both share a commitment to universalism, but translating the principle into practice requires a conceptualisation beyond states. Those national governments and intergovernmental organisations that are part of IHG continue to have an important, and indeed, core role in GHG. It is not an issue of hurrying the end of the state. On the contrary, the state remains central to strong public health systems built from the ground up. Nonetheless, it must also be recognised that state actors alone are increasingly insufficient. States must take into account the views and actions of non-state actors, in particular NGOs and the business sector, that are emerging to shape GHG.

There lies the friction. As the globalisation of health continues, health governance will have to become more global in scope. Yet the enigma of how to achieve a more pluralist, yet cohesive, system of GHG stands before us. The proto forms of GHG that are presently emerging (such as the FCTC and GPPPs) might be seen as examples of improving practice as they open up participation in health governance to a wider range of actors. Nonetheless, a critical evaluation of the quality of participation is yet to be undertaken, nor is it yet clear whether these emerging forms of GHG will achieve their objectives.

The task of moving forward this complex, yet much needed, debate can be facilitated by a number of further tasks. The first would be to better understand the 'nitty gritty' of global governance in terms of what, in concrete terms, it looks like in practice. Based on this initial conceptual review, an examination of what currently exists within the health field, as well as other fields such as trade and environment, may shed light on future possibilities. While such a review can only be selective in nature, it can point to lessons for building mechanisms for GHG.

A second task is to better understand the historical context of IHG and GHG, and how this can inform the transition from one to the other. Many different types of governance mechanisms for health purposes have been tried and tested since the end of the Second World War, and it would be useful to explore these in relation to the criteria set in this paper.

A third task is to define more clearly the potential role of non-state actors, both civil society groups and the private for-profit sector, in a system of GHG. Relations, patterns of influence and agreed roles among state and non-state actors within an emerging system of GHG are still evolving. This myriad of different actors, each with individual spheres of activity, types of expertise, resources, interests and aspirations, cannot yet be described as a 'global society'. As defined by Fidler, a global society is 'made of individuals and non-state entities all over the world that conceive of themselves as part of a single community and work nationally and transnationally to advance their common interests and values'.[37] The *ad hoc* nature of GHG so far, however, suggests that a more concerted effort to define and describe existing and potential roles would contribute to policy debates on possible future directions.

Notes

1 James Rosenau, 'Governance, Order and Change in World Politics', in James Rosenau and Ernst-Otto Czempiel (eds) *Governance without Government: order and change in world politics* (Cambridge: Cambridge University Press, 1992), p. 4.
2 L. Finklestein, 'What is Global Governance?', *Global Governance*, 1: 3, pp. 367–72.
3 Early regional health organisations include the Conseil Superieur de Santé de Constantinople (*c.* 1830), European Commission for the Danube (1856) and International Sanitary Bureau of the Americas (1902).
4 David Fidler, 'International Law and Global Public Health', *International Colloquium on Public Health Law*, Durban, South Africa, 22–24 November 1998. Craig N. Murphy, *International Organisation and Industrial Change: global governance since 1850* (Cambridge: Polity Press, 1994), pp. 64–71.
5 Fidler, 'Microbialpolitik: Infectious diseases and International Relations', *American University International Law Review*, 14: 1, pp. 1–53.
6 Murphy, *International Organisation and Industrial Change*, p. 48.
7 M. Roemer, 'Internationalism in Medicine and Public Health', in D. Porter (ed.) *The History of Public Health and the Modern State* (London: Clio Medical/ Wellcome Institute, 1994).
8 N. Goodman, *International Health Organizations and Their Work* (London: Churchill Livingstone, 1971).
9 F. Antezana, C. Chollat-Traquet and D. Yach, 'Health for All in the 21st Century', *World Health Statistics Quarterly* 51: 1 (1998), pp. 3–4.
10 A. Lucas, S. Mogedal, G. Walt, S. Hodne Steen, S. E. Kruse, K. Lee and L. Hawken (1997) *Co-operation for Health Development, The World Health Organisation's support to programmes at country level* (London: Governments of Australia, Canada, Italy, Norway, Sweden and the UK, 1997).
11 S. Bennett, B. McPake, and A. Mills (eds) *Private Health Providers in Developing Countries: serving the public interest?* (London: Zed Books, 1997).

12 M. Zacher, 'Uniting Nations: Global Regimes and the United Nations System', in R. Vayrynen (ed.) *Globalization and Global Governance* (Oxford: Rowman and Littlefield, 1999), p. 59.

13 K. Lee, 'The Impact of Globalisation on Public Health: Implications for the UK Faculty of Public Health Medicine', *Journal of Public Health*, 22: 3 (2000).

14 M. Zacher, 'Global Epidemiological Surveillance: International Co-operation to Monitor Infectious Diseases', in I. Kaul, I. Grunberg and M. Stern (eds) *Global Public Goods: international co-operation in the 21st century* (Oxford: Oxford University Press, 1999), pp. 266–81.

15 D. Fidler, 'The Globalisation of Public Health: Emerging Infectious Diseases and International Relations', *Indiana Journal of Global Legal Studies*, 5: 1 (1997), pp. 11–51.

16 UNDP, *Reconceptualising Governance* (New York: UNDP Management Development and Governance Division, 1997).

17 I. Kaul, I. Grunderg and M. Stern, 'Introduction', in Kaul, Grunberg, and Stern (eds) *Global Public Goods* (Oxford/New York: Oxford University Press/UNDP, 1999), pp. xxv–xxvii.

18 Fidler, 'International Law and Global Public Health'.

19 Lee, 'The Impact of Globalisation on Public Health: Implications for the UK Faculty of Public Health Medicine'.

20 I. Kickbusch, 'Global Public Health: Revisiting health public policy at the global level', *Health Promotion International*; P. Farmer, 'Social Inequalities and Emerging Infectious Diseases', *Emerging Infectious Diseases*, 2: 4 (1996), pp. 259–66.

21 J. A. Scholte, 'Globalization and Social Change', *Transnational Associations*, 2: 62 (1998).

22 Commission on Global Governance, *Our Global Neighbourhood* (Oxford: Oxford University Press, 1995).

23 J. P. Vaughan, S. Mogedal, G. Walt, S. E. Kruse, K. Lee and K. de Wilde, 'WHO and the effects of extrabudgetary funds: is the Organization donor driven?', *Health Policy and Planning*, 11: 3 (1996), pp. 253–64.

24 C. Chen, T. Evans, and R. Cash, 'Health as a Global Public Good', in Kaul, Grunberg and Stern, *Global Public Goods*, p. 285.

25 K. Lee, S. Collinson, G. Walt and L. Gilson, 'Who Should be Doing What in International Health: a confusion of mandates in the United Nations?', *British Medical Journal*, 312 (3 February 1996), pp. 302–7.

26 R. Beaglehole, *Global Trade and Health Manual* (Geneva: WHO/WTO, 2001); G. Brundtland, 'Speech of the WHO Director-General', *Ad hoc Working Group on Revised Drug Strategy*, Geneva, 13 October 1998.

27 P. Jareg and D. C. Kaseje, 'Growth of Civil Society in Developing Countries: Implications for Health', *The Lancet*, 351 (14 March 1998), pp. 305–10.

28 R. Dodgson 'The Women's Health Movement and the International Conference on Population and Development', unpublished PhD dissertation, University of Newcastle-upon-Tyne, UK, 1998.

29 S. D. Krasner, *International Regimes* (Ithaca, NY: Cornell University Press, 1983), p. 3.

30 Kickbusch, 'Global Public Health: Revisiting health public policy at the global level'.

31 J. N. Rosenau, 'Governance in the Twenty-first Century', *Global Governance*, 1: 1 (1995), p. 9.

32 K. Buse and G. Walt, 'Global Public–Private Health Partnerships: Part I – a new development in health?', *Bulletin of the World Health Organization*, 78: 5 (2000), pp. 549–61.

33 Buse and Walt, 'Global Public–Private Health Partnerships: Part I – a new development in health?', p. 549.

34 Interview with J. Ann Zammit, The South Centre, 9 December 1999. 'UNICEF: Bellamy warns against partnership with private sector', *UN Wire*, 23 April 1999.
35 Rosenau, 'Governance in the Twenty-first Century', p. 11.
36 Kaul, Grunderg and Stern, 'Introduction', p. xxviii.
37 Fidler, 'Microbialpolitik', p. 28.

Part III

Human security and global governance

7 Global governance and human security

Caroline Thomas

> When we think about security, we need to think beyond battalions and borders. We need to think about human security, about winning a different war, the fight against poverty.
>
> (James Wolfensohn, President of the World Bank, addressing the United Nations Security Council meeting on HIV/AIDS in Africa, *World Bank News Release*, 2000/172/5, 10 January 2000)

> Poverty is the ultimate systemic threat facing humanity. The widening gaps between rich and poor nations . . . are . . . potentially socially explosive.
>
> (Michel Camdessus, Managing Director of the IMF, speaking at the UNCTAD X meeting in Bangkok, February 2000)

The global landscape of the 1980s and 1990s was marked by pervasive poverty and deepening inequality within and between states. Over that same period, the agents of global governance promoted worldwide a model of development premised on the philosophy of political and economic liberalism. Global economic integration was presented as the best, the most natural and universal path towards growth and therefore development for all humanity. This was to be achieved by the application of neoclassical free market economic principles, but had important political components as well. The role of the state was minimised, and trade, finance and investment were systematically liberalised. The market, rather than the state, was to determine entitlement to fundamental material aspects of human security. This represented a fundamental ideological shift with the previous period. Economic liberalisation proceeded hand in hand with political liberalisation, and Western-style democratic reform and the prioritisation of civil and political rights was the order of the day. Neoliberal political and economic philosophy defined the dominant notion of human security.[1] In important respects, however, the achievements of these policies did not live up to expectations. Neoliberal economics did not result in the trickle down of wealth to those at the bottom, nor did neoliberal political liberalisation result in real empowerment of voters or respect for economic, social and cultural rights.[2] For the majority of humankind, human security remains elusive. Wolfensohn's statement above indicates that the key agents of global governance understand the necessity of doing things differently.

This chapter examines the evolving relationship between global governance and human security. First, it begins with a brief discussion of the notion of human security, illustrating its roots and significance in International Relations but importantly locating the concept at the confluence of many disciplinary rivers. It is argued that material sufficiency is a necessary, though not sufficient condition, of human security. Confines of space require discussion in this chapter to be confined largely to that material dimension of human security. Hence the problems of pervasive poverty and deepening inequality which characterise the global social landscape, and which are affected directly by global governance via global development policy, are central to the discussion. Second, therefore, the chapter looks briefly at the global governance institutions that set global development policy. Questions are raised about the appropriateness and legitimacy of these institutions for setting global social policy that impacts on human security across the globe. Those neoliberal development policies, based on the Washington consensus, have been widely rehearsed, and familiarity with them is assumed here. Third, the chapter examines the growing recognition by global governance institutions of deepening inequalities, mounting opposition to global development policies and the potentially explosive link with instability arising from the application of the neoliberal development vision. Accordingly, these governance institutions are revisiting global development policy and mapping a reformist pathway to take us beyond the current material predicament of deepening human insecurity. Assessing this pathway, the chapter concludes that the realisation of human security requires at minimum not only different development strategies to those reformist approaches currently favoured by global governance institutions; it requires a significant reform of those institutions themselves.

Human security

The concept of human security involves a fundamental departure from an orthodox, International Relations security analysis that has the state as the exclusive primary referent object. Instead, human beings and their complex social and economic relations are given primacy with or over states. In the words of Heinbecker, human security is about 'the ability to protect people as well as to safeguard states'.[3] In some human security formulations, such as that of Canadian Foreign Minister Lloyd Axworthy, human needs rather than state needs are paramount. For Axworthy, 'Human security includes security against economic privation, an acceptable quality of life, and a guarantee of fundamental human rights.'[4]

The concept of human security pursued here differs fundamentally from notions of 'security of the individual', conceived in the currently fashionable neoliberal sense. Human security is very far removed from liberal notions of competitive and possessive individualism (that is, the extension of private power and activity, based around property rights and choice in the market place). Rather, human security describes a condition of existence in which basic material needs are met, and in which human dignity, including meaningful participation in the life of the community can be realised.[5] Human security is oriented towards an active and substantive notion of democracy, one that ensures the opportunity of all for participation in decisions that affect their lives. Therefore it is engaged directly with discussions of democracy at all levels, from the local to the global. Such human security is indivisible; it cannot be pursued by or for one group at the expense of another.

Therefore, while material sufficiency lies at the core of human security, the concept also encompasses non-material dimensions to form a qualitative whole. In other words, material sufficiency is a necessary, but not sufficient, condition of human security that entails more than physical survival. For simplicity we can refer to these different aspects in terms of a quantitative/ qualitative distinction, which broadly refer to income poverty and human poverty – to which we return below.

Human security is pursued by the majority of humankind as part of a collective: most commonly the household, sometimes the village or the community defined along other criteria such as religion, ethnicity, gender or caste. Often it is pursued through a combination of these. At the global level, states have the authority and responsibility to attend to the human security needs of their citizens. Weak state–society relations mean that states often hinder rather than help the achievement of human security by all their citizens. Global governance institutions also play a crucial role. They set global development policy and set, apply and monitor the global entitlement rules. Importantly they drive and legitimise global economic integration.

In the context of this emerging global economy, a consideration of human security requires us to consider humanity embedded not simply within discrete sovereign states, but within a global social structure, the capitalist world economy that has been developing since the sixteenth century. A proper understanding of the process of global economic integration and of the distribution of associated costs and benefits is crucial. This involves an appreciation of the patterns of systemic inclusion and exclusion of people in the global economy, which can be mapped with reference to the means of economic sustenance. Cox provides a useful categorisation of the world's producers in the global economy.[6] He identifies a core workforce of highly skilled people integrated into the management process. A second level of precarious workers is located where business is offered the greatest incentives in terms of lowest labour costs or environmental costs. The third level comprises the rest, the expanding pool of people globally who are excluded from international production – the 37 million unemployed plus the low skilled in the rich countries; and one billion under- or unemployed, the marginalised in the Third World and within the economies in transition.

In a way, the work of the United Nations Development Programme (UNDP) has leaned in the direction of considering human security within the context of humanity embedded within a global social structure, the capitalist world economy. The late Dr Mahbub Ul Haq first drew global attention to the concept of human security in the UNDP's Human Development Reports. In 1994, the Human Development Report focused explicitly on human security. The Report argued that:

> For too long, the concept of security has been shaped by the potential for conflict between states. For too long, security has been equated with threats to a country's borders. For too long, nations have sought arms to protect their security. For most people today, a feeling of insecurity arises more from worries about daily life than from the dread of a cataclysmic world event. Job security, income security, health security, environmental security, security from crime, these are the emerging concerns of human security all over the world.[7]

The 1994 Report, by focusing on human security, sought to influence the UN's 1995 World Summit on Social Development in Copenhagen. Over the late 1990s the UNDP's annual reports built upon and refined this concept. In 1997, the focus was on human development, which refers not simply to the income aspects of poverty, but to poverty as a denial of choices and opportunities for living a tolerable life.[8] Importantly, the 1997 Report further disaggregated what we referred to earlier as the quantitative and qualitative dimensions of human security. It made a distinction between income poverty (US$1 a day and below) and human poverty (illiteracy, short life expectancy and so forth). Income poverty and human poverty are often, but not always, linked; for example in the Gulf States, people may suffer human poverty without being income poor. These two aspects tally broadly with the quantitative and qualitative aspects of human security discussed earlier.

The UNDP played a crucial agenda setting role at an early stage with its focus on human security. It was noted earlier that development and human security are receiving more attention now from the key global governance institutions such as the IMF and World Bank, partly because poverty and inequality are increasingly considered to be national, regional and global security threats. Indeed, there seems to be a correlation between the level of entitlement to human security and the propensity for conflict, defined not in orthodox interstate terms but in the wider sense to include the most frequent form of warfare, intrastate. Over the period 1990–5, 57 per cent of countries experiencing war were ranked 'low' on the UNDP's Human Development Index, while only 14 per cent were ranked 'high', and 34 per cent were ranked 'medium'. There may be a causal relationship between lack of material entitlement, health and education, and war.[9]

One explanation of this tragic outcome may be that fundamental economic and social structures allow a privileged global and national elite to control a disproportionate share of available resources. This impacts directly on security. In the words of Smith:

When a privileged elite defends its too large share of too few resources, the link is created between poverty, inequality and the abuse of human rights. The denial of basic freedoms – to organise, to express yourself, to vote, to disagree – forces people to choose between accepting gross injustice and securing a fairer share by violent means. As conflict unfolds, the political leaders that emerge often find that the easiest way of mobilizing support is on an ethnic basis. Thus do the various causes of conflict weave in and out. War will only end if, and when, and where its causes are removed.[10]

Smith elucidates the poverty, inequality and security link clearly. With one-sixth of the world's population receiving 80 per cent of global income, and 57 per cent of the global population consuming only 6 per cent of global income, the concerns about poverty and security expressed at the outset of this chapter by Camdessus and Wolfensohn appear legitimate.[11]

Yet it is important to remember that issues of poverty and inequality matter to human beings in the most potent way, irrespective of whether global governance organisations categorise them as security issues. It is also worth recalling that the total number of people killed during the First and Second World Wars is estimated as having been about 30 million. Compare this figure with the number of people who currently die of hunger-related causes each year: some 15 million. Consequently we can say that every two years the number of people who die of hunger is roughly equivalent to the number killed in eleven years of world war.[12]

In its new concern with human security, the discipline of International Relations is converging with other disciplines such as social policy and development studies. This is long overdue. The increasing concern of all these disciplines with the process and impact of globalisation is fuelling mutual concern with global social policy.[13] This has the potential to generate policy responses greater than the sum of the parts. We turn now to a discussion of global governance, raising some general issues, before turning to a discussion of the nature of reforms proposed by global governance institutions to better meet the human security challenge.

Global governance: in whose interest?

As we enter the twenty-first century, the lack of autonomy which has always been a defining characteristic of Third World states is being felt by all states, to varying degrees. Rapid global economic integration has been accompanied by the erosion of national control over economic decision-making and associated social policies. Global economic governance has concentrated power in fewer and fewer hands. Increasingly, the overwhelming problem of poverty and the broader problem of human insecurity are being tackled by the implementation of global social policies developed and promoted by global governance institutions. An increasingly co-ordinated array of public and private governance institutions, and recently, public/private partnerships, are influential here in promoting the neoliberal vision. This is problematic, not least because those institutions have no formal mandate from global citizenry. Moreover, while the reach of the governance structures referred to may be global, those institutions are hardly global in membership or legitimacy. Exactly who or what is governing the globe, with what authority, and in whose interest? Who has a voice in 'global governance'? Are all voices heard equally? Third World states have long been distinguished by, among other factors, their perception of themselves as vulnerable to external factors beyond their control, and in particular to decisions and policies – primarily economic – which they do not own. Do these Third World states, which now arguably include the former Second World states within their ranks, perceive themselves as having a say in global governance?[14] Or is someone speaking for them?

Here, most attention is paid to the public agencies of global governance, especially the IMF, the World Bank and the WTO. (See Box 7.1 for an illustration of the broad range of global economic governance institutions, and their respective memberships and remits.) The reason for this focus on public agencies is simple: they are supposed to be representing the interests of global citizens and promoting global public goods.

However, this should not be taken to suggest the lesser importance of private groupings that operate alongside states and international institutions in the global governance fraternity. Transnational Corporations (TNCs), for example, have a powerful influence on global economic agenda setting. They work with a range of private business interests through forums such as the International Chamber of Commerce (ICC) and the annual World Economic Forum (WEF) at Davos. As Gill notes:

> At the heart of the global economy there is an internationalisation of authority and governance that not only involves international organisations (such as the BIS, IMF, and World Bank) and transnational firms, but also private consultancies and private bond-rating agencies . . .[15]

Sinclair[16] and Van der Pijl[17] develop ideas about the roles of private bond-rating agencies and management consultancies respectively in global governance. Sinclair refers to these as 'private makers of global public policy'.[18]

Increasingly, business interests are co-operating not only with individual governments but also with international organisations. This is evident in the sudden proliferation of *public/private partnerships*, such as in UN Secretary-General Kofi Annan's Global Compact. Public/private partnerships are also seen in the field of global health. The rise in collaboration between agencies mandated to provide public goods, with private interest based agencies, is clearly visible. For example, even international organisations such as the UNDP increasingly seek collaboration and funding from private businesses. Private companies played an important role in funding global conferences in the 1990s. This closeness between the private and public spheres raises

Box 7.1 **Major agencies of global economic governance** (with membership figures as of the mid-1990s)

BIS Bank of International Settlements. Established in 1930 with head-quarters in Basle. Membership of 40 central banks. Monitors monetary policies and financial flows. The Basle committee on Banking Supervision, formed through the BIS in 1974, has spear-headed efforts at multilateral regulation of global banking.

G7 Group of Seven. Established in 1975 as the G5 (France, Germany, Japan, UK and USA) and subsequently expanded to include Canada and Italy. The G7 conducts semi-formal collaboration of world economic problems. Government leaders meet in annual G7 Summits, while finance ministers and/or their leading officials periodically hold other consultations.

GATT General Agreement on Tariffs and Trade. Established in 1947 with offices in Geneva. Membership had reached 122 when it was absorbed into the WTO in 1995. The GATT co-ordinated eight 'rounds' of multilateral negotiations to reduce state restrictions on cross-border merchandise trade.

IMF International Monetary Fund. Established in 1945 with head-quarters in Washington DC. Membership of 182 states. The IMF oversees short-term cross-border money flows and foreign exchange questions. Since 1979 it has also formulated stabilisation and systemic transformation policies for states suffering chronic difficulties with trans-border debt or transitions from communist central planning.

IOSCO International Organisation for Securities Commissions. Estab-lished in 1984 with headquarters in Montreal. Membership of 115 official securities regulators and (non-voting) trade associa-tions from 69 countries. The IOSCO develops frameworks for transborder supervision of securities firms.

OECD Organisation for Economic Co-operation and Development. Founded in 1962 with headquarters in Paris. Membership of 29 states with advanced industrial economies. Drawing on a staff of 600 professional economists, the OECD prepares advisory reports on all manner of macroeconomic questions.

UNCTAD United Nations Conference on trade and Development. Estab-lished in 1964 with offices in Geneva. Membership of 187 states. UNCTAD monitors the effects of cross-border trade on macro-economic conditions, especially in the South. It provided a key forum in the 1970s for discussions of a New International Eco-nomic Order.

WBG World Bank Group. A collection of five agencies, first established in 1945, with head offices in Washington DC. The Group pro-vides project loans for long-term development in poor countries.

	Like the IMF, the World Bank has since 1979 become heavily involved in structural adjustment programmes in the South and former East.
WTO	The World Trade Organisation. Established in 1995 with head-quarters in Geneva. The WTO is a permanent institution to replace the provisional GATT. It has a wider agenda and greater powers of enforcement.

Source: Jan Aart Scholte, 'Global Trade and Finance', in John Baylis and Steve Smith (eds) *The Globalization of World Politics* (Oxford: Oxford University Press, 1997), p. 431.

important issues, especially about agenda-setting and also the democratic process. The work of Sharon Beder on corporate influence on environmental policy is indicative.[19]

The inclusive language of global conferences, such as the UN Conference on Environment and Development (UNCED) in 1992, and the UN Social Summit in 1995, and their associated declarations, raises some important questions. Whose globe are we talking about? Who is to manage it? With what authority? In whose interest? Global management assumes a common understanding of a particular problem and agreement about how it is to be addressed. These global conferences have undoubtedly played an important and positive role in raising awareness of pressing problems, and have helped to create the space in which debate can occur. Yet the debate has been neatly circumscribed. These conferences have lent legitimacy to a broad neoliberal framework for understanding development, and thus they have a direct bearing on human security. The liberal ideology espoused by powerful states and institutions, and accepted by the majority of governments, has offered a blueprint for global development. This model of development, with its associated methods and objectives, is assumed to be in the interest of all humanity, and it is assumed to have unquestionable authority as it is presented as common sense.

Global governance is increasingly reflected in a conscious co-ordination of policies between the IMF, the World Bank, other regional multilateral development banks, the WTO and a growing number of other arms of the UN system. Recently, it has been seen in aspects of the work of the UNDP and the United Nations Conference on Trade and Development (UNCTAD). The most recent of all these policy co-ordinations is evident perhaps in the integration of the International Labour Organisation (ILO) – a tripartite body in which employers, labour and states are represented. An increasing closeness between the ILO and the WTO is apparent.[20] To different degrees and in different ways, these key institutions have been adapting their general orientation, and their respective institutional structures and policies, to facilitate movement towards a world in which for capital, if not for citizens, national economic sovereignty is an anachronism.

Table 7.1 Global economic governance, 1997

Title	Institutional grouping	Membership	% world GDP	% world population
G7	Western economic powers	Canada, France, Germany, Italy, Japan, UK, US	64.0	11.8
G77	Developing and some transition countries (not Russian Federation or Poland)	143 members	16.9	76.0

Source: Adapted from UNDP, *Human Development Report* (Oxford: Oxford University Press, 1999).

Influence within the public institutions of global governance directly reflects the material inequality of states. Only a handful of states exert meaningful influence in institutions such as the IMF, World Bank or WTO. While the Group of 7 (G7) has been transformed into the Group of 8 (G8) with the addition of Russia, it is the case that the G7 sets the norms and rules of global economic policy. As Sachs points out:

> The G7 countries, plus the rest of the European Union, represent a mere 14 per cent of the world's population. Yet these countries have 56 per cent of the votes in the IMF Executive Board . . . The rest of the world is called upon to support G7 declarations, not to meet [them] for joint problem solving.[21]

From where does the G7 derive the authority and legitimacy to do so? Particularly, given that the G7 is not very representative in terms of global population or indeed number of states. (See Table 7.2.) This is striking when compared with the Group of 77 (G77) – see Table 7.1.

In this context, it is interesting to ponder for a moment on the source of the democratic legitimacy of the IMF and the World Bank. As key institutions pushing the neoliberal development model that favours the private rather than the public sector, *they* are not models of democratic representation. This is evident in Table 7.2.

With regard to the IMF, it is important to remember that the only member state able to exert unilateral veto power is the US. The very existence of the veto is enough to ensure that the US does not need frequent recourse to its use.

Another important forum for global economic governance is the Organisation for Economic Co-operation and Development (OECD). In reality, this is a negotiating body for the industrialised democracies, though membership during the 1990s extended to include South Korea, the Czech Republic, Hungary, Poland, and Mexico (interestingly, Turkey was a founding member in 1961). The overwhelming majority of developing countries do not belong

Table 7.2 Formal distribution of voting power in the IMF, 2000

Country	Population (millions)	% IMF executive vote
US	276	17.68
UK	59	5.1
Germany	82	6.19
France	59	5.1
Japan	126	6.33
Saudi Arabia	21	3.27
Countries: 6	623	44.27
Other Countries: *c*. 190	5.4 billion	43.4

Source: Compiled from IMF data, April 2000, IMF website, and UN Population Division, *Charting the Progress of Populations, 2000*, www.undp.org/popin/wdtrends/chart/15/15.pdf.

to the OECD, and therefore a question arises as to its legitimacy as the negotiating forum for policies and agreements of global reach. The choice of the OECD as the negotiating forum for a Multilateral Agreement on Investment (MAI) comes to mind here.

The scepticism and cynicism of developing countries and global citizens regarding global governance is understandable. From their vantage points, global governance has all the hallmarks of being 'organised under US hegemony and the international institutional structure that conforms to the interests of, broadly speaking, the G7 core capitalist states and their corporations'.[22] Democratic potential at all levels, from the local to the global, is diminished by placing key decisions over policy-making in the hands of ever further removed officials and institutions. It is also reduced by the influence of private interests on the public process, referred to above.

Leaders of those governance institutions are becoming more aware of the failure of neoliberalism to deliver economic and political benefits to everyone. They are also more aware of potential social and political obstacles to the broadening and deepening of global economic integration, on which they continue to pin their hopes for the maximisation of global welfare. Thus they are tentatively beginning to address the nature of global governance, as well as the direction of global development policies. It is to this that we now turn.

Global governance and human security: moving beyond the impasse?

The debate on globalisation and its effects on the poor is legitimate and necessary. No one has a monopoly on the truth. Everyone should have a voice, particularly the poor themselves.

(James Wolfensohn, President of World Bank, *International Herald Tribune*, February 2000)

A new paradigm of development is progressively emerging ... A key feature of this is the progressive humanisation of basic economic concepts. It is now recognised that markets can have major failures and that growth alone is not enough and can even be destructive of the natural environment and of social and cultural goods. Only the pursuit of high-quality growth is worth the effort . . . growth that has the human person at its center . . . A second key feature is the convergence between respect for ethical values and the search for economic efficiency and market competition.

> (Michel Camdessus, Managing Director of the IMF,
> speaking at UNCTAD X in Bangkok, February 2000)

These words may appear very unexpected from the lips of the President of the World Bank and Managing Director of the IMF respectively, who have been at the forefront of these key global governance institutions as they have striven to implement the Washington consensus. But something new is happening. At the outset of the twenty-first century, largely in response to the global financial crises that spread from East Asia in mid-1997, to Russia in 1998, and to Brazil in 1999, the level of debate among concerned champions of the neoliberal project is increasing rapidly. This stands in stark contrast to the 1980s and 1990s, when the neoliberal supporters formed a more cohesive grouping and when the overwhelming number of critiques originated from outside of the development orthodoxy. A new uneasiness is developing within the neoliberal camp, as awareness is heightened of the risks as well as the opportunities posed by global economic integration.[23]

In response, neoliberalism is being *reformed from within*. Reformist views, specified in the above sense, emanate from the global governance institutions such as the G7, the World Bank, the IMF and the WTO, and various other arms of the UN family. They are also developed and supported by various academics, particularly in the US, who move easily between global governance institutions and governments and their academic obligations. While other actors, such as TNCs, are also playing an influential role, the concern in this chapter is mainly with reform responses in the public global governance agencies.

The reformists are not a monolithic group. Yet they have enough in common for us to identify a *reformist pathway*. In particular, reformists have realised the need to secure broad-based support from an increasingly alert 'global public'. Without this, the policy prescriptions of neoliberalism will not enjoy the requisite degree of legitimacy for their continued application. Popular opposition could obstruct – even derail – the neoliberal project. Thus, reformists seek to alter both the process of global governance for development, and global development policies, but in a highly circumscribed way.

While discussion within the neoliberal camp *is* flourishing, it is still located firmly within the parameters of the Washington consensus. Thus, its scope and focus remain constrained in terms of the core assumptions of neoliberal politics. These entrenched commitments – depoliticisation of the economic system, immunisation of the private sphere from demands in the name of the public; the efficacy of market efficiency in allocating social goods – remain unchallenged by the reform proposals which we are witnessing now. The latter are best understood as evolutionary *adaptations within neoliberalism at the tactical level*. For reformists, the end goal remains the same: global economic integration via the free market. This project is meeting with certain challenges. Thus reformists are committed to meeting these challenges by the modification of existing governance structures and modification of neoliberal policies.

The reformist response can best be interpreted with reference to the challenges at which it is directed. Two challenges are especially significant in terms of shaping the reform agenda. The first is the popular opposition to neoliberal policies given that global economic integration has not delivered on its promise of benefiting everyone through 'trickle down'. This elicits reformist responses that are well captured by rhetoric about institutional learning, such as the importance of 'listening to the voices of the poor'. This is clear in Wolfensohn's statement, cited above, calling for a more inclusive sort of decision-making process, and Camdessus' call for a more inclusive approach to development. The second is the challenge of technical obstacles to the smooth running of global economic integration. These include market distorting subsidies, financial instability, and even the role of International Financial Institutions (IFIs) as agencies interfering in the 'ideal market'.

Despite heated debate within the reformist grouping, which is by no means monolithic, three core elements can be abstracted that, taken together, amount to an identifiable whole:

1   Far from abandoning the liberalisation agenda, reformists are seeking to expand it.
2   They want to introduce policy modifications to tackle challenges.
3   They want to broaden ownership of the liberalisation agenda by reaching out to potential opponents, states or civil society groups, and tying them into the project.

Whether we choose to consider trade, finance or investment – the three key areas of liberalisation in the 1980s and 1990s – we can identify an extension of the liberalisation agenda, policy modifications to accommodate problems and challenges, and a new degree of focus on broadening ownership of liberalisation policies to dampen opposition. In each area, the central thrust of the Washington consensus is being maintained under reformist policy changes. Continuity is the name of the game. Here, the focus will be on the third element, as that relates most directly to the nature of governance. Some examples will be drawn from trade, investment and finance as a basis for assessing the adequacy of the strategy of inclusion.

Trade: civil society as the key to expanding ownership?

The migration of the trade liberalisation agenda into new areas is a key aim of the current agents of global economic governance. This will be facilitated by the expansion of ownership of the agenda. Reformists believe a key lesson of the breakdown of negotiations at the WTO Seattle Summit in November/December 1999 was the importance of developing a broader consensus in support of further liberalisation. This had been recognised earlier, but not acted on with serious commitment.

At its May 1998 Ministerial Meeting, the WTO 'recognised the importance of enhancing public understanding of the benefits of the multilateral trading system in order to build support for it'.[24] To this end, most G7 governments, the WTO and the EU, have undertaken consultations or discussions with civil society groups (mostly from the G7 countries) active in the trade debate. Former Director-General of the WTO, Renato Ruggiero, has initiated outreach activities by the Organisation. All these exchanges with civil society are designed to increase support for further trade liberalisation (and in the case of the US, to promote support for fast-track negotiating authority). The EU issued a statement on improving the transparency of WTO operations that stated:

> Transparency should be part of a wider communication strategy to convey the benefits of an open multilateral trading system, explain the function and role of the WTO, as well as the interactions between trade policy and broader concerns in a global economy.[25]

The objective of these reformist moves is to enhance the acceptability of neoliberal economic integration, as well as to pre-empt political resistance to the agenda based on arguments about the legitimacy of neoliberal global governance. Upon closer investigation, the purported concessions can be seen in themselves to advance the agenda to de-politicise the problem of the social distribution of goods.

It is important at this juncture to stress the expansion of *meaningful state involvement* in global governance. The standard reformist response to the need to broaden participation is to widen the involvement of civil society, as illustrated above. Yet although influential figures such as the former Director-General of the WTO, Renato Ruggiero, call for more civil society involvement in trade rules that are increasingly affecting day-to-day lives of the majority of global citizenry, this increased pluralism does not address the fundamental problem of the structure of social power within the WTO. Who sets the WTO's agenda, and in whose interests? While there is a role for civil society groups, they too are unelected representatives of citizenry. In contrast, national governments are mandated to represent citizens, they are accountable to citizens, and they are responsible for the human security of citizens. They must be able to exercise judgements with the goal of human security in mind. They must be able to make the case for developmental and social imperatives in all international forums, confident that they will be heard and that their voices will count. While developing countries are in a majority in the WTO, this does not mean they can exert significant influence on the trade agenda or on outcomes. What matters is not the exercise of numerical strength, but the exercise of social power.[26] Decisions are made in the WTO by the 'consensus of the Quad' – that is, the US, Europe, Japan and Canada. This was exemplified at the Seattle Ministerial Meeting in the exclusive 'Green Room' meetings which did not have the mandate of the full membership, which were not officially announced, and the results of which were not generally made known.[27] The reformist agenda, in identifying civil society involvement as the key to broadening ownership of the liberalisation agenda, is both limited and misconceived. There is a place for such involvement, but as a supplement to, rather than in place of, meaningful state participation.

Finance: broadening ownership by expanding representation

The financial crises of the late 1990s spawned several *ad hoc* groupings of states intent on discussing the reform of the global financial architecture. One important theme that recurred in various incarnations was that of representation. As we saw with trade, those committed to liberalisation are keen to expand ownership of that agenda in order to ease its application. Jeffrey Sachs has suggested that what is needed is 'a dialogue of the rich and the poor together, not just a communion of the rich pretending to speak for the world'.[28]

Some efforts are being made in this direction. The importance of including the emerging economies in the governance structure from the point of view of the G7 was very apparent in the context of the Asian, Russian and Brazilian financial crises. Financial liberalisation meant that the stability of the entire international system could be affected by developments in a range of countries outside of the traditional G7 grouping. If those countries could be brought into the governance structure, the structure itself would gain greater legitimacy. From the viewpoint of the non-G7 countries, especially the emerging economies, it was inappropriate not simply for reasons of sovereignty but for reasons of economic weight that key decisions were made by an exclusive grouping of states.

In September 1999, at the annual meeting of the IMF, a new grouping – the G20 – was agreed upon to consider the restructuring of global finance. The idea of this grouping had originated with Prime Minister Mahathir of Malaysia, and been taken up by US President Clinton. Membership included the G8 countries, the EU, plus eleven emerging market countries chosen for their significance in the global economy. These included, for example, China, India and Brazil. The IMF and the World Bank were also invited to attend the first meeting of the group held in Berlin in December 1999.

Some commentators, such as Randall Germain in this volume (Chapter 2), see the establishment of the G20 as a significant step towards a more inclusive governance of the international financial system. The G20 membership represents 86.7 per cent of global GDP, and 65.4 per cent of global population. However, it is important to raise a note of caution: *the body has no decision-making power*. How significant then is the G20 in bringing even the emerging markets, let alone the 140 or more other states, into the governance of global finance? Germain argues that we can take heart from this, as at least the politics of inclusion is back on the financial agenda in a way it has not been for several decades.

But the establishment of the G20 must be seen against the backdrop of other ongoing discussions which are potentially highly influential and very exclusive indeed. Discussions ongoing in the US, the largest IMF shareholder, and the only state with veto power, need to be taken very seriously. The ideas of US Treasury Secretary Lawrence Summers are noteworthy here, as is the work of the Meltzer Commission.[29] Some commentators, such as Alan Greenspan, Chairman of the US Federal Reserve Board, have gone so far as to suggest that 'financial markets are far too complex for public regulators to oversee'.[30] For him, and many others, self-regulation of private finance is appropriate. Against the backdrop of these debates, the G20 is at best a small step along the road to a more inclusive, representative debate.[31]

Investment: public/private partnerships

Reformists recognise that the globalisation project may be impeded by social challenges. Thus, they are concerned about the bad press targeted at the activities of TNCs in the 1990s. They accept that it is important to address any significant tensions between corporate practice and society's values. The method advocated is *private, not public, regulation*. They believe the circle can be squared by the *voluntary actions* of companies to develop responsible business practice. This is best achieved through *partnerships* between companies, governments, international organisations, employees and local communities.

Reformists set great store on the value of partnerships. These serve a dual function: they help make business practice compatible with society's social values, and they expand ownership of the investment liberalisation agenda. A number of such partnership initiatives have achieved a high profile. At the global level, UN Secretary-General Kofi Annan's Global Compact is one example. In February 2000, Annan remarked:

> I propose that you, the business leaders gathered in Davos, and we, the United Nations, initiate a global compact of shared values and principles, which will give a human face to the global market . . .[32]

At the WEF in Davos, in January/February 1999, the UN Secretary-General called on corporations to abide by core values – human rights, environment and labour standards[33] via participation in a Global Compact. The Global Compact took forward Annan's previous calls at earlier WEF meetings for the UN to form a 'creative partnership' with the private sector, on the basis that the two share mutually supportive goals, and because without such action the course of globalisation will be challenged. Annan pleaded: 'I call on you – individually through your firms, and collectively through your business associations – to embrace, support and enact a set of core values in the areas of human rights, labour standards, and environmental practices.'[34]

Annan's choice of human rights, labour standards and environmental practices was not arbitrary. It was a direct response to the fact that interest group campaigns in these three areas were having an impact on trade and investment liberalisation. The Multilateral Agreement on Investment (MAI), for example, had been derailed at the OECD largely the result of NGO campaigning. Concerned that the result might be restrictions attached to further liberalisation agreements, Annan declared: 'restrictions on trade and impediments to investment flows are not the best means to use when tackling [these legitimate concerns] . . . Instead, we should find a way to achieve our proclaimed standards by other means'.[35]

Annan did *not* suggest a binding international code of behaviour. Rather, *self-regulation* was the way forward for business, especially transnational business. Annan sees private regulation as serving all those affected by a company, that is the stakeholders – shareholders, employees, suppliers, customers, NGOs, business partners and the community. The Secretary-General is calling on businesses to work with a variety of other partners to develop programmes in the three specified areas. These include NGOs, workers' organisations such as the International Confederation of Free Trade Unions (ICFTU) and business associations such as the World Business Council on Sustainable Development (WBCSD), the International Chamber of Commerce (ICC), and the European Business Network for Social Cohesion (EBNSC).

Not all of these partners agree with the exclusive self-regulation of businesses. The ICFTU, for example, argues that 'Global and binding rules are necessary to protect people, not just property'. However, it believes that 'Voluntary initiatives can make a difference', and sees the Global Compact as potentially contributing by encouraging companies to engage in a dialogue with their global social partners.[36]

In addition to the broad agenda of the Global Compact, reformists are developing and supporting a variety of methods to facilitate responsible corporate behaviour. An ILO study available on the Global Compact website offers a good overview of these tools as they relate to labour, for example codes of conduct, social labelling and investor initiatives.[37] A UNEP study accessed via the same site offers an overview of possibilities as they relate to the environment. These codes share two key features: they are *voluntary*, and they are *private*.[38]

Existence of these codes does not guarantee their application. To be effective, codes must be adhered to. However, independent assessments have revealed significant gaps between policy and practice.[39] Mark Thomas' investigations on Nestlé suggest that the company is failing to adhere to the World Health Organisation (WHO) Code of Conduct on powdered baby milk.[40] The problem of lack of adherence to codes is not confined to operations in the developing world. Forcese's study[41] reveals that Canadian cigarette manufacturers, having been criticised for violating the code of conduct which forbade advertising close to schools, changed the code rather than their practice. This is not an isolated incident of non-compliance. A recent study of 360 US companies revealed that 71 had their own code of practice, but less than a third of these codes are monitored, and virtually none are monitored by independent third parties.[42]

A key weakness of the reformist pathway regarding investment was highlighted in April 2000, when in an unprecedented move, UK Prime Minister Blair asked the British company Premier Oil to downsize its operations in Burma. The reason given was that the human rights record of the Burmese government is one of the worst in the world. The company immediately refused, saying that it preferred the path of positive engagement and felt better able to monitor human rights in Burma by operating in the country. The British government had no sanction under law to require a change in the policy of the company. Ultimately, private regulation does not work in the interests of the global citizenry: its origin is private, it is non-binding, it has no mandatory, publicly constituted independent verification process, and it is without automatic punitive sanctions.

Conclusion

This chapter has argued that basic material needs are a necessary but not sufficient condition of human security. The achievement of human security rests firstly on the achievement of those needs. World Bank figures available at the IMF/World Bank annual spring summit in April 2000, indicated that the UN target of a 50 per cent reduction in the absolute poor by 2015 will not be met.[43] In an increasingly co-ordinated fashion, key global governance institutions, and the interests they represent, are overseeing a process of increased economic, political and social stratification. They are complicit in this outcome.

The reformist pathway for development in the twenty-first century, which forms the foundation stone of human security policy, by continuing along the trajectory of the Washington consensus, represents business as usual. It will not make significant inroads into the *distributional* problems of global poverty or global inequality. Neither will it engage with the grim global unemployment situation. The sort of growth which Camdessus is advocating now, that is growth with 'the human person at the center', is not occurring. Likewise, the sort of ownership of global governance which Wolfensohn calls for, is not happening. Without this, the other qualitative aspects of human security, such as respect for social and cultural rights, will remain elusive.

In the short-term, the reformist pathway may temper opposition from within its own ranks. Over the medium to long-term, its failure to address poverty, inequality and unemployment, as well as other social issues, will make it increasingly more difficult to expand ownership of the reformist vision. In turn, this will impact on its ability to achieve its primary goal, that of expanding the liberalisation agenda. Ultimately, the reformist pathway carries the seeds of its own destruction: reform of the governance institutions and of global development policies is not proceeding quickly or deeply enough.

Notes

1 C. Thomas, *Global Governance, Development and Human Security* (London: Pluto, 2000).
2 T. Evans, *The Politics of Human Rights: A Global Perspective* (London: Pluto, 2001).
3 P. Heinbecker, 'Human Security', *Headlines*, 56: 2 (1999), p. 6.
4 L. Axworthy, 'Canada and Human Security: the need for leadership', *International Journal*, LII: 2 (Spring 1997), p. 184.
5 C. Thomas, 'Where is the Third World Now?' *Review of International Studies*, Volume 25, Special Millennium Edition, December 1999.
6 R. W. Cox, 'Civil Society at the Turn of the Millennium: prospects for an alternative world order', *Review of International Studies*, 25: 1 (January 1999), p. 1.
7 UNDP, *Human Development Report* (Oxford: University Press, 1994), p. 3.
8 UNDP, *Human Development Report* (Oxford: Oxford University Press, 1997), p. 2.
9 D. Smith, *The State of War and Peace Atlas* (London: Penguin, 1997), p. 48.
10 Smith, *The State of War and Peace Atlas*, p. 15.
11 *World Bank Development News*, 14 April 2000.
12 C. Thomas and M. Reader, 'Development and Inequality', in B. White, R. Little and M. Smith (eds) *Issues in Global Politics* (Basingstoke: Macmillan, 1997), p. 109.
13 B. Deacon, *Global Social Policy* (Sage: London, 1997).
14 C. Thomas, 'Where is the Third World Now?', p. 228.
15 S. Gill, 'Globalisation. Market Civilisation, and Disciplinary Neoliberalism, *Millennium*, 24: 3 (Winter 1995), p. 418.
16 T. Sinclair, 'Between State and Market: Hegemony and Institutions of Collective Action under Conditions of International Capital Mobility', *Policy Sciences*, 27: 4 (1994).
17 K. Van der Pijl, *Transnational Classes and International Relations* (London: Routledge, 1998).
18 Sinclair, 'Between State and Market', p. 448.
19 S. Beder, *Global Spin: The Corporate Assault on Environmentalism* (Devon: Green Books, 1997).
20 For an alternative perspective see N. Haworth and S. Hughes, 'Trade and International Labour Standards: Issues and Debates over a Social Clause', *Journal of Industrial Relations*, 39: 2 (1997); and R. Wilkinson, 'Peripheralising Labour: the WTO, ILO and the Completion of the Bretton Woods Project', in J. Harrod and R. O'Brien (eds) *Globalized Unions? Theory and Strategy of Organised Labour in the Global Political Economy* (London: Routledge, 2002).
21 J. Sachs, 'Stop Preaching', *Financial Times*, 5 November 1998.
22 P. Wilkin, 'Solidarity in a Global Age – Seattle and Beyond', paper presented to the International Studies Association Annual Conference, Los Angeles, March 2000.
23 J. Rubin, US Treasury Secretary, 'Remarks on the Reform of the International Financial Architecture to the School of Advanced Studies', Princeton University, 21 April 1999.

24 EU, 'Improving the Transparency of WTO Operations', 13 July 1998, sent to WTO for circulation on 14 July as WTO Document WT/GC/W/92.
25 EU, 'Improving the Transparency of WTO Operations'.
26 Wilkin, 'Solidarity in a Global Age'.
27 M. Khor, 'The Revolt of Developing Nations', *Third World Resurgence*, 112/113, January 2000, pp. 9–12; M. Khor, 'Initiate Reform of WTO, Says G77 Chairman', *Third World Resurgence*, 112/113, January 2000, pp. 24–6.
28 J. Sachs, 'Stop Preaching', *Financial Times*, 5 November 1998.
29 L. Summers, 'The Right Kind of IMF for a Stable Global Financial System', US Treasury Secretary remarks to the London School of Business, UK (Washington DC Treasury News from the Office of Public Affairs, US Treasury), 14 December 1999; M. Wolf, 'Between Revolution and Reform: The Meltzer Commission's vision for the IMF and World Bank moves in the right direction but is too simplistic', *Financial Times*, 8 March 2000. Thomas, *Global Governance, Development and Human Security*.
30 A. Greenspan, *American Banker* (October 1998) cited in M. Chossudovsky, 'The G7 "solution" to Global Financial Crisis: a Marshall Plan for creditors and speculators' (Department of Economics, University of Ottawa, 1998).
31 *World Bank Development News*, 15 December 1999.
32 K. Annan, 'Secretary-General Proposes Global Compact on Human Rights, Labour, Environment, in address to World Economic Forum in Davos', *UN press release*, SG/SM/6881, 31 January 1999 (UN Secretary-General Kofi Annan, Davos Forum, January 2000).
33 Annan, 'Secretary-General Proposes Global Compact'.
34 Annan, 'Secretary-General Proposes Global Compact'.
35 Annan, 'Secretary-General Proposes Global Compact'.
36 http://www.icftu.org/english/tncs/glcindex.html.
37 http://www.unglobalcompact.org/gc/unweb/nsf/content/ilostudy.htm.
38 C. Forcese, *Commerce with Conscience* (Ottawa: International Centre for Human Rights and Democratic Development, 1997); A. Ross (ed.) *No Sweat* (London: Verso, 1997); D. Justice, 'The New Codes of Conduct and the Social Partners' ICFTU', 1999, available at http://www.icftu.org/english/tncs/glcindex.html; and Panos Institute, 'Globalisation and Employment', Briefing No. 33 (London: Panos Institute, 1999).
39 Committee of Inquiry, *A New Vision for Buisness* (London: Forum for the Future, 1999), p. 24.
40 http://www.channel4.com/mark_thomas/nestle.10.html.
41 Forcese, *Commerce with Conscience*.
42 A. Marlin, 'Visions of Social Accountability: SA8000', *Visions of Ethical Business*, No. 1 (London: Financial Times Management, October 1998), p. 40.
43 *World Bank Development News*, 14 April 2000.

8 Global governance and poverty reduction

The case of microcredit

Heloise Weber

At the dawn of the twenty-first century the material polarisation of global society is clearly evident. This situation has been aptly described by the Development Assistance Committee (DAC) of the Organisation for Economic Co-operation and Development (OECD) as a 'crisis of global poverty'.[1] Key global institutions have begun to respond to this: in the context of their enhanced efforts to co-ordinate policy for poverty reduction, microcredit has become one of the key targeted institutional responses. However, contrary to popular images of the poverty impact of microcredit, research has shown the adverse social implications for many of the targeted recipients. An understanding of the political-economic embeddedness of microcredit in the context of globalisation offers crucial insights in terms of accounting for this discrepancy. I argue that the global institutional appropriation of microcredit is motivated primarily by its capacity to both facilitate globalisation as well as extend the global governance agenda – in terms of disciplinary neoliberalism – to the level of local communities.

Critical questions about the impact of globalisation on social justice have been raised.[2] In the development context, particular attention has been directed towards the neoliberal orthodoxy of the 1980s and 1990s, especially as it came to be implemented via the World Bank and the International Monetary Fund (IMF) through Structure Adjustment Programmes (SAPs). In some circles this orthodoxy came to be referred to as the Washington Consensus. In many cases, the direct or indirect consequences of SAPs were adverse social impacts, and the Washington Consensus was itself challenged to 'adjust' to bear a human face.[3]

Key international institutions have now begun to respond to 'the crisis of global poverty'. Poverty has become a central focus of global institutions and actors, from the World Bank to the IMF, to Regional Development Banks and Bilateral and Multilateral Development Agencies. Moreover, the IMF and the World Bank have enhanced policy co-ordination for poverty reduction.[4] The renewed focus on issues of social (in)equality has been identified as reflecting a 'mood swing' away from the Washington Consensus towards a *post*-Washington Consensus.

To summarise briefly, under the post-Washington Consensus the global institutional response to the crisis of global poverty has been both distinctive and clear: the focus of the World Bank's World Development Report 2000/ 2001 is on *Attacking Poverty*.[5] These efforts have entailed the making of new patterns of policy co-ordination (or policy harmonisation) across key global institutions and actors, and may be seen to construct the rules and norms of an emerging global development architecture.[6] These concerted efforts must, according to the DAC, be embedded within the process of globalisation and an associated policy framework of economic liberalisation.[7]

Against this background it becomes possible to locate the 'poverty reduction' agenda of the post-Washington Consensus in global political economy. That is, in the context of the *unification* of the rules and norms of the emerging global development architecture with those of neoliberal steered globalisation (reflected in, for example, the values and policies of the World Trade Organisation (WTO)). The global trend towards policy convergence and harmonisation in this logic is representative of what has been referred to by Claire Cutler as the global *unification movement*.[8] Central to the unification movement is *lex mercatoria* or private international trade law.[9] Given the way in which it is embedded in global political economy, the poverty reduction agenda becomes an extension of the global unification movement to the level of local communities. This is the context in which the microcredit strategy to poverty alleviation takes on its significance. The associated widespread adoption of microcredit as a targeted strategy for poverty reduction on a global scale is then best seen as an extension of the global unification movement to the local level. An understanding of the global political-economic embeddedness of microcredit provides important insights in terms of accounting for the disjunction between its purported virtuous outcomes and actual experiences at the community level. The chapter proceeds by first explaining, and then critically evaluating microcredit and microfinance.

Microcredit and poverty reduction

The microcredit approach to poverty reduction is the provision of small loans to poor individuals usually within groups as capital investment to enable income-generation through self-employment. Microcredit programmes are usually complemented by the extension of microfinancial services, which include, for instance, options for insurance schemes or savings. The microcredit approach differs significantly from other approaches to poverty reduction in that it is embedded in a commercial framework. It is, therefore, important to understand the shift in the conception as well as implementation of local development efforts of the 'new' poverty reduction agenda. In this chapter, the focus is on microcredit projects with either formal or informal links to the approach endorsed and structured by global institutions.[10] This is referred to below simply as microcredit or microfinance.

The global microcredit approach to poverty reduction relies on the provision of *credit only*. No skills advancement or training schemes (capabilities enhancement) accompany the packages. The approach has come to be termed 'microcredit minimalism'. Microcredit is innovative in the sense that credit is provided to the poor in the absence of conventional forms of collateral (such as assets of financial value against which credit can be raised). Instead, group (mutual) guarantee mechanisms, such as peer monitoring and peer pressure are employed as a form of social collateral. Policy recommendations have been made however, to establish relevant collateral laws for microcredit where appropriate. This allows for the appropriation of 'movable' property in lieu of monies outstanding.[11]

The underlying assumption of the microcredit approach is that the credit input will result in investments that would generate profits, thus enabling an increase of capital accumulation and asset creation. Typically, however, microcredit steered poverty reduction is anticipated to result not from one-off credit interventions (that is, one loan), but rather through several credit cycles. Therefore, ideally, new and bigger investments should follow each profit cycle, for which new credit interventions (that is, new loans) will always be needed. The envisaged outcome – 'credit, investment, profits, more credit, more investments, bigger profits' – is assumed to result in the transformation of the conditions of the poor from a 'vicious circle' to a 'virtuous cycle'.[12]

Given the above assumption, microcredit focuses on increasing the *supply* of credit to the poor. Since this entails the removal of access barriers to credit provision, microcredit has crucial policy implications in terms of facilitating the liberalisation agenda at all levels, from the global to the level of local communities.[13] In particular, it has direct policy implications for financial sector liberalisation as well for the setting of interest rates. Following the logic of the liberalisation agenda, the preferential interest rates for microcredit are the optimal market rates, and typically range from 20–45 per cent. In some cases it is even made conditional that non-governmental organisations (NGOs) or Microfinance Institutions do *not* lend to the poor at a rate below given commercial rates.[14]

Microcredit has now been widely adopted by key global financial institutions, such as the World Bank and Regional Development Banks. It has also been incorporated by Multilateral and Bilateral Development Agencies (such as, USAID, DFID, CIDA, AusAID), United Nations (UN) Agencies, and NGOs.[15] In February 1997, it was given global coverage through the Microcredit Summit in Washington which inaugurated an action plan to reach 100 million of the world's poorest families – and particularly the women of those families – with microcredit by the year 2005.[16] The Summit's agenda was publicly endorsed and supported through declarations made by various global actors and institutions. Among these declarations, the 'Joint Declaration of the Councils of International Financial Institutions and Donor Agencies' stood out as an important agenda setting pledge.[17]

In short, the envisaged *potential* 'virtuous' outcomes serve as the normative basis for microcredit intervention as a targeted strategy for poverty reduction. Based on this reasoning, it has been argued that credit ought to be guaranteed for life to all persons, and even be declared as a fundamental human right.[18] Thus, popular images and conventional wisdom maintain a positive correlation between microcredit and poverty reduction. These popular representations and discourses have been referred to as the 'public transcripts' of microcredit and poverty reduction.[19] The public transcripts represent microcredit not only as an innovative approach that empowers the poor – and poor women in particular – but also as an *alternative* to neoliberal policy prescriptions. It is often thought of as a 'local', bottom-up approach that results in self-sufficiency, rather than dependency.[20] Thus, microcredit has been, and continues to be, presented as a panacea for poverty reduction.

The 'hidden transcripts' of microcredit and poverty reduction

However, against the public transcripts of its 'virtuous' outcomes, are rich 'hidden transcripts' regarding the poverty impact of microcredit. These hidden transcripts comprise the less *publicly* known facts about the adverse poverty impacts that also result as a consequence of the implementation of microcredit programmes. The hidden transcripts substantially challenge the salience of microcredit as an effective approach to poverty reduction globally. For many of its targeted recipients, microcredit is, in practice, reinforcing poverty and survival insecurities rather than ameliorating these conditions or resulting in self-reliance through self-employment as the public transcripts maintain.[21]

The strategic embedding of microcredit in global political economy

A crucial explanation for the discrepancies between its purported virtuous outcomes as sustained by the public transcripts, and its actual experiences at the local level, may be found in the global political-economic embeddedness of microcredit. In this context, evidence suggests a hidden agenda underpinning the global microcredit approach to poverty reduction. By hidden agenda I mean that the appropriation of microcredit at the level of policy by key institutions of global governance may be motivated by strategic objectives, rather than by substantive concerns, about poverty reduction and development. The *strategic* appropriation of microcredit by institutions of global governance may be underpinned by the conduciveness of the approach to perform a dual function in the context of attempts to both consolidate as well as accelerate the process of globalisation. These two aspects are the following:

1   *Microcredit functions as a catalyst for financial sector liberalisation.* Microcredit as a financially steered poverty reduction strategy by policy implication *facilitates* financial sector liberalisation at the various levels of policy implementation – particularly at the national or macro level. Microcredit also advances financial globalisation. This means the facilitation of an expansion of the trade in financial services: microcredit, as the provision of money *via* credit at the local level, can thus be seen to be an extension of the global trade in financial services agenda.[22] In addition

to achieving financial sector liberalisation through policy implication, the normative force of making financial liberalisation a prerequisite for poverty reduction serves to legitimate this outcome. Thus, the normative agenda is a particularly useful tool to legitimate advances in financial sector liberalisation in a climate of growing disquiet with the associated volatility and hence potentially adverse development implications of a liberal financial order.[23]

2   *Microcredit is an important political safety-net.* Microcredit programmes typically accompany the implementation of economic liberalisation programmes and/or austerity measures, better known as Structure Adjustment Programmes (SAPs). Microcredit employed in such contexts offsets 'income insecurity' that may, for example, result as a consequence of SAPs. In this sense, it absorbs surplus labour in the growing informal sectors (labour rationalisation may also be a consequence of SAPs). The targeted credit intervention sustains continued entitlements to basic resources in the absence – or upon the withdrawal – of the state as guarantor of basic public goods and services. In these contexts, microcredit is envisaged to dampen resistance to the implementation of global policy trends, particularly through SAPs at the national level because of its adverse implications for social justice.

To corroborate the argument about the dual function of microcredit, the chapter now turns to a more detailed discussion of two cases of microcredit in practice: The Grameen Bank in Bangladesh, and the 1986 Emergency Social Fund (ESF) for Bolivia. These two examples have been chosen for the following reasons. The case of Grameen is considered important here because it has been held up as a model of 'success' in the operation of microcredit and poverty reduction. Normative discourses of the poverty impact of Grameen have provided legitimacy to both sustain and expand the global microcredit agenda. The Bolivian ESF, on the other hand, constituted a large microcredit component. It was the first 'experiment' of microcredit's potential to function as a political safety net. The Bolivian experiment has since come to serve as a 'model' for replication in other countries under similar political conditions on a global scale. Both these examples are important in understanding the critique of the global microcredit agenda advanced here.

The Grameen Bank in Bangladesh

The Grameen Bank in Bangladesh has enjoyed a global reputation as a minimalist microfinance institution that has been successful in lifting many families out of abject poverty. It has also had a special reputation for empowering, particularly the women of those families. There is a vast amount of literature supporting these public transcripts, many of which have been published by Grameen itself and/or advocates/practitioners of microfinance minimalism.[24]

However, against the broadly construed favourable presentation of Grameen's role in poverty reduction, there are several critical impact assessment studies, based on participant observation which challenge the dominant discourses broadly on two counts.[25] First, with regard to Grameen's benign effects on the situation of the rural poor; and second, with regard to Grameen claims to 'empower' poor rural women through 'self-employment'.

Grameen's impact on poverty: a critical overview

Several explanations may prevail with reference to the issue of Grameen's adverse impact on the livelihoods of many of its members as well as non-members at the community level. Of these, perhaps one of the most common is that Grameen loans are not always utilised as investment capital for self-employment. Rather, in practice, the loans are actually used for a variety of other reasons and mainly for 'consumption purposes'. Rahman's findings posit the discrepancy between real and projected use of loans to be around 78 per cent.[26] Examples of loans used for purposes other than investment include the purchase of food and clothing, and for re-building or repairing basic dwellings. Loans may also be used to pay for medical treatment. In some cases, loans may even be simply misused by male family members (for purposes such as gambling). It is also common practice to use loans as payment of *dowries* for female family members.[27] Loans are also used for money-lending purposes and in many cases also to repay previous loans.[28] In these circumstances, repayments are usually sustained through a reliance on other sources (or through new loans) or by tapping into any existing but often vulnerable household incomes.

There are some cases when loans used 'indirectly' for investment purposes have been successful. For example, loans have been used by the rural poor as payments to employment agencies as a fee to secure work in the Middle East or in Malaysia, mostly as factory workers or domestic labourers.[29] But these investments are not risk free; even these successes may be easily turned around, as Rahman's examples have illustrated.[30] As a result, there are many cases of the loan input actually resulting in negative social and economic consequences for poor households, with particularly harsh repercussions for the women members.[31] Furthermore, given that the concept of the household in Bangladesh generally refers to the extended family, the social costs of 'downward mobility' are extensive.

Even in circumstances when loans have been invested in a proposed project, they have often resulted in the generation of liabilities rather than assets. Since loans in most cases are used for agricultural or related activities, these investments are often vulnerable to natural disasters (such as floods and cyclones) and other natural calamities, such as the death of farm animals. Insurance policies are not offered to cover these risks.

Other reasons for loans actually being a liability rather than an asset result from the marginal nature of most of the investments. Since the Grameen approach is minimalist, investments tend to be in familiar marginal activities. This is problematic on at least three accounts. First, one consequence is market saturation (engaging in similar investments), which means either a low level of returns on the investment, or a total loss. Second, the interest rate charged by Grameen is so high that 'it is incompatible' with the profit made on these investments.[32] As Rahman has shown, contrary to the public transcript that the Grameen interest rate is 20 per cent, in 1994–95 'the actual annual interest realized from borrowers was 31.68 per cent'.[33]

Third, the loan repayment schedule tends to create bottlenecks for many borrowers, who by definition live in precarious circumstances. Loan repayments commence a week after disbursement. While this affects all borrowers it is particularly harsh for those members who invest the loan as proposed but who do not anticipate failure, or who need time before any profits can be accrued. In such cases, repayments must be made from any other existing household income. This is often done through recourse to the already vulnerable survival strategies, and in many instances at the expense of a further 'downward mobility'[34] of livelihoods. There are many documented cases of households losing their meagre belongings, such as their tin roofs and/or having to take out additional loans from Grameen, sell their fruit trees, or 'borrow cash from all available sources to keep up the installment payments'.[35] In many cases, it has become common practice to either sustain repayments through taking out second or third loans, by borrowing from other NGOs operating similar credit programmes in the community (this process is referred to as 'overlapping' or 'cross-borrowing'), or indeed by resorting to local money-lenders.[36] Through these options of last resort, repayments to the Grameen Bank have been sustained and many have done so through a process of 'credit cycling' that has resulted in the emergence of a 'debt-trap'.

Loan repayments in many circumstances have been sustained under conditions of hardship primarily through the social implications of employing peer pressure, a key strategy that ensures Grameen's institutional success. Rahman's study has revealed that peer-pressure has led to an escalation of violence in Grameen villages stemming from the strategies applied to recover instalments.[37] In my own experience, I encountered a woman who worked for an NGO as a labourer in order to repay her sister-in-law's outstanding loans. This woman explained to me that she, like many others, were too fearful of the social consequences that may follow if repayments were not maintained.

Grameen's impact on women's empowerment

On the issue of the empowerment of destitute women through microcredit, Grameen once again falls short: the micro-loans are said to enable marginalised and destitute women to engage in income generating activities which will result in their economic self-sufficiency. On the issue of the actual loan users, however, it has been revealed that although women take the credit, and are responsible for the debt, a majority of them do not utilise the credit themselves. These findings differ from between 25 and 97 per cent of the proportion of women borrowers who utilise the credit themselves.[38] This means, according to one study, that only 3 per cent of women borrowers actually use the loans themselves.

On raising this issue with senior Grameen Bank officials, rather than dispute these findings, I was provided with a 'new' explanation of what they mean by empowerment: given the cultural context of Bangladesh, they explained, the fact that women *take* the loans is in itself a process of empowerment. This is contrary to the many public images and the rhetoric sustained on Grameen, both by the institution itself and by other official development agencies and institutions.

Furthermore, Rahman's analysis of Grameen's gender bias points to strategic objectives associated with the targeting of women. The targeting of women as credit recipients in this context, Rahman argues, is strategic, because the safeguard of women's *ijjat* (honour) 'by men in the society gives the lending institution an unwritten guarantee of getting back regular installments from its women borrowers'.[39]

Rahman's argument points to the fact that Grameen's gender bias is based on the assumption that, given the cultural context, women are easier to discipline, and therefore pose less of a (default) risk to the Bank's practices and operations. This is substantiated by Helen Todd's analysis which finds that the shift toward a focus on women by Grameen in the mid-1980s was 'mainly in response to increasing repayment problems within male centers'.[40] These findings have led to conclusions that 'women have taken over the task of securing loan instalments for their male relatives, but not of managing new economic initiatives. In effect, they have become an unpaid intermediary for credit institutions'.[41]

As an institution of local financial intermediation, Grameen can lay claim to considerable success, with an impressive 98 per cent loan repayment rate often cited as a reflection of this. However, in evaluating the success of Grameen it is important to desegregate its *institutional* success from a corresponding social impact. Indeed, an analysis of the hidden transcripts of Grameen suggests that its institutional success may well be sustained at the cost of the social and economic regression of the livelihoods of many of its members. These critical findings are not unknown among the policy community, both in Bangladesh[42] and among global institutions. As a World Bank study observes,

> [I]n Bangladesh, for example, microfinance programmes sponsored by the Grameen bank and other organizations – with increasing support from donors – are emerging as a strong instrument for poverty reduction. The available literature does not, however, indicate whether microfinance can reduce, if not eliminate poverty ... programmes benefit only the portion of the poor that [are] able to use loans productively. The ultrapoor who lack this ability as well as land (a source of employment)

do not join microcredit programmes, and thus targeted wage employ-ment schemes or other transfer mechanisms are more appropriate.[43]

Another World Bank analysis cautions on the limitations of microcredit *minimalism* especially in the context of globalisation.

> Relying primarily on the credit demand of the poorly-educated entre-preneurs may prove too costly for the Grameen Bank. As the economy grows, commercial banks and other development financial institutions could finance projects that produce similar non-farm goods on a larger and more profitable scale. The low cost production of large-scale enter-prises may drive down the profit margins of small-scale projects financed by the Grameen Bank, eventually forcing them out of this sector.[44]

These critical findings and cautionary advice have yet to stem the global drive to replicate the core features of Grameen and microfinance minimalism. The appeal of Grameen to the global policy community lies in its optimism of achieving poverty reduction through 'grass-roots capitalism'.[45] However, the 'reality' of Grameen's poverty impact does not stand up to its 'rhetoric'. Yet, the rhetoric of Grameen has been a powerful force in contributing to legitimating the political shift of development policy to the imperatives of the post-Washington Consensus. This has been a useful instrument in the context of appropriating microcredit primarily because of its capacity to function as a political safety net. The next section engages this issue through the example of the Bolivian ESF.

The Bolivian ESF and microcredit

The ESF was implemented in the context of Bolivia's adoption of a New Economic Programme (NEP). This entailed the widespread implementation of liberalisation policies as well as the adoption of austerity measures. The adverse social impact of the NEP was enormous and threatened to become politically unsustainable, thus endangering the entailed adjustment pro-gramme.[46] The ESF was implemented as a temporary measure to counter this political risk. In December 1986 the World Bank, with the support of eminent local business groups, set up the ESF.[47] The ESF, as noted above, had a strong microcredit component.[48]

Designed as a 'quick-disbursing mechanism for financing small, technically simple projects'[49] operating in the informal sector, the ESF approach pro-vided a departure from traditional public welfare programmes which suited well the objectives of the NEP. Thus a World Bank evaluation concluded that 'the ESF philosophy was consistent with the macroeconomic frame-work'.[50] That is, it was primarily conceived of in terms of an economically cost-effective political safety net to see through the implementation of the NEP. It was based on the assumption that,

The *perception* that the government is doing something to make the adjustment process less painful or costly is important to the political process of sustaining adjustment . . . If this did not create direct support, it at least reduced potential opposition to the government and its programme . . .[51]

The ESF was relatively successful in achieving its objectives at that time. As a consequence, the World Bank pursued its potential to be replicated in other countries under similar political prerogatives. The following observations and conclusions were drawn:

> In a nation where the organized base of opposition was relatively larger, or where resources were more limited, the political dynamic might not be the same, and the issue of who the programme targeted might have to take very different criteria into account, if contributing to the political sustainability of adjustment was a major goal of the compensation programme.[52]

Thus, although the ESF in Bolivia had come about under quite specific circumstances it was concluded that its basic patterns – given certain contextually contingent amendments and modifications – were salient enough to provide a framework for more general applications. Moreover, the financial embedding of the ESF and its cost effectiveness as an approach to welfare provision, at least from the perspective of the World Bank, made it an attractive model for replication. It was concluded that,

> the basic principle of a financial intermediary that provides grants to local groups on a demand-driven basis using flexible and well designed management strategies is more *globally applicable*.[53]

The ESF was designed as a temporary measure to bridge a period of economic adjustment and recovery. It was politically astute, but it also enabled the World Bank and the IMF to repackage their innovative response to local social and political resistance to SAPs as though they were responding to the widespread criticisms of the social cost of adjustment and the calls for 'adjustment with a human face'.[54]

The Bolivian ESF thus informed the design of Social Funds, which has come to be a popular and targeted lending strategy within the World Bank's lending portfolio. Other ESFs were soon created, especially in Latin America and sub-Saharan Africa.[55] On one reading of the Bolivian ESF, it has been observed that '[m]ost importantly [it] . . . encouraged the international development banking system to experiment with funding projects that addressed the social costs of adjustment'.[56]

The next section addresses the replications of the Bolivian ESF in its relation to the targeted poverty reduction agenda that subsequently emerges in the World Bank. This poverty reduction agenda is then evaluated in the context of the wider policy objectives of both the World Bank and IMF.

The IMF and the World Bank: financial framework setting for poverty reduction

The ESF policy framework, adopted by the World Bank under the rubric of its Social Funds approach, has been recognised as a long-term functional necessity. This is because it has been acknowledged that the social cost of adjustment might well be long term rather than temporary.[57] Since the Bolivian case, the World Bank has rapidly increased its portfolio of Social Fund type programmes. At the end of fiscal year 1996, it had approved 51 Social Funds in 32 countries.[58] The controversial issues surrounding Social Funds[59] are concealed through public discourses of commitments to poverty reduction. Poverty reduction in this sense means 'add on' strategies to facilitate and sustain the objectives of liberalisation and fiscal austerity. In 1998 the World Bank stated that,

> the amount lent under the Programme of Targeted Interventions increased from 29 to 40 per cent of total investment lending. The amounts lent for poverty-focussed adjustment operations also increased, from 52 to 64 per cent of total adjustment lending.[60]

In practice, an increase in 'poverty targeting' has meant an increase in the application of Social Funds. It is in this context, that the appropriateness of microcredit as an intervention into poverty reduction has been placed on the agenda of global development finance institutions, particularly that of the World Bank.

In addition to the capacity of microcredit to be appropriated as a political safety net in the context of SAPs, it also provides an added fillip to realising the policy objectives assigned to the World Bank in the division of labour between itself and the IMF.[61] In this institutional division of labour, the World Bank has responsibility to focus in practice on financial sector development (this includes the liberalisation of financial sectors).[62] The capacity of microcredit to function as a catalyst for financial liberalisation has made it a particularly pertinent tool in the form of the poverty reduction strategy.

For example, the World Bank has, since the early 1990s, adopted proactive policy guidelines through which to pursue these financial sector objectives. A notable advancement in this direction was the adoption of Operational Directive 8.30 for the Financial Sector. However, because of uncertainty about how to implement the guidelines in practice,[63] it was recast as an Operational Policy (OP 8.30) on Financial Intermediary Lending (FIL).[64] This document sets out policies for financial sector operations within a liberal financial framework. It makes explicit reference to microcredit and microfinance, and can be seen to tie in microcredit to wider financial sector objectives. For example, crucial policy implications of OP 8.30 entail the removal of barriers to the supply of credit. It can thus be seen to directly facilitate financial sector liberalisation. OP 8.30 incorporates microcredit into the financial sector objectives by anchoring the FIL approach in the context of poverty reduction. At the same time, it can be seen to legislate the call for 'enabling environment' at the macro level for microcredit. It is interesting to note how OP 8.30 progresses towards its policy on microcredit. For instance, it states that the World Bank will not accept a member country's wish to pursue state intervention in the setting of interest rate policy, which includes interest rate subsidies.

> However, under certain circumstances, the Bank may support programmes that include *directed credit or subsidies*.[65]

Micro-credit steered poverty reduction programmes fall within the Bank's rubric of *directed credit* under its Programmes of Targeted Intervention. A detailed exposition of directed credit, is explicit in its micro-finance focus:

> In many borrowing countries, increasing access to credit by specific sectors (e.g *micro-finance institutions* or the rural sector) is a major policy objective of the government, and some use directed credit to pursue this objective. A Bank FIL may support directed credit programmes to promote sustained financing for such sectors, *provided the programmes are accompanied by reforms to address the underlying institutional infrastructure problems and any market imperfections that inhabit the market-based flow of credit to these sectors*. Such reforms include measures to (a) address obstacles that impede the flow of funds to the credit recipients, or (b) *enhance the creditworthiness of the intended beneficiaries through appropriate approaches such as mutual group guarantees*.[66]

While OP 8.30 sets the precedent for targeted poverty reduction strategies and openly quotes the microcredit approach, the World Bank has yet to officially co-ordinate it with its Operational Policy on Poverty Reduction (OP 4.15). It is anticipated, however, that OP 4.15 would complement OP 8.30 and cite microcredit as a key targeted intervention for poverty reduction.[67] Meanwhile, such co-ordination is already reflected in practice through the Social Funds strategy.

The capacity of microcredit to facilitate the conducive 'enabling environments' for the financial services sector has been well recognised. For example, in 1995 the World Bank created the Consultative Group to Assist the Poorest (CGAP). The CGAP has a specific mandate to advance microfinance globally, and particularly to work towards legislature changes for financial sector operations at the macro-level.

The CGAP and microfinance

Housed in the World Bank's Finance and Private Sector Development Vice-Presidency, the CGAP is a multi-donor initiative created 'to reduce poverty by increasing *access* to financial services for very poor households through financially sustainable institutions'.[68] The CGAP was initially established for a three-year period, but was renewed by its member donors for an additional five years, starting from 1 July 1998.[69] The objectives of the CGAP make clear its role as a catalyst for the expansion of microfinance programmes as well as financial sector liberalisation.[70] One role of the CGAP is to work towards co-ordinating the global microfinance agenda with the World Bank's financial sector objectives. According to the CGAP this has resulted in,

> *expedited financial sector reform* in such countries as Angola, Argentina, Armenia, Benin, Brazil, Cambodia, China, Ethiopia, Ghana, Guatemala, Honduras, India, Jamaica, the Kyrgyz Republic, Lao PDR, Mexico, Moldova, Mozambique, Pakistan, Panama, Peru, Sri-Lanka, Tajikistan, Tanzania, Togo, and Vietnam.[71]

Co-operation between the World Bank and the CGAP is tantamount to a form of 'cross-conditionality'. The CGAP through a co-ordination of policy between informal donor consortiums, the financial markets and country specific financial objectives, offers recommendations for potential strategies to the World Bank to achieve its financial sector objectives. The World Bank, in turn, offers support for poverty reduction through microfinance programmes (targeted interventions) to respective countries on the condition that those states agree to improve the overall macro-economic environment. This would specifically entail the liberalisation of national financial sectors. Most countries adopting microcredit-based poverty reduction programmes have had accompanying financial sector policy changes. Thus, by making poverty reduction one of the motives for financial liberalisation, the strategic imperative has been inverted and legitimated through normative appeal. In doing so, obstacles toward financial liberalisation have been overcome by making them untenable both practically and morally. They have been made harder to sustain against the moral force *for* poverty reduction.

Social Funds and the dual function of microcredit

According to a CGAP report, the most popular means for implementing microcredit programmes are through Social Funds.[72] Through Social Funds the dual function of microcredit is consolidated and legitimated on the grounds of a poverty reduction agenda. The strategic political objectives underpinning the Social Funds agenda are reflected in the fact that research has uncovered links between 'safety net' programmes (or targeted poverty reduction programmes) and local political outcomes (including electoral ballot-based outcomes).[73] In terms of achieving any substantial impact on poverty reduction, however, microcredit has not delivered on its purported 'virtuous' outcomes.[74]

A study by the World Bank's Sustainable Banking for the Poor (SBP) initiative stated that the microfinance sector does not dominantly service microenterprises, but rather provides credit for 'consumption smoothing'.[75] It points to the widespread problems of 'pyramid loans' and 'overlapping' or 'cross-borrowing'. The SBP study backtracks on the role of microcredit as a panacea for alleviating the economic conditions of the *poorest*, and cites it as purposeful virtually only in the limited sphere of small enterprise development rather than for income-generation purposes.

These critical findings have not, however, contained or cautioned the outreach efforts (individuals being targeted).[76] The SBP study does draw attention to the fact that 'the seeds had been planted for a shift to microcredit aimed at very poor people whose activities were not so much businesses as "livelihood activities" '.[77] An explanation for this may be found in what the study does not address: within the framework of a Social Funds approach these outcomes might be integral to the motivations underpinning the microcredit agenda.[78]

Global governance and poverty reduction: concluding observations

The global microcredit and poverty reduction agenda is significant in terms of both its function as a tool that facilitates the imperatives of globalisation, as well as for its global governance implications. In the sense of the latter, the appropriation of microcredit as a political safety net, as with the case in Bolivia and its many replications under similar political conditions, reveals a disciplinary potential underpinning the strategy. This potential of microcredit applied at the level of individuals within local communities can be seen to reflect what Stephen Gill has identified and referred to conceptually as disciplinary neoliberalism at the global level.[79]

The disciplinary component of microcredit might be essential to the objective of extending the socially disembedding logic of the global unification movement to the level of local communities. This is because, as Cutler has argued,

> The global unification movement privileges the private sphere and, in so doing, facilitates the further denationalization of capital and *the disembedding of commercial activities from governmental and social control*. Unification thus operates as a corporate strategy designed to assist the reconfiguration of authority in the global political economy in line with the disciplinary neoliberal agenda.[80]

Thus, from the perspective of the architects of global development the harmonisation of local social policy at the global level along the rules and norms of the unification movement provides for a coherent set of tools that may facilitate as well as govern the globalisation agenda. The microcredit agenda is significant in that it is conducive to facilitating policy changes at the local level according to the logic of the globalisation agenda while at the same time advancing its potential to discipline locally in the logic of the global governance agenda.

An exposition of the global political economy of microcredit and poverty reduction elucidates *how* the 'poverty reduction' agenda is implicated in strategies of global governance. Microcredit, although implemented at the level of local communities, is a policy initiated not at the national (or even local) level but at the level of global institutions. It is thus also an explicating example of what Deacon has referred to as the 'supranationalization of local social policy'.[81] In this sense, the politics of development of most Southern states – local politics – has now come to be pre-framed at the level of global institutions. This has critical implications for political struggle and undermines the 'democractic provision'.[82]

The example of microcredit also points to the changing conceptions of development policy, as well as to the changing nature and patterns of governance precisely at a point when political legitimacy for neoliberalism is waning in the social 'life-world'. What is discernible is the manner and extent by which the global governance agenda seeks to consolidate the crises and contradictions of capitalism through a normatively sustained 'politics of inclusion'. This has entailed a particular strategy that has sought to govern the 'local' in a manner that aims at social closure.[83] In this sense, the 'poverty reduction' agenda of the post-Washington Consensus seems rather a mechanism of social control through disciplinary neoliberalism. The normative discourses of 'poverty reduction' appropriated in the public transcripts may be instrumental to efforts to manage or offset, what Sinclair has identified as the contest between global governance and local governance.[84] Thus, understanding the political significance of 'the dialectical potential of the commonplace arena in which these pressures compete'[85] is as important as understanding the political significance of strategies *actually* targeted towards poverty reduction. The agenda may well be aimed at commanding 'consensus' for what Gill has called the 'new constitutionalism'[86] from those engaged in political struggle for a more democratic and just global polity.

Notes

1 OECD, 'Development Co-operation 1999 Report', *The DAC Journal – International Development*, 1: 1 (2000) p. 119.
2 See for example, Samir Amin, *Capitalism in the Age of Globalisation* (London: Zed Books, 1997); Julian Saurin, 'Globalisation, Poverty and the Promises of Modernity', *Millennium*, 25: 3 (1996); Richard Higgott and Richard Devetak, 'Justice Unbound: Globalisation, States and the Transformation of the Social Bond', *International Affairs*, 75: 3 (1999); James H. Mittelman, *The Globalization*

Syndrome: Transformation and Resistance (Chichester: Princeton University Press, 2000); Caroline Thomas, 'Where is the Third World Now?', *Review of International Studies*, Special Issue 25 (1999).

3 For a discussion of these issues see for example, Caroline Thomas, *Global Governance, Development and Human Security* (London: Pluto, 2000).

4 This is most evident in the new 'poverty focussed' conditionalities, prepared jointly by the IMF and World Bank. See for example the 'Poverty Reduction Strategy Papers – Operational Issues' (10 December 1999); see also the World Bank Group, Operations Policy and Strategy, 'Poverty Reduction Strategy Papers, Internal Guidance Note'. Both documents are available at www.worldbank.org/poverty/strategies/keydocs.htm.

5 World Bank, *World Development Report 2000/2001: 'Attacking Poverty'* (Oxford: Oxford University Press, 2000).

6 An outline of such an architecture is evident in World Bank President, James Wolfensohn's, *A Proposal For A Comprehensive Development Framework* (Washington, DC: World Bank, 1999). For the various policies adopted in this context see OECD, 'Development Co-operation 1999 Report'; see also OECD, 'Development Co-operation 2000 Report', *The DAC Journal – International Development*, 2: 1 (2001).

7 OECD, 'Development Co-operation 1999 Report', p. 3.

8 Claire Cutler, 'Public Meets Private: The International Unification and Harmonisation of Private International Trade Law', *Global Society*, 13: 1 (1999).

9 Claire Cutler, 'Locating "Authority" in the Global Political Economy', *International Studies Quarterly*, 43: 1 (1999) p. 59. See also Jarrod Wiener, *Globalization and the Harmonization of Law* (London: Pinter, 1999), esp. pp. 151–83.

10 See, for example, *Micro and Small Enterprise Finance: Guiding Principles for Selecting and Supporting Intermediaries*, (pink book) produced in 1995 by the 'Committee of Donor Agencies for Small Enterprise Development' and the 'Donors' Working Group on Financial Sector Development'. Available from the CGAP, World Bank. The 'pink book' rules have been endorsed across the board among the donor community.

11 See the CGAP, *Focus No. 4* (Washington DC: the CGAP Secretariat, World Bank, 1994) p. 3.

12 For more of an institutional perspective on issues and case studies of microcredit and microfinance see Maria Otero and Elisabeth Rhyne (eds) *The New World of Microenterprise Finance: Building Healthy Financial Institutions for the Poor* (London: Intermediate Technology Publications, 1994); and Hartmut Schneider (ed.) *Microfinance for the Poor* (Paris: IFAD/OECD, 1997). For a general overview see David Hulme and Paul Mosley, *Finance Against Poverty*, Volumes 1 and 2 (London: Routledge, 1996); and Geoffrey D. Wood and Iffath A Sharif, *Who Needs Credit? Poverty and Finance in Bangladesh* (London: Zed Books, 1997).

13 These policy implications can be discerned from statements made by the G7 and G8. See for instance their following statements: G7, 'Confronting Global Economic and Financial Challenges' (1997); G8, *Communique, Denver*, 22 June 1997 (both documents available at www.library.utoronto.ca/g7/denver.htm); G8, *Communique, Okinawa*, 2000 (available at www.g8kyushu-okinawa.go.jp/e/documents/commu.html) p. 3.

14 For example, the Palli Karma-Sahayak Foundation (PKSF) an apex financial institution in Bangladesh has clear policy on this issue. In lending to its Partner Organisations (that is, NGOs and Microfinance Institutions) to onlend microcredit at the level of individuals it 'imposes a minimum lending rate of 16% to ensure that POs do not lend below commercial bank rates'. See World Bank, *Bangladesh, Poverty Alleviation Microfinance Project* (Washington, DC: World Bank, 1996) p. 51.

15 See the respective websites of these institutions and agencies for policy documents and programmes on microcredit.

16 *The Microcredit Summit Report, February 2–4 1997* (Washington, DC: RESULTS Educational Fund, 1997), p. 1.

17 *The Microcredit Summit Report*, pp. 47–9.

18 M. Yunus, *Credit For Self-Employment: A Fundamental Human Right* (Dhaka: Grameen Bank, 1996).

19 Aminur Rahman, 'Micro-credit Initiatives for Equitable and Sustainable Development: Who Pays?', *World Development*, 27: 1 (1999), p. 68.

20 An oft mistaken assumption that has indirectly contributed to the legitimation of the expansion of microcredit programmes has been the uncritical conception (at least among most circles) of the 'local' as a social life-world sphere to be somehow more democratic and ethically consolidated. Thus the assumption that microcredit is a 'grassroots' and 'locally' bounded approach has often reinforced perceptions of it being 'alternative' to neoliberal politics. The understanding that microcredit results in self-sufficiency rather than dependency informed the Hearing before the (US) Subcommittee on International Economic Policy and Trade of the Committee on International Relations House of Representatives (105th Congress, Session I). See the report of this hearing, *Microcredit and Microenterprise: The Road to Self-Reliance* (Washington, DC: US Government Printing Office, 1997).

21 See for example, Benjamin McDonald and Joanna Ledgerwood, 'Case Studies in Microfinance, Non-Governmental organizations (NGOs) in Microfinance: Past, Present and Future – An Essay, May 1999 (http://www-esd.worldbank.org/sbp/end/ngo.htm). This study is based on research conducted by the World Bank under the Sustainable Banking with the Poor (SBP) project, other literature on microfinance and their (authors) own experience over the last 15 years. On the issue of loan use, this study confirms that cross-borrowing is a part of survival strategies of the poor (that is, where money is borrowed from one NGO to pay off the other); Shahidur Khandker, *Fighting Poverty with Microcredit* (World Bank, Poverty and Social Policy Department – unpublished research document), p. 2. Khandker has also noted that 'microcredit induced self-employment is a complement to child labor and that self-employed activity financed by a microcredit programme may facilitate child employment', p. 48. Also Aminur Rahman, *Rhetoric and Realities of Micro-Credit for Women in Rural Bangladesh: A Village Study of Grameen Bank*, unpublished PhD thesis, Department of Anthropology, University of Manitoba, Canada, 1998; Rahman, 'Micro-credit Initiative'; Mubina Khondkar, *Women's Access to Credit and Gender Relations in Bangladesh*, unpublished PhD thesis, University of Manchester, UK, Institute for Development Policy and Management, 1998; Jude L. Fernando, 'Empowerment Through Indebtedness: NGOs, 'Gender Politics' and the Political Economy of Microcredit', paper presented at the International Studies Association, 42nd Annual Conference, Chicago, February 2001. See also Helen Todd, *Women at the Centre: Grameen Bank Borrowers After One Decade* (London: Westview Press, 1996).

22 For a general overview of this issue see Sydney J. Key, 'Trade Liberalisation and Prudential Regulation: The International Framework for Financial Services', *International Affairs*, 75: 1 (1999).

23 For example, see the discussion in Nicola Bullard, Walden Bello and Kamal Mallhotra, 'Taming the Tigers: the IMF and the Asian Crisis, *Third World Quarterly*, 19: 3 (1998).

24 For literature supporting these public discourses see for example the many writings by Muhammad Yunus, the founder and Managing Director of the Grameen Bank. Some examples of these are: Muhammad Yunus, *Credit for Self Employment for the Poor*; Muhammad Yunus, *Combating Poverty Through Self-Help:*

German Parliamentary Committee Hearing (Dhaka, Bangladesh: Grameen Bank, Re-print January 1996); Muhammad Yunus, *Grameen Bank – Does the Capitalist System have to be the Handmaiden of the Rich?* (Dhaka, Bangladesh: Grameen Bank, 1996). See also Andreas Fuglesang and Dale Chandler, *Participation as Process – Process as Growth* (Dhaka, Bangladesh: Grameen Bank, 1993); David S. Gibbons (ed.) *The Grameen Reader*, 2nd Edition, Reprint (Dhaka, Bangladesh: Grameen Bank, 1995); Helen Todd, *Women at the Centre: Grameen Bank Borrowers After One Decade* (Westview Press, 1996).

25 Rahman, *Rhetoric and Realities of Micro-Credit*; Rahman, 'Micro-credit Initiative'; Mubina Khondkar, 'Micro-Finance and Women's Economic Empowerment', paper presented at the Development Studies Association, Norwich, 1997; Mubina Khondkar, 'Socio-Economic and Psychological Dynamics of Empowerment of Grameen Bank and BRAC Borrowers', paper presented at the Institute of Development Studies, Sussex, 1998; M. Goetz and R. Sen Gupta, 'Who Takes the Credit? Gender Power and Control over Loan Use in Rural Credit Programmes in Bangladesh', *World Development*, 24: 1 (1996), pp. 44–64; Khondkar, *Women's Access to Credit and Gender Relations in Bangladesh*; Fernando, 'Empowerment Through Indebtedness'; see also, Todd, *Women at the Centre*. My own participant observation in Bangladesh supports these conclusions.

26 Rahman, 'Micro-credit Initiatives', p. 75.

27 A *dowry* is a 'gift' paid for the marriage of women to their male partners.

28 Khondkar, 'Micro-Finance and Women's Economic Empowerment', pp. 6–7. See also Rahman, 'Micro-credit Initiatives' p. 75; Rahman, *Rhetoric and Realities of Micro-Credit*, pp. 123–40.

29 Khondkar, 'Micro-Finance and Women's Economic Empowerment', pp. 6–7; Rahman, 'Micro-credit Initiatives', pp. 75–8.

30 Rahman, *Rhetoric and Realities of Micro-Credit*, pp. 121–68. See also Khondkar, 'Women's Access to Credit and Gender Relations in Bangladesh', pp. 137–68. While clearly an opportunity to work in the Middle East has helped many rural families, the insecurities and physical and emotional abuse that may come with this option are clear. See 'Fuses are burning all over the Gulf', *Financial Times, Weekend* 10 June/11 June 2000, p. i.

31 Rahman, *Rhetoric and Realities of Micro-Credit*, p. 147.

32 See for example, Rahman, *Rhetoric and Realities of Micro-Credit*, p. 132.

33 Rahman, *Rhetoric and Realities of Micro-Credit*, p. 154 (see note 54).

34 Rahman, 'Micro-credit Initiatives'; Rahman, *Rhetoric and Realities of Micro-Credit*, esp. pp. 133–68; Khondkar, 'Women's Access to Credit and Gender Relations in Bangladesh', pp. 137–68, 253–78.

35 Rahman, 'Micro-credit Initiatives', p. 77.

36 Rahman, *Rhetoric and Realities of Micro-credit*, pp. 162–3.

37 Rahman, 'Micro-credit Initiatives', pp. 71–2; Rahman, *Rhetoric and Realities of Micro-credit*, pp. 115–48.

38 See Todd, *Women at the Centre*; Khondkar, 'Micro-Finance and Women's Economic Empowerment', p. 14; Khondkar, *Women's Access to Credit and Gender Relations in Bangladesh*, p. 275; the findings of my own participant observation suggest the ratio to be within the latter category.

39 Rahman, 'Micro-credit Initiatives', p. 70; Rahman, *Rhetoric and Realities of Micro-Credit*, pp. 86–90.

40 Todd, *Women at the Centre: Grameen Bank Borrowers After One Decade*, pp. 159–60; Rahman, 'Micro-credit Initiatives', p. 69.

41 Mubina Khondkar, 'Socio-Economic and Psychological Dynamics of Empowerment of Grameen Bank and BRAC Borrowers', p. 8.

42 See, for example, Dewan A. H. Alamgir, *Microfinancial Services In Bangladesh: Review of Innovations and Trends* (Dhaka: Credit and Development Forum, 1999)

p. 37. Here Alamgir references his 1998 study of the 'Impact of Poverty Allevia-tion Programme of the Palli Karma-Sahayak Foundation' (PKSF). The PKSF is the apex financial institution in Bangladesh for microfinance. Funding for the PKSF comes from the World Bank among other donors. See also M. D. Hasan Khaled, 'Overlapping Problems in Microcredit Operations', *The Microcredit Review*, 1: 1 (December 1998), pp. 43–7. *The Microcredit Review* is produced by the PKSF.

43 Khandker, *Fighting Poverty with Microcredit*, p. 2. Khandker has also noted that 'microcredit induced self-employment is a complement to child labor and that self-employed activity financed by a microcredit programme may facilitate child employment', p. 48.

44 Shahidur R. Khandker *et al.*, *Grameen Bank, Performance and Sustainability* (Washington: World Bank, 1996), p. 86.

45 See Muhammad Yunus (with Alan Jolis), *Banker to the Poor: The Autobiography of Muhammad Yunus* (London: Arum Press, 1998), p. 194.

46 For more on this see, James Dunkerley, *Bolivia: Political Transition and Economic Stabilization, 1982–1989* (London: Institute of Latin American Studies, UCL, 1990); and Jeffrey D. Sachs (ed.) *Developing Country Debt and Economic Perform-ance: Volume 2, Country Studies: Argentina, Bolivia, Brazil and Mexico* (London: The University of Chicago Press, 1990) esp. pp. 157–266. See also Devesh Kapur *et al.*, *The World Bank – Its First Half Century* (Washington, DC: Brookings Institution Press, 1997), p. 365.

47 Steen Jorgensen *et al.*, *Bolivia's Answer to Poverty, Economic Crisis, and Adjust-ment: The Emergency Social Fund*, (Washington, DC: World Bank, 1992) p. 26.

48 Jorgensen *et al.*, *Bolivia's Answer to Poverty*, p. 6.

49 Jorgensen *et al.*, *Bolivia's Answer to Poverty*, p. 6.

50 Jorgensen *et al.*, *Bolivia's Answer to Poverty*, p. 120.

51 Jorgensen *et al.*, *Bolivia's Answer to Poverty*, p. 51.

52 Jorgensen *et al.*, *Bolivia's Answer to Poverty*, p. 51.

53 Jorgensen *et al.*, *Bolivia's Answer to Poverty*, p. 114 (emphasis added).

54 See, for example, Giovanni Andrea Cornia *et al.*, (eds) *Adjustment With a Human Face: Protecting the Vulnerable and Promoting Growth Vol. 1* (Oxford: Oxford University Press, 1987).

55 Devesh Kapur *et al.*, *The World Bank – Its First Half Century*, p. 365.

56 See, for example, Lourdes Beneria and Breny Mendoza, 'Structural Adjustment and Social Emergency Funds', in Jessica Vivian (eds) *Adjustment and Social Sector Restructuring* (Geneva: UNRISD, 1995), p. 56.

57 Helena Ribe *et al.*, *How Adjustment Programmes Can Help the Poor* (Washington, DC: World Bank, 1990).

58 Deepa Narayan and Katrinka Ebbe, *Design of Social Funds: Participation, Demand Orientation, and Local Organizational Capacity* (Washington, DC: World Bank, 1997), pp. 2–3.

59 Frances Stewart and William van der Geest, 'Adjustment and Social Funds: Polit-ical Panacea or Effective Poverty Reduction?', in Frances Stewart, *Adjustment and Poverty – options and choices* (London: Routledge, 1995), pp. 108–37.

60 World Bank, *Poverty Reduction and the World Bank: Progress in Fiscal 1998* (Washington, DC: World Bank, 1999), p. 3.

61 See Key, 'Trade Liberalisation and Prudential Regulation: The International Framework for Financial Services'.

62 E. Denters, *Law and Policy of IMF Conditionality* (The Hague: Kluwer Law International, 1996), p. 160. See also The World Bank Group Operations Policy and Strategy, 'Poverty Reduction Strategy Papers Internal Guidance Note', p. 4.

63 On this see, CGAP, 'A Review of the World Bank's Microfinance Portfolio' (Washington, DC: World Bank, 1997 – An Internal Document), p. 3.

64 World Bank, 'Operational Policy 8.30, Financial Intermediary Lending' (World Bank Operational Manual, July 1998).

65 World Bank, 'Operational Policy 8.30', see paragraph 6 (emphasis added).

66 World Bank, Operational Policy 8.30', see paragraph 7 (emphasis added).

67 Authors interview with the Director of the World Bank's 'Poverty Reduction and Economic Management' network, Michael Walton, Washington, DC, February 1999.

68 'About CGAP' – see http://www.worldbank.org/html/cgap/about.htm, p. 1, (emphasis added).

69 CGAP, *Focus No. 1*, p. 2.

70 CGAP – *A Policy Framework for the Consultative Group to Assist the Poorest: A Microfinance Programme* (Washington: World Bank, 1995), p. 1.

71 CGAP, *Status Report: Consultative Group to Assist the Poorest* (Washington, DC: CGAP Secretariat, Word Bank) No publication date stated. However, the report summarises CGAP's activities from its inception in June 1995 to May 1998, p. 24.

72 CGAP, 'A Review of the World Bank's Microfinance Portfolio', p. 17.

73 See for example, Jessica Vivian, 'How Safe are "Social Safety Nets"? Adjustment and Social Sector Restructuring in Developing Countries', in Vivian (eds) *Adjustment and Social Sector Restructuring*. See also in this volume Beneria and Mendoza, 'Structural Adjustment and Social Emergency Funds', and Samual K. Gayi, 'Adjusting to the Social Costs of Adjustment in Ghana: Problems and Prospects'. In general, all the essays in this collection have some relevance to this issue.

74 Despite initial enthusiasm about Bolivia's successful experiment with microfinance and the NEP, eighteen years on the incidence of poverty and human insecurities have significantly worsened. See *Financial Times*, 'Anger in the Andes', 26 April 2000.

75 Benjamin and Ledgerwood, 'Case Studies in Microfinance, Non-Governmental organizations (NGOs) in Microfinance: Past, Present and Future – An Essay'.

76 There is a rapid and vigorous process to reach the Microcredit Summit target: the recent case of microfinance in the Philippines is a clear example. President Estrada doubled the outreach target of the People's Credit and Finance Corporation (PCFC) from one million poor families to two million to be reached by 2000. At December 1998 PCFC had reached a target of 100,000.

77 Benjamin and Ledgerwood, 'Case Studies in Microfinance, Non-Governmental organizations (NGOs) in Microfinance: Past, Present and Future', p. 10.

78 The CGAP did not wish to discuss the role of microcredit in the context of social funds. Authors interview with a member of the CGAP, Washington, DC, February 1999.

79 Stephen Gill, 'Globalisation, Market Civilisation, and Disciplinary Neoliberalism', *Millennium*, 24: 3 (1995), pp. 399–424.

80 Cutler, 'Public Meets Private', p. 48 (emphasis added).

81 Bob Deacon, 'Social Policy in Global Context', in Andrew Hurrell and Ngaire Woods (eds) *Inequality, Globalization, and World Politics* (Oxford: Oxford University Press, 2000), p. 213.

82 See Robert Latham, 'Globalisation and Democratic Provisionism: Re-reading Polanyi', *New Political Economy*, 2: 1 (1997).

83 See Ronen Palan, 'Global Governance and Social Closure *or* Who Is to Be Governed in the Era of Global Governance?', in Martin Hewson and Timothy J. Sinclair, *Approaches to Global Governance Theory* (Albany, NY: SUNY, 1999), pp. 55–70.

84 Timothy J. Sinclair, 'Synchronic Global Governance and the International Political Economy of the Commonplace', in Hewson and Sinclair, *Approaches to Global Governance Theory*, pp. 157–71.

85 Sinclair, 'Synchronic Global Governance', p. 158.

86 Gill, 'Globalisation, Market Civilisation, and Disciplinary Neoliberalism'.

Part IV

Organised labour and global governance

9 Coming in from the cold

Labour, the ILO and the international labour standards regime

Steve Hughes

Introduction

In surveying the galaxy of international organisations the International Labour Organisation (ILO) stands out in two respects: it is one of the oldest existing intergovernmental organisations, and it is unique among these organisations in its tripartite system of governance. In many respects this tripartism helps explain the ILO's longevity. Since its founding in 1919, interest accommodation – between government, business and labour – has defined ILO decision-making and guided the development of an international organisation dedicated to labour protection and social justice. Significantly, this tripartite structure links domestic and international interests in a way that influences, and in important respects determines the *modus operandi* of ILO activity – the development and maintenance of the international labour standards regime. Much of the debate over trade and labour standards, for example, has been brokered by the ILO through this system of interest accommodation. This has helped carry forward an often stale and polarised deliberation and nurtured alternate paths for the development of labour protection.

While the Bretton Woods institutions have come under increasing pressure to reform and the future of the World Trade Organisation (WTO) is clouded by concerns over new trade rounds and executive transition, the ILO seems to have been revitalised. The very issues which have been raised in some of the contributions to this volume – global inequality; strategic responses to the Asian crisis; trade and social protection; human rights – have helped push the ILO to the centre stage of alternative models of global governance. Executive leadership within the ILO has been quick to try to fill the international social strategy vacuum exposed by the limitations of International Monetary Fund (IMF) and World Bank responses to the Asian crisis and the non-resolution of the Social Clause debate. ILO Director-General Juan Somavia was elected on a mandate that, in effect, sought to build upon the work of his predecessor Michael Hansenne. As the ink dried on the 1996 WTO Singapore Declaration, Hansenne seized upon the last-minute compromise that became paragraph 4 by highlighting how the ILO's standard-setting activities and its tripartite structure of governance were central to any resolution of the trade and labour standards debate.[1] For Hansenne, it provided the opportunity for the Organisation to lift itself from the shadows of the Cold War and construct a new sense of common purpose among its tripartite constituents and a more visible relevance to those increasingly concerned about the social costs of globalisation. In a key speech to the International Labour Conference two years later, the twinned themes of opportunity and renewal were echoed by Somavia:

> At this juncture, the ILO therefore finds itself well positioned. Business, labour and governments sit at its table. Its instruments are social dialogue and strategies to promote fundamental principles and rights at work, employment, and people's security. All this gives new public relevance to the facilities the ILO provides to the international community: the global reference point for knowledge on employment and labour issues; the centre for normative action in the world of work; a platform for international debate and negotiation on social strategy; and a source of services for advocacy, information and strategy formulation. It is a moment when the ILO must once again display its historic capacity for adaptation, renewal and change. The moment of opportunity will not last indefinitely.[2]

I argue in this chapter that these responses represent a return to the strategies that informed and structured the early development of the ILO and the international labour standards regime. This return marks the end of the Cold War agenda which had been influential in structuring ILO activity following the Second World War, but which had set it adrift as well as contributed to its marginalisation following the collapse of Soviet Communism. In doing so, I demonstrate the importance and influence of patterns of interest representation that have again combined to place the ILO at the heart of contemporary global governance. I argue also that a combination of domestic and international interests have historically mediated the activities of international organisations, yet not all efforts at international co-operation take this sufficiently into account. In this respect, as regimes shift from their initial formation to their development, domestic factors such as public opinion and interest mobilisation become critical considerations in the formation and enactment of intergovernmental activity. This is in line with the view that international co-operation is not only an outcome of relations among states, but of the interaction between convergent domestic and international interests.

In examining the institutional development of the ILO a number of key questions are identified: how did the ILO go about engaging opinion in its member states during its formative years and how did this aid in the development of the international labour standards regime?; how do regimes influence national strategy choices and the interests of national actors?; and relatedly, in those instances where political decision-makers have been reluctant to engage in international co-operation, can the pressure and support of external actors tip strategy in favour of those who seek engagement? I conclude that the evolution of global governance will be increasingly dependent upon the interaction of convergent domestic and international interests of which the ILO remains the international exemplar in the management of this dependency. I begin by examining the beginnings of the international labour standards regime as this provides the foundation for our understanding of ILO longevity and the root-strategies which have governed it. Moreover, it helps explain how the geo-politics of the Cold War shifted the ILO away from these root-strategies, raising questions about its relevance to the multilateral trade agenda and domestic market liberalisation.

The formation of an international labour standards regime

One of the main tasks of regime analysis is to explain the determinants of regime formation and its persistence or demise. The success or failure of regime building can be explained partially by the extent to which a regime provides information, monitoring capabilities and focal points for its members. In this respect, regime creation and maintenance can be a function of the distribution of power and interests among its members. Despite the proselytising efforts of humanitarian philanthropists such as Robert Owen and Daniel Le Grand and Liberal reformists such as Charles Hindley, the formation of an international labour standards regime was largely driven by the political self-interest of European states. Confronted by rising levels of worker unrest, and disturbed by the revolutionary potential of labour, European states proposed the convening of periodic conferences to examine labour issues and the construction of an international organisation to collect and distribute information on labour legislation. Powerful states, such as Great Britain, only agreed to the proposals on the understanding that international co-operation would not extend to binding agreement. This action determined that the retention of state sovereignty over labour issues remained a critical factor in regime formation.

When at the turn of the twentieth century the International Association for Labour Legislation was set up, its functional capacity remained restricted. It did not have any intergovernmental authority, its function was limited to the gathering and dissemination of information, and it relied for its administration on the voluntary activities of essentially, middle-class social reformers. Nonetheless, in 1906 the Association was successful in bringing into existence the first international labour conventions – covering the prohibition of the use of white phosphorus in industry and the prohibition of night-work for women. These conventions, coupled with the Association's research activities, provided the foundation for international co-operation on labour protection.

The existence of three other influences can be noted in this respect. First, by the time of the 1906 Conventions, countries were already engaging in bilateral agreements on labour protection. Second, the research work of the Association helped breakdown the protectionism that followed the economic crises of the late nineteenth century. Its work on social security and labour protection systems aided the process of liberalisation by making governments more aware of how much they would gain or lose under a new trade regime. A growth in the number of official government representatives attending the Association's International Assemblies reflected a desire to support measures that helped address unfair competition. From this, it can be determined that the political interest in regime formation increased as trade competition intensified at the turn of the twentieth century. Third, the increasing importance of the Association highlighted its weaknesses. To a large extent the trade unions and employers were suspicious of the middle-class reformers who ran the Association and largely remained indifferent to its activities. Meanwhile, government interest seemed proportional to the amount of labour unrest and trade competition being experienced. In essence, the Association had no firm constituency on which it could rely for support and co-operation. Without the co-operative and consistent support of government, employer and labour organisations, regime formation remained limited.

The influences which brought into existence the International Association for Labour Legislation were again evident in the construction of the ILO. The political fears concerning the revolutionary potential of labour became more pronounced following the Bolshevik revolution in 1917. Organised labour had become more global in its aspirations. It demanded a role in the peace settlement and called for the creation of an international labour office to study and co-ordinate the development of post-war labour legislation. To the political leaders of the key powers – Britain, the United States and France – the new organisation was an acknowledgement of these demands and by extension, a buttress against the spread of Bolshevism. Moreover, for many countries, international competition was just as much a reason for supporting the labour provisions of the Peace Treaty as the threat of labour unrest and the ideal of social justice.

When the ILO was created under Part XIII of the Treaty of Versailles, four principal ideas underpinned its establishment. The first was the creation of an intergovernmental organisation to deal specifically with labour issues. The second was the convening of periodic conferences for the conclusion of international agreements on labour protection. The third was the maintenance of the Conventions arising from the conferences. And the fourth was a decision-making process based on tripartism. Using Krasner's definition of a regime as 'implicit or explicit principles, norms, rules and decision-making procedures around which actors' expectations converge in a given area of international relations',[3] it can be determined that the principle of social justice, norms requiring ILO member nations to recognise and protect the rights of labour, rules requiring the ratification of international labour standards, and a tripartite decision-making process, combined to form an international regime dedicated to the introduction and maintenance of international labour standards. In the final instance, the power to ratify international labour standards still rested with national governments.

Haas observes that all international organisations are designed by their founders to solve problems that require collaborative action.[4] However, beyond the 'grand gesture' of Part XIII, governments had developed little clear strategy toward the ILO apart from retaining sovereignty over the ratification process. Without their support and legislative sanction, the future of the international labour standards regime remained uncertain. This uncertainty prompted the first Director of the ILO, Albert Thomas, to embark on a radical programme of regime building in which he intended to develop a dynamic profile for the ILO that would see it engage proactively with its tripartite constituency and distinguish it from what he perceived as the static bureaucracy of the League of Nations.

The development of an international labour standards regime

Thomas's radical programme rested on three substantive strategies. These strategies governed ILO activities during its formative years and laid the foundation for the development and survival of the international labour standards regime to the present day. First, a strategy of autonomy sought to establish the ILO's independence from the League of Nations and articulate its own role as an international organisation. Second, a strategy of presence informed the research activities of the Organisation based upon regular contact with worker, employer and government organisations of member countries. Third, a strategy of relevance sought to ensure that the ILO's activities remained germane to the aspirations of labour and the political and economic interests of governments.

A strategy of autonomy

A strategy of autonomy established the independence of the ILO and became critical in influencing political opinion towards the ILO in later years – particularly that of the United States. The key lay in Albert Thomas' view of the League of Nations as a moribund political bureaucracy 'divorced from peoples'. The League's principal European members – Great Britain and France – saw it as a way of institutionalising older methods of managing international relations based on the Concert of Europe. They were more or less free to do so because the United States remained outside the League for the duration of its existence, and other significant powers, for example, Germany, Japan, Italy and the Soviet Union, were members only periodically. The frustrated attempts by smaller nations to gain greater representation on the League's Council served to underline the self-interested dominance of European powers in its affairs and an inability to reflect changes in the international order.

The European dominance of the ILO's Governing Body merely served to reflect the make-up of the League's Council and ran the risk of being subject to the same creeping disillusionment infecting the League. Moreover, Thomas remained keenly aware that the locus of ratification was the national political process. An important task, therefore, was to activate a strategy designed to persuade governments, employers and workers in member countries that there existed an international dimension to nationally determined labour standards. The ILO needed two vital ingredients to succeed: the continuing and active support of workers and the increased involvement of countries outside of Europe.

Thomas defined the ILO in strict, pro-labour terms: 'The Organisation is labour, and nothing that concerns labour is alien to it'. With the reforming of the International Federation of Trade Unions (IFTU) in 1920, labour had become an organised and powerful force in the international system. Moreover, the IFTU dominated worker representation on the ILO Governing Body and had warned the League against ignoring the interests of workers. Thomas recognised that without a positive and proactive approach to fulfilling workers interests, the ILO risked isolation and abandonment not only by workers, but also by a significant number of employers and governments already sceptical of the Organisation's role.

In the early years, many non-European countries viewed the ILO with a distant detachment and made only a limited contribution to regime development. While many responded positively to the information-gathering activities of the ILO – by furnishing it with information on legislative and labour practices – the International Labour Conference remained largely the exclusive preserve of the European powers. This rendered ILO membership a passive and reactive process. In this respect, its regime exercised only a limited compliance pull.[5] Beyond simply responding to requests for information, there was little interest in co-operating in the development of international labour standards. A number of reasons can be determined for this. First, the aims and objectives of the ILO were not generally understood among political, employer and worker organisations outside of Europe. Second, booming economies such as Australia and New Zealand questioned the relevance of a distant organisation whose purpose seemed to be the promotion of labour standards lower than those prevailing in their own countries. Third, a consistent refrain was that the time and expense of sending a tripartite delegation to Geneva was considerable. Fourth, colonial governments were often content to defer to imperial interests in the governance of the ILO. For a regime to have an impact on state behaviour, and for this impact to have significant political implications, subscribing to regime norms has to be more than an automatic and immediate reflection of self-interest. To paraphrase Andrew Hurrell, there has to be some notion of being bound by a regime even when a state's self-interest seems to suggest otherwise.[6]

In attempting to overcome this apathy, engaging and influencing public opinion became a critical factor in regime development. To this end, ILO staff, encouraged by their Director-General, would make regular field trips to member states outside of Europe. Particular effort was focused on arranging meetings with newspaper editors. The purpose was to influence the editorial content of leading newspapers and procure greater press interest in the activities of the ILO and, consequently, greater discussion on international issues within the countries visited. In attempting to engage public opinion and raise the profile of the ILO, the importance of the print media stood out. Newspapers were the only medium through which most of the general public could be reached and, thus, they remained the primary mechanism for moulding public opinion on regime membership. Thus as the depression of the 1930s deepened the ILO took the opportunity to provide an alternative forum to the League for international discussion on the crisis. Apart from the drive to influence public opinion within member states, three things played a critical part in the ILO's ability to position itself in this regard. First, the emphasis by ILO staff on gathering and collating information on national responses to the depression informed much of the debate within the International Labour Conference and placed greater credence on its outcomes. Second, new fears of working-class unrest promoted the role of the ILO as the principal international platform on labour issues. Worker radicalisation occupied the minds of political decision-makers throughout the industrialised world as the economic depression, and its most visible face – mass unemployment – became a world-wide phenomenon. The perception of unemployment as a breeding ground for political unrest prompted greater effort toward international collaboration. Third, the International Labour Conference provided a vital forum for the ILO's unique tripartite structure to examine and debate the critical issues associated with the depression. If the Organisation was to retain the support of labour it had to demonstrate a vitality that made the prospect of an international labour standards regime a real and dynamic one. The International Labour Conferences remained a critical part of this process. It was the forum in which government, employer and labour representatives of ILO member states examined the research, debated and finally voted. Thomas viewed this process of interaction, collaboration, and tripartism as the life-blood of the Organisation. Its function was to generate support for social justice and worker rights through international Conventions and Recommendations.

A strategy of presence

The strategy of presence drew on the ILO's attempt to construct a dynamic and autonomous role for itself in the international system. The strategy had two objectives: to make the ILO ideologically relevant, by linking its efforts to promote social justice at the international level with activities of social reformers and trade unions at the national level; and to maintain a profile of the Organisation in the minds and strategies of those in a position to influence public opinion. Regular contact with government, employer and worker organisations – through letters, Reports, Missions and Conferences – constituted the heart of the strategy.

The world beyond Europe was growing in importance economically and politically. The post-war European powers were increasingly challenged by the industrial growth of the United States and Japan. However, despite changes in the international economic landscape, the ILO Governing Body continued to be dominated by European interests. Following the death of Albert Thomas in 1932, Harold Butler was appointed executive head of the ILO. While both Thomas and Butler stressed the importance of building an organisation of universal and not just European relevance, it was Butler who designated the task a priority of his office. Goldstein has emphasised the extent to which international regimes reflect the views of dominant states at the time of their formation.[7] In the ILO's case, dominant European interests continued to be reflected in the activities of the Governing Body. This led non-European members of the ILO to question the relevance of a regime whose norms and decision-making continued to reflect these interests. On this basis, not only did ILO claims to universality ring hollow but also the relevance, and therefore the existence, of the regime was under threat. If regime creation and maintenance are a function of the distribution of power and interests among states,[8] then these functions were heavily weighted in favour of the European powers.

During the economic crisis of the 1930s, the ILO demonstrated its competence in gathering and collating information on national responses to the depression and used this competence to take a lead in finding an international solution to its social effects. This competence influenced the US's decision to join the ILO in 1934. This decision was significant for the international labour standards regime in a number of respects. It signalled the end of European dominance; it suggested that changes in the underlying structure of power would become more visible; and, it also suggested that broader, more inclusive international coalitions would gradually emerge. However, the rationale for US entry into the ILO stemmed less from 'abstract humanitarian concerns' and more from the economic costs of Roosevelt's New Deal programme and their impact on the US's trade position. The message Harold Butler took from the US and the general condition of the world under the depression would have far-reaching regime implications. The economic crisis saw the rise of alternatives to the political and economic orthodoxies of the imperialist powers. Communism offered one alternative, Fascism another. The corrosive effects of the depression and the implications for peace, social stability and the maintenance of the international labour standards regime were not lost on Butler. He suggested a radical shift in the ILO's emphasis from the purely social to the economic sphere. In this, he sought to build on the Organisation's research competence and create a 'body of coherent thought' on the relationship between economic and social strategy.

Butler's directive underlines Kratochwil and Ruggie's[9] point on the significance of the epistemic dimension to regimes. They argue that knowledge in the international arena, its accumulation and its comprehension, are neither passive nor automatic processes, but intensely political. In this respect international organisations 'manoeuvre' themselves into the position of being the vehicle through which knowledge emerges on the international agenda and from which the future demand for international regimes lie. Their argument forces us to recognise that international organisations can feed the process of regime change through the information and ideas that they are able to mobilise. It follows that one of the most important functions of regimes is the collection and dissemination of knowledge.

The importance of these functions were underlined when issues of state sovereignty often rendered the ratification of international labour standards a politically sensitive process. This was as true for powerful economies such as the US as it was for smaller, empire-subservient countries. In both instances, the catalyst for a shift from a passive to a proactive strategy on regime membership was internal political change and the space created by the diminishing interest of European powers in the activities of the ILO. The election of a more internationally oriented Labour government in New Zealand for instance, marked a turning point in relations with the ILO. The success of the new government's programme rested on the co-operation of the trade unions. Part of the price of this co-operation was closer, more active engagement with the ILO as both labour and government struggled with the depression and looked to the ILO for a more internationally co-ordinated response. Thus, seeking to understand why and how states co-operate and bargain in regimes must be addressed with reference to the changing nature of state engagement domestically and internationally. As Hurrell points out, state interests are not fixed but vary according to the institutional context, to the degree of organisation of competing political forces within the state and wider political system, and to the leadership capacities of the major actors.[10] We can, therefore, determine that domestic politics matter in shaping responses to international regimes.

A strategy of relevance

In the analysis of the ILO's early years, it seems clear that the leadership and strategy initiatives of its Director-Generals played a critical part in regime development. This follows Robert Cox's argument that knowledge, in the form of political personality and elite group interests, is a primary factor in the formation, development and continuity of international organisation.[11] More specifically, Cox argues that the ILO has survived since 1919 partly, though significantly, through the activities and initiatives of its own elite of executive leaders. The increasing discontent among non-European members of the ILO over the dominance of European interests in its structures threatened to render the organisation of regional rather than global relevance. Developing countries, such as those in Latin America, were actively examining the possibility of establishing their own labour organisations with the capacity to develop regionally-specific labour conventions. Both issues posed serious threats to the ILO's functional capacity to maintain the international labour standards regime and fixed the political terrain on which the ILO directors needed to engage.

Through a mixture of shrewdness and tenacity on the part of Thomas and the capacity of Butler to interpret nuance and change in the wider political terrain, the Director of the ILO occupied an eminent international position, in many respects more important than the Secretary-General of the League of Nations. Thomas and Butler were able to influence the course of action of the ILO to a far greater extent than their counterpart in the League. Thomas's vision of the Organisation as a 'living thing' whose autonomy gave it the freedom to develop a relevance to workers all over the world, provided it with the impetus to action rather than the status of a passive collector of information. The ability to use this information proactively, in influencing national strategy, developing international labour legislation, and in bringing the US into its fold, proved vital in first developing and then shifting the ILO's 'centre of gravity' away from Europe.

As personalities and as directors, the two were very different. Thomas was a politician who revelled in the political battles that established the ILO's autonomy from the League of Nations. Significantly, his background in French industrial relations, and the socialism that constituted the core of his politics, helped him earn the respect of national and international worker organisations. Thus the critical variable that influenced the direction in which Thomas guided the ILO most explicitly was labour. Without its support in the immediate years following the end of the First World War, the ILO would have fallen victim to the same political inertia that dogged the League of Nations. In contrast, Harold Butler was a former British civil servant whose reserve and shyness created a somewhat enigmatic figure who nonetheless possessed an acute ability to interpret changes in the political environment. At the time of Thomas's death in 1932, the balance of power in the ILO had switched from labour to government and employer interests as organised labour weakened in the face of the depression. A problem faced by Butler was the increasingly antagonistic nature of these interests and their challenge to the ILO and regime development. In response, Butler focused on the development of the ILO's research competence. He commissioned reports that underlined the importance of international action to combat the depression; the value of regime membership in ensuring equity and transparency in this action; and the economic as well as the social role of regime development. In essence, Butler's investment in strengthening ILO research activities was geared toward convincing governments that it lay in their economic interests to support the international labour standards regime.

In the absence of some form of world authority or hegemony to direct or constrain its activities, both Directors engaged in a 'conscious strategy of leadership'.[12] It was the recognition that international organisations are not merely passive reflectors of power and preference but can actively seek to shape these through executive action, institutional arrangements, and the enforcement of rules.[13] Their foresight and executive activities ensured that the ILO not only survived the Depression but became an organisation of universal relevance in the future. One of Thomas's first actions was to organise the International Labour Office into three main Divisions – a Diplomatic Division to deal with member governments; a Scientific Division to undertake research work; and a Political Division to deal with employer and workers organisations. Structuring the ILO in this way, Thomas signalled a strong rejection of a British suggestion that the ILO be modelled on the British Civil Service – which would have rendered the fledgling organisation an administrative arm of the Governing Body. Instead, Thomas proposed that the ILO become an 'instrument of action'.[14] What he meant by this became evident in the functions he assigned to each of the proposed Divisions. While the research activities of the Scientific Division seemed in line with the expectations of the Governing Body, Thomas's underlying ideas for an 'instrument of action' became clear in the functions he proposed for the other two Divisions. The Diplomatic Division would organise an inspection branch and approach member states to secure or hasten the ratification of Conventions. The Political Division would be responsible for branch offices set up 'in all important centres' to liaise with employers and workers and collect information on social and economic change. Thomas underlined the importance of the Political Division when he said, '[t]his local organisation should be undertaken immediately. The very life of the Office depends on its success'.[15]

For Thomas and Butler, the energy and dynamism of the ILO was derived to a large degree from its tripartism, particularly the 'masses of the workers and the employing classes'. By emphasising workers and employers as 'the strength of the Organisation' and structuring the activities of the ILO on the basis of 'keeping in close touch with the organisations upon which its strength depends', Thomas distanced the ILO from a criticism made of the League of Nations that it 'was nothing but a meeting of Government delegates with no proper mandate'.[16] While politicians were content to prevaricate on the activities of the League in the aftermath of the war and constrain it in a web of political indifference and national self-interest,[17] they found themselves subject to much more pressure for action within the ILO. For one thing, its tripartite structure provided a more transparent platform for change and a forum on which worker interests and to a significant extent, worker power, could be articulated. Thomas recognised the importance of this platform in giving life to his own vision of the ILO but he also saw how it was vital to provide workers with a sense of ownership and responsibility in the ILO and the development of an international labour standards regime.

Root ideology and the management of dependency

The world following 1945 was very different from that experienced by Thomas and Butler. If, as Robert Cox argues, the inter-war period was non-hegemonic, then the world following the Second World War was defined by tensions between two competing hegemonies – that of the Soviet Union and the United States. These tensions articulated themselves in the growing number of intergovernmental organisations that structured the international environment. The ILO was not immune to the chill wind of the Cold War blowing through its corridors. Bi-polar politics conditioned debate over key conventions such as freedom of association; it institutionalised itself in the two peak international labour unions, the Soviet-sponsored World Federation of Trade Unions (WFTU) and the US-dominated International Confederation of Free Trade Unions (ICFTU); it influenced the resignation of an ILO Director-General;[18] and, for a period, it led to the withdrawal of US funds to the ILO.[19]

Gradually, as in-fighting and power politics fractured the Organisation it drifted from the root strategies devised and employed by its founding Directors. For many, the ILO became an irrelevance, detached from the lives of ordinary workers it was set-up to serve, and important only to those whose agendas were determined by the imperatives of the Cold War. While it continued to add to the number of International Labour Conventions, the ratification of these Conventions by national governments – an important measure of regime relevance – continued to decline.

This state of regime drift changed with the conclusion of the Uruguay Round of the General Agreement of Tariffs and Trade (GATT) in 1994. Acrimonious debate over creating a social dimension to multilateral trade at the conclusion of the talks had seen entrenched positions quickly materialise and threaten the signing of the Uruguay provisions. The establishment of the WTO allowed a compromise that required the new Organisation to seek a definitive position on the issue at its first Ministerial Meeting held in Singapore in 1996. The outcome of this meeting for the labour standards debate is now well documented both in this book and elsewhere. If for the ILO, the collapse of the Soviet bloc had marked one turning point from its post-war past, then renewed international tension over trade and labour standards offered an opportunity to determine its future.

The speeches of ILO Director-Generals have always been defined by their commentary on major social and economic issues and their emphasis on institutional action – a practice first employed by Albert Thomas and followed in spirit by his successors.[20] In his Report to the 81st Session of the International Labour Conference in 1994, Michael Hansenne marked the 75th Anniversary of the ILO by moving the ILO centre stage in the debate over the social costs of globalisation. It was a time when hard questions were being asked about the Organisation's relevance in the face of a continuing decline in trade union membership, rising unemployment and the global spread of market liberalism.

Hansenne argued that these changes underlined the importance of the ILO in balancing the needs of the state, society and the market at time when tensions between these institutions were no longer subsumed beneath geopolitical agendas:

the ILO would seem to have lost a lot of its appeal to those who no longer feel their interests threatened by communism . . . For nearly 50 years we functioned under a system of international relations that predetermined alliances within the Governing Body and the Conference. This system has now disappeared, and what we are left with is a revival of the underlying tension which presided over the creation of our Organisation and which the Organisation is responsible for managing at the International level: the tension that has always existed and will always exist between workers and employers . . .[21]

Hansenne's speech came two months after the debate over a linkage between trade and labour standards had threatened the signing of the GATT Uruguay Agreements. As the first post-Cold War Director-General of the ILO, Hansenne was attempting to renew the ILO's commitment to its tripartite roots and call for a greater role in international structures concerned with economic and social development. The ILO *Declaration on Fundamental Principles and Rights at Work and its Follow-up* adopted in 18 June 1998, represented the most visible outcome of Hansenne's efforts to shift the ILO agenda toward a more comprehensive, and encompassing approach to addressing the social costs of globalisation. The Declaration represented a commitment by its signatories to core labour Conventions such as Freedom of Association and the Right to Collective Bargaining, and a follow-up requiring:

- those who had not ratified the core Conventions to submit a yearly report on progress in implementing the principles enshrined in the core Conventions;
- a four yearly report by all ILO member that provides an overview of national efforts in promoting and implementing the core Conventions.

The Declaration institutionalised attempts to reconverge domestic and international interests on globalisation and social protection displaced by the Cold War agenda. The debate on trade and labour standards and growing domestic concerns over the social costs of open markets and the pursuit of free trade had influenced much of this reconvergence. In addition, a greater emphasis on its international activities by organised labour and the political defeats of centre-right governments in key economies such as the UK and the US, shifted political opinion toward a more positive engagement with the ILO.

An archipelago of unconnected islands

Hansenne's successor, Juan Somavia, was elected on a mandate to pursue much of the agenda put in place by his predecessor. The twin themes of modernisation and renewal attempt to carry this agenda further. In this regard, a number objectives are pursued:

- to focus the ILO's energies on 'Decent Work' as a major demand of the time;
- to strengthen cohesive tripartism and collective action among the ILO constituents;
- to instigate the reform and modernisation of the ILO;
- to develop a clearer policy identity that will help define a closer engagement with other [intergovernmental] institutions and actors.[22]

The Decent Work agenda consolidated the move toward the root strategies that had informed the early development of the international labour standards regime. Engagement with public opinion and the mobilisation of domestic interests around globalisation and social justice has seen a renewal of political investment in the machinery of tripartism. A significant influence on this, of course, was the desire to shift the social clause (trade and labour standards) debate away from the regulatory instruments of the WTO and into the ILO. However, an added dimension to this shift is the emphasis on a parallel engagement with the institutions of global governance as the ILO seeks a greater role in the multilateral system and with it a more considered and proactive approach to social issues arising from the process of globalisation. Both Hansenne and Somavia have sorted out this engagement on the basis of the renewal of political commitment to the ILO and the mounting criticism of the failure of the multilateral system to engage in a cohesive and systematic approach to these issues. For Somavia – taking a more overtly critical stance in this regard than his predecessor – the tendency for the institutions of this system to operate as autonomous, inwardly-protective and self-serving entities, has rendered multilateralism 'an archipelago of basically unconnected islands'.[23] He argues,

> Decent work . . . offers a way of combining employment, rights, social protection and social dialogue in development strategies. The difficulties faced by the traditional structural adjustment polices of the Bretton Woods institutions lie in part in their failure to incorporate these goals, and poverty reduction strategies will not succeed unless the same goals are built into them. At present, the Poverty Reduction Strategy Papers produced under the auspices of those institutions do not frontally address these issues. Reducing the decent work deficit is the quality road to poverty reduction and to greater legitimacy of the global economy.[24]

The search for common ground on which to build a more institutionally inclusive system of global governance is grounded in the belief that in order to thrive, markets must be embedded in broader frameworks of social values and shared objectives. The piecemeal and fragmented approach of the Bretton Woods institutions to these frameworks and the failure to engage in any real system-wide dialogue in this regard, underlines the task facing Somavia. To a large extent, and while labour and civil movements are dealt with via arms-length diplomacy outside of the ILO, the onus lies in the political commitment of governments to build a new consensus within and among the institutions of multilateralism. The sophisticated forms of activism employed by NGOs to garner support and influence public opinion and the increasingly confrontational strategies employed by the global protest movements, demands a more considered response than has hitherto been employed by the targets of these protests. The convergence of domestic and international interests around issues of globalisation, regulatory transparency, human security and social justice, places new demands on the system of global economic governance. The ILO, unshackled from the bi-polar politics of the Cold War and with a renewed commitment to the machinery of tripartism, remains the international exemplar in the accommodation of these interests. Its success in this regard (and the resilience of its regime) is founded upon strategies first devised and employed during the inter-war period. The challenge for Somavia and the multilateral institutions he is seeking to engage with, is to nurture these root strategies as a foundation for a reconfiguration of the system of global governance. As the institutions of multilateralism search for a new legitimacy in response to demands for a more inclusive and transparent system of governance, lessons from the ILO could be a starting point for this engagement.

Conclusion

I began this chapter by examining the formation and development of the international labour standards regime. The activities of the founding Director-Generals of the ILO were important conduits in forging links between domestic and international interests and evolving a predominantly European organisation into one that sought a more globally inclusive governance based upon tripartism. The strategies of autonomy, presence and relevance formed the pillars which guided the formation and development of the ILO and international labour standards regime. The regime-drift experienced by the ILO in the post-war period was an outcome of the marginalisation of these root strategies in favour of the bi-polar politics which influenced its agenda and conditioned its institutional activities. The reconfiguration of alliances in the wake of post-colonial development; the emergence of new economic powers in Asia and Latin America; the end of the Cold War and the rise in domestic challenges to the doctrine of market liberalism has forged a more complex form of multilateralism that the institutions who inhabit it are struggling to adapt. Sceptics will argue that any change will be essentially cosmetic and the Washington Consensus which has informed the multilateralist agenda will continue to prevail. Yet this struggle and its internal and external manifestations suggests that this complexity and the pressures which manipulate it will require new frameworks to manage it. In the debate over global governance, the emphasis on the Bretton Woods institutions and the GATT/WTO has only recently shifted towards a broader understanding of institutions outside of these configurations. A more considered examination of the ILO and the international labour standards regime offers possibilities in taking the global governance debate into new domains hitherto considered politically infertile. The challenge then, is to demonstrate that the multilateral institutions have the wherewithal to explore these possibilities and offer a new framework of coherence and legitimacy to the multilateralist system.

Notes

1 Michel Hansenne, 'The ILO, Standard Setting and Globalisation', Report of the Director-General to the International Labour Conference, 85th Session, Geneva (June 1997). See also Steve Hughes and Rorden Wilkinson, 'International Labour Standards and World Trade: No Role for the World Trade Organisation?', *New Political Economy*, 3: 3 (November 1998), pp. 375–89.
2 Juan Somavia, 'Decent Work', Report of the Director General to the International Labour Conference, 87th session, Geneva (June 1999).
3 Stephen Krasner, 'Structural Causes and Regime Consequences: Regimes as Intervening Variables', *International Organisation*, 36: 2 (Spring 1982).
4 Ernst Haas, *Beyond the Nation State: Functionalism and International Organisation* (Stanford: Stanford University Press, 1964).
5 M. Koskenniemi, *From Apology to Utopia: The Structure of International Legal Argument* (Helsinki, 1989).
6 Andrew Hurrell, 'International Society and the Study of Regimes: A Reflective Approach', in Volker Rittberger and Peter Mayer (eds) *Regime Theory and International Relations* (Oxford: Clarendon Press, 1993), p. 53.
7 Judith Goldstein, 'The Political Economy of Trade: Institutions of Protection', *American Political Science Review*, 80 (1986), pp. 161–84. See also Robert Keohane, 'The Analysis of International Regimes: Towards a European-American Research Programme', in Volker Rittberger and Peter Mayer (eds) *Regime Theory and International Relations*, p. 45.
8 Stephen Krasner, 'Sovereignty, Regimes, and Human Rights', in Volker Rittberger and Peter Mayer (eds) *Regime Theory and International Relations*, p. 141. See also Joseph Grieco, *Co-operation Among Nations: Europe, America, and Non-Tariff Barriers to Trade* (Ithaca, NY: Cornell University Press, 1990); Robert Gilpin, *War and Change in World Politics* (Cambridge: Cambridge University Press, 1981); and Stephen Krasner, 'State Power and the Structure of International Trade', *World Politics*, 28: 2 (1976), pp. 317–47.
9 Friedrich Kratochwil and John Gerard Ruggie, 'International Organisation: The State of the Art and Art of the State'. *International Organisation*, 40: 4 (1986), pp. 772–4.
10 Hurrell, 'International Society and the Study of Regimes. A Reflective Approach', in Rittberger. and Mayer (eds) *Regime Theory and International Relations*.
11 See Robert Cox, 'Labor and Hegemony', *International Organisation*, 31: 3 (Summer 1977).
12 Haas, *Beyond the Nation State*, pp. 144–50.
13 See Robert Keohane, 'International Institutions: Two Approaches', *International Studies Quarterly*, 32: 4 (1988). Also J. March and J. Olsen, 'The New Institutionalism: Organisational Factors in Political Life', *American Political Science Review*, 79 (1984).
14 Edward Phelan, *Yes and Albert Thomas* (London: Cresset Press, 1936), p. 38.
15 Phelan, *Yes and Albert Thomas*, p. 42.
16 Phelan, *Yes and Albert Thomas*, p. 41.

17 D. Armstrong, L. Lloyd and J. Redmond, *From Versailles to Maastricht: International Organisation in the Twentieth Century* (London: Macmillan, 1996), chapter 2.

18 David Morse, an American, resigned as Director-General of the ILO in 1970. His political skills (of which there were many) had largely been employed avoiding a confrontation between the superpowers over Soviet representation in ILO governance. His resignation was interpreted by some as a recognition that these skills had been exhausted and he had 'reached the limit of his ability to avoid a crisis'. See Robert Cox, 'Labor and Hegemony', pp. 385–424.

19 In 1970 the US suspended payment to the ILO for two years when the Director-General Wilfred Jenks appointed a Soviet citizen to the post of Assistant Director-General.

20 See Robert Cox, 'The Executive Head: An Essay on Leadership in International Organisation', *International Organisation*, 23: 2 (Spring 1969), pp. 205–30.

21 Michael Hansenne, 'Defending Values, Promoting Change: Social justice in a global economy: An ILO agenda', Report of the Director-General, International Labour Conference, 81st Session, Geneva, June 1994.

22 See Juan Somavia, 'Decent Work'.

23 Juan Somavia, 'Reducing the Decent Work Deficit – a Global Challenge', Report of the Director-General, International Labour Conference, 89th Session, Geneva, June 2001.

24 Juan Somavia, 'Reducing the Decent Work Deficit – a Global Challenge'.

10 International labour and its emerging role in global governance

Regime fusion, social protection, regional integration and production volatility

Nigel Haworth

The 1999 Seattle Ministerial Meeting of the World Trade Organisation (WTO) fails to reach accord, in part the result of an unresolved clash over the trade–labour standards issue. Meanwhile, in the aftermath of the 1997 Asian financial crisis, issues of social protection and the participation of civil society in growth models take centre stage at the intergovernmental level and in International Financial Institutions (IFIs). Labour-related issues become increasingly significant in the major models of regional integration. Elsewhere, Adidas–Salomon advertise a post as head of their Asian regional 'standards of engagement' programme, in charge of ensuring that plants contracting to supply Adidas–Salomon meet established International Labour Organisation (ILO) standards in their operations. What ties these disparate processes together and how do they relate to the role of labour in global governance? In simple terms, the answer is that each is a defining context in which labour transcends national boundaries and seeks to establish a role in global institutions. In combination, they provide a basis for an analytical understanding of the emergence of labour in global governance debates, and an insight into the supranational institutional frameworks open to the international labour movement.

At the heart of the relationship between labour (and its institutions) and global governance is the possibility of a global accommodation between international institutions of governance, international capital and labour. Mirroring the national accommodations struck in sovereign states during the original consolidation of capitalist social and production systems, this international accommodation was inconceivable, even as late as the 1980s. However, in the combination of the trade–labour standards debate, the contemporary international focus on social protection, regional integration and the demands of global production, the basis of an international accommodation is now discernible. For labour, the accommodation opens up once unforeseen opportunities. In the debates about internationalisation and labour in the 1970s and 1980s, the prospect of labour playing a substantial, international role was generally thought to be poor.[1] The power and capacity of capital's internationalisation appeared to have left far behind the reach of national labour movements. International labour organisation was fundamentally divided on ideological grounds, and largely ineffectual on the international stage. This bleak perspective may now be replaced by the opportunities offered to labour by an international accommodation.

This chapter offers an examination of this accommodation. In doing so, it suggests that this accommodation defines a relatively positive, and historically unique, context for international labour's engagement with global governance. The chapter then briefly discusses international labour's response to this challenge and concludes accordingly.

Regime fusion: the trade–labour standards debate[2]

Trade is simultaneously a primary feature of internationalisation and the site of conflict about the role of international labour and international labour relations regimes. In the recent period, a combination of governments, union bodies and NGOs brought the conclusion of the Uruguay Round (and the formation of the WTO) into question around the issue of the trade–labour standards link. Neat diplomatic footwork was required to shift the trade–labour standards debate off to a joint committee between the WTO and the ILO, thus averting possibly insuperable problems for the completion of the Uruguay Round. At the same time, the Social Clause debate established the trade–labour standards relationship as a major global issue, in which governments (for example, the US and the EU), unions and the ILO supported trade sanctions as a means of establishing and maintaining appropriate inter-national labour standards.

From its inception, the WTO displayed little sympathy for the linkage. Beneath the usual intergovernmental and inter-agency pleasantries, the WTO argued that the proper location for the discussion of labour standards was the ILO. It was, went the argument, not the job of the WTO to address this issue, because the WTO was a trade organisation in which no consensus was possible around a trade–labour standards link, even if enough support could be raised within the WTO to consider the idea. Courteous but distant relations between the ILO and the WTO (and particularly between their Director-Generals) reinforced the WTO's distance from the linkage.[3]

Despite this, the labour standards debate emerged at the WTO's Singapore Ministerial Meeting in December 1996. The US and other states once again raised the issue and were opposed by a mixed group of developed and developing states. In Singapore, the WTO agreed that all its members were committed to the observance of core labour standards; the ILO was the appropriate body to establish and maintain such standards; standards and their observance were improved where economic growth took place; and developing states should not see their comparative advantage undermined by the arbitrary application of such standards. The Singapore outcome signalled a firm attempt once again to distance the WTO from the general issue of labour standards. It also echoed much of the orthodox economic commentary on the trade–labour standards link. Nevertheless, despite the demise of the Social Clause campaign,[4] pro-link states and agencies sustained international pressure for a trade–labour standards link in numerous international forums. Singapore was simply a further skirmish in a long campaign.

Changes in the ILO then came to play a significant role in the debate. Director-General Michel Hansenne retired, to be replaced by Juan Somavia. Two aspects of this transition are important. The first is that Hansenne, in his last years in office, recognised that the Social Clause debate had run its course. He therefore shifted ground within the ILO to recapture the broader social agendas originally at the heart of the ILO, while also giving focus to core labour standards in the ILO's Declaration on Fundamental Principles and Rights at Work (1998).[5] These were epitomised in the 1944 Philadelphia Declaration and, more generally, in the role anticipated for the ILO in the post-Second World War settlement. Somavia has taken this message and developed it further. Somavia was, of course, a key participant in the 1995 Copenhagen Social Summit, which, among other outcomes, strongly supported the trade–labour standards relationship in the context of the mobilisation of civil society in response to economic internationalisation and its consequences. We should note here that the relationship between Somavia and the new Director-General of the WTO, Mike Moore, is considerably more open than was the case for their predecessors.[6] In mid-2000, relationships between the ILO and WTO were still somewhat distant, but there is growing common ground between the two around social development agendas. For its part, the ILO is seeking to establish itself as a dynamic leader in social mobilisation in a 'globalised' world. The WTO, as we explain in detail below, is similarly concerned that trade is not seen as separate from (and in opposition to) social development. Hence, there is informal discussion, particularly in Geneva, about the possibility of a third location in which agencies such as the ILO and WTO can legitimately share agendas without compromising institutional consensus. 'Development' is the context that appears to provide that safe ground for shared initiatives.[7]

Thus, we arrive at Seattle with the trade–labour standards issue 'parked' in a side street, but with the engine ticking over strongly.[8] The sense in holding a WTO Ministerial in the US during an election year is now widely questioned.[9] The potential for the WTO meeting to become the focus of domestic politics was great. The quality and comprehensiveness of the preparatory work for the meeting was also an issue. The unexpected difficulties in appointing a successor to Renato Ruggiero resulted in the truncation of the groundwork for Seattle. Location and preparation were two important factors in what is broadly accepted to have been a major setback for the WTO.

In the meeting, a number of specific problems emerged. These included:

- The scope of multilateral trade negotiations, including the treatment of investment, competition policy, transparency in government procurement and trade facilitation (the so-called Singapore issues).

- US opposition to the re-opening of anti-dumping and subsidies agreements.
- Developed country opposition to the wish of textile exporting states to liberalise trade in that sector.
- The future rate of reduction of agricultural tariffs and domestic and export subsidies.
- Some technical aspects relating to peak tariffs on industrial goods.
- The status of future TRIPs negotiations within the WTO process.
- Procedural questions around both internal and external transparency.

However, the labour standards issue created the deepest divisions. We have already noted the attempt in Singapore to exclude this issue from WTO discussions. Nevertheless, both the US and the EU insisted on the re-opening of the issue and the setting up of a process to consider further trade–labour standards linkages. It is widely accepted that, by the latter stages of the Seattle meeting, a compromise was in place based on the establishment of a joint WTO/ILO working forum on globalisation, trade and labour issues. The intention was to promote discussion between governments on these issues, in the expectation that other international agencies would also participate. The compromise was fragile. Developed states offered support, notionally on the basis that it would be an important way of disarming anti-liberalisation unions, while many developing states saw protectionism in both the issue and the compromise – a view exacerbated by the US government and Presidential comments.

From a trade perspective, Seattle was a failure, but it can be reversed. None of the trade issues is *a priori* insuperable. In particular, the emergence in Seattle of a North–South division is not seen by trade specialists as necessarily permanently damaging. More problematic, but perennial issues in the WTO and since the formation of General Agreement on Tariffs and Trade (GATT), are the power relations between the US, Japan and Europe and the traditional areas of conflict such as agriculture. Trade specialist wisdom broadly argues that the gains made in international trade by the outcome of the Uruguay Round and its predecessors are such that governments will overcome the Seattle legacy. In other words, the legitimacy and the sustenance of the WTO as the institutional manifestation of the global trade regime is guaranteed despite Seattle.

However, if trade specialists are confident that a better prepared meeting will overcome the problems faced in Seattle, they also recognise that the role of civil society in relation to the global trade regime is now a volatile issue. The stalling of the Multilateral Agreement on Investment (MAI), the popular protests in Seattle and elsewhere, and the international flowering of a popular discourse critical of unquestioning trade liberalisation have worried WTO officials and their governmental allies. They feel themselves to be trapped between the mandate given to the WTO by its member governments and the growing pressures for a modified trade regime emerging from popular debate. They also feel that their technical arguments for the WTO trade regime are not well understood (if more coherent than those of their opponents).

The popular mobilisations for and against a link between trade and labour standards are central to that questioning discourse. Unions in India and Pakistan may disagree fiercely with the International Confederation of Free Trade Unions' (ICFTU) support for the linkage, but neither grouping shares a view of trade with the WTO and the trade liberalisation lobby. They oppose that view with their commitment to the establishment and maintenance of a global industrial or labour relations regime, in which effective, supranational labour organisation is able to confront the power of internationalised capital.[10] At the heart of the debate about trade and labour standards is the relationship between these two regimes – the one grounded in neo-classical trade theory and market forces, the other in the extension of labour standards and bargaining regimes as social protection. Institutionally, the WTO stands proxy for the former, the ILO for the latter. Proponents of the linkage are seeking at least a partial fusion of the two regimes, an intersection of regimes in which social considerations are not perceived to be located in a separate, unrelated sphere of human endeavour, but to be integral to trade and, by extension, all international economic relations. Somavia's agenda for the ILO, in its harking back to the Philadelphia Declaration (1944) and its focus on a broad social role for the ILO, is one element of this potential fusion. The activity of the international labour movement is another.[11]

We should note that there are examples already in place where trade relations are tied in with the observance of labour standards. In the Generalised System of Preferences (GSP) of the EU and the US, measures exist that permit trade sanctions in the case of non-observance of labour standards. In the case of the US, the 1974 GSP measure allows for the withdrawal of duty free treatment for goods arriving in the US from countries that do not permit rights such as freedom of association and collective bargaining. Countries in Central America and the Caribbean have been subject to such measures, or the threat of such measures, and, as a result, have amended domestic legislation. In the case of the EU, measures are in place to link core labour standards with trade relations under the GSP. In 1997, for example, Burma lost its trade privileges with the EU, primarily because of government-sanctioned use of forced labour. This noted, we now turn to the issue of social protection, economic crisis and regional integration, arguing that it constitutes a second dynamic towards a new international accommodation.

Crisis and social protection

The concept of social protection has a long history in market-based societies. It has, however, taken on new meaning in the late 1990s.[12] Social protection's recent entry on to the global stage was precipitated by the scale of the 1997 Asian financial and economic crisis and its subsequent global impact. As numerous reports have analysed,[13] the precipitate end of a generation of high growth in Asia resulted in massive economic and social dislocation. Women, young people, migrant labour and older men were particularly badly hit. All sectors, including primary commodity production, were dislocated. This dislocation carried longer term implications. People lost educational opportunities, thus threatening the long-term basis for economic growth. Health systems decayed. The existing minimal social security measures were generally inadequate to deal with the level of dislocation. In sum, the social infrastructure upon which future growth was to be based, and in which populations had built significant expectations, threatened to fail.

The economic and financial reforms instituted in response to the crisis were supported by major initiatives in the social protection area. They had two dimensions. Domestic policies sought to alleviate the immediate impacts of sudden large-scale unemployment. An array of government interventions across Asia sought to modify the pace of lay-offs, while attempting to maintain economic activity wherever possible. Educational provision was funded to take the unemployed and re-skill them, often focusing on the growth of new small and medium sized enterprises (SMEs). Meanwhile, social provision was introduced in the hope that family structures would remain intact. Examples of measures include subsidies of essential commodities, provision of medical support and the funding of relocation to more promising domestic labour markets.

Complementing domestic responses were the actions of the international agencies, particularly the International Monetary Fund (IMF) and the World Bank. It is important to understand how dramatic was the change of orientation of the International Financial Institutions (IFIs) in the face of the Asian crisis. By 1998, that is, within a year of the crisis hitting, the IFIs had in place detailed *social* strategies, coupled with explicit recognition of the need for dialogue with civil society and NGOs.[14] The social protection agenda of the IFIs takes a different form from the domestic policies enacted by the affected states. It is seen as complementary to the economic and financial reform process deemed necessary as a consequence of the crisis. Moreover, in its stress on the need for 'ownership' by the affected economy of the social protection process, it also proposes an important shift of responsibility for social protection from the domestic state to the family and the individual. This follows from the logic of recent (1970s onwards) IFI interventions in the development process, in which a reduced role for the state and the increased role of individuals in the market have been proposed.

Thus, social protection is contentious, not in terms of its importance upon which all seem to be agreed, but in terms of its configuration. A modern, market-driven social protection agenda is counterposed to classical state interventions to smooth the cyclical effects of the market. From a social mobilisation perspective, the important aspect of the contemporary social protection debate is its global reach. Hitherto, with, perhaps, the exception of regional integration in the European Union (EU), social protection policies have been the province of the sovereign state, in recent years a state likely to be wedded to a reduction in social provision. The impact of the 1997 crisis has propelled social protection onto a global stage. The institutions with overarching global responsibilities in financial and development matters are seized with its significance. The political and social stability of the international economic order are now seen to be lodged in part in effective global social protection measures. It has become an international arena for participation and debate, particularly for the international labour movement.

Regional integration[15]

Regional integration has provided a similar opportunity for international labour. Commencing with the European Union (EU) and its foundation in the 1950s, we observe the North American Free Trade Agreement (NAFTA), El Mercado Común del Sur (MERCOSUR) and the Asia Pacific Economic Co-operation forum (APEC) all emerging during the 1980s and 1990s. The EU is the outlier, in terms of history, process and impact. Its origins, bound up in complex ways with regional security relations as well as economic co-operation for nearly fifty years, sets it apart from the more recent regional blocs. The defining difference is that, while trade is important to the EU, it is not its primary *raison d'être*. In the case of the other three blocs, trade liberalisation is the primary driver of co-operation. In part this is a historical effect. The origins of the EU lie in the 1950s redevelopment of the European economy. The other three blocs are the outcome of trade considerations emerging in the 1970s and 1980s – precisely those decades in which Keynesian thinking was in decline and the rhetoric of international competitiveness became ubiquitous. Moreover, European integration is a political process in which contending economic and political philosophies are played out in high-level regional institutions, often with profound policy impacts on member states.

This is not so for the other regional blocs. APEC, NAFTA and MERCOSUR focus on trade liberalisation, a purpose usually explicitly counterposed to any deeper political purpose. Thus, while it is possible for the social democratic tradition embodied in Jacques Delors to sustain and implement interventionist policies in Europe, this is far less the case in other regional groupings. Neither the institutional framework for, nor the political commitment to, such interventionism is found in NAFTA, APEC or MERCOSUR. Also, the different dynamics of supranational regionalisation combine protectionism and liberalising tendencies in different measure, depending on the regional bloc. In the case of the EU, support for the WTO exists, but it is constrained by, for example, the desire to sustain the Common Agricultural Policy (CAP). Similarly, the stalled MAI finds mixed support within the EU. In contrast, the rhetoric of APEC wholeheartedly supports the WTO and the attempt to create an international investment regime equivalent to the WTO's trade regime. However, the EU, APEC and other regional blocs are committed to international competitiveness in an integrated global economy. Hence, if all blocs share a common view of the desirable end – international competitiveness – they subscribe to different means of achieving that end. In the EU, tripartite, pluralist traditions are broadly accepted to contribute to competitiveness and are the subject of EU-wide legislation. An example of this is the establishment of European Works Councils (EWC). In the other major regional blocs, international commitments are limited primarily to trade arrangements. The governments that commit to these blocs accept the argument that liberalised trade impels domestic efficiencies and, consequently, improves competitiveness. Other means of achieving international competitiveness – for example, labour relations measures, industry policy and education and training – remain the prerogative of the participating sovereign economy and are not usually subject to international integration.

The EU and its social agendas, particularly its EWC model, have assisted the internationalisation of labour's activities.[16] The EWC model interacts with previously established supranational bargaining or information exchange mechanisms between unions and companies in Europe and beyond. Cases such as Danone and Accor capture this complexity. Danone employs 80,000 workers in 120 countries and 200 companies world-wide. Since 1986, annual meetings have been held between trade unions and Danone. The purpose of the meetings is primarily information exchange. However, there are international agreements in place between the International Union of Foodworkers (IUF) and Danone on information exchange, equality at work, skills training, union rights and responses to changing business activities, which are monitored at the annual meeting. Danone's reasons for this arrangement lie in a commitment, spelt out in the 1970s, to social progress and economic development. In practice, this translates to an IUF view that Danone takes seriously its social responsibilities and a commitment to 'constructive workplace relations between employers and representative, democratic and independent trade unions'.[17] The ICFTU notes a range of successes for the unions participating in the Danone EWC (for example, in cases of threatened restructuring in France), but also points to areas in which progress is still to be made (for example, in relation to child labour in sub-contractors).[18]

A similar story may be told for Accor.[19] Operating in the international hotel, catering and tourism industry, Accor employs over 120,000 in 142 countries, mainly in SMEs. The IUF signed an agreement with Accor management in 1995 in relation to trade union rights. This has been activated in dispute settlement with some success in Australia, Indonesia, Canada and the US. The Accor EWC now includes delegates from thirteen countries and builds on meetings in place since 1994.

Trade unionists are careful not to make too much of the EWC model and the examples of international company-level agreements such as Danone and Accor. For some, they are developments that are at best first steps towards a model of international collective bargaining. They depend on two factors: the institutional environment created by the EU and, for activities including but also transcending the EU, company commitment to such activities. Notwithstanding sober assessments, cases such as Danone and Accor intimate one possible mode of supranational labour intervention. In terms of the other major trading blocs (APEC, NAFTA and MERCOSUR), such developments are less likely. In particular, despite the side agreement on labour associated with the NAFTA agreement, a tradition of effective action consequent on the side agreement has still to arise.[20]

Production volatility, new technology and internationalisation

Economic internationalisation, driven by trade expansion, the movement of foreign direct investment (FDI) and the emergence of new centres of international production, provides a further opportunity for international labour, but in an unexpected manner. Traditionally, internationalisation is associated with labour movement weakness. Mobile international capital is generally portrayed as setting insuperable challenges for labour movements relying on national identities and bargaining systems for their effectiveness. Meanwhile, new centres of international production, particularly in the developing world, are usually presented as difficult to organise by trade unions as a result. Above all, internationalisation has, by its creation of global markets and global supply chains, created challenges for capital that, in turn, have resulted in further adverse conditions for labour. Internationalisation has resulted in market fragmentation and volatility, accompanied by ever-shorter production cycles, increasing cost competition and rising quality expectations. For companies, flexibility has been the key response, incidentally giving rise to the hydra-like flexibility debate. Leaving that debate to one side, the key elements of flexible production have been flexible production capacity, cost flexibility, constant quality improvement, timeliness in output and shorter product cycles. Labour has been an important dimension of flexibility, as have been production systems based on sub-contracting, networks and alliances. Labour has found it difficult to respond effectively to this dynamic production system, particularly as government policy has usually seen economic growth to depend upon integration into global markets and their associated production systems.

However, there are aspects of these production systems not wholly antithetical to labour's international activities. To illustrate this, we begin with Adidas–Salomon, the international producer of sporting goods. Adidas–Salomon have defined a policy on social and environmental affairs that includes what are termed 'standards of engagement'.[21] These standards are explicitly modelled on ILO conventions and on the code of conduct laid down by the World Federation of the Sporting Goods Industry (WFSGI).[22] Contractors, sub-contractors and other suppliers are required to observe these standards, which are monitored by a team of twenty-three specialists, who in turn are subject to independent audit. Independent audit is also a requirement of membership of the Fair Labour Association (FLA), which Adidas–Salomon joined in 1999. The FLA – a non-profit alliance of companies and NGOs – has designed a code of practice and monitoring procedures in relation to the international apparel industry's labour practices.[23] Adidas–Salomon includes in its standards of engagement a commitment to work for freedom of recognition of workers' organisations in suppliers in line with domestic laws and ILO convention.

The WFSGI has been working on related issues since the mid-1990s, especially in relation to child labour in the football industry. Sialkot in Pakistan produces over 75 per cent of the world production of hand-stitched footballs. In a series of international conferences and related missions to Sialkot, the WFSGI, with the Soccer Industry Council of America (SICA) and other agencies (including the ILO, UNESCO and NGOs such as Save the Children), created the Atlanta Agreement (1997). This agreement seeks to eliminate child labour in the soccer ball industry by means of two programmes, the first in prevention and monitoring, the second in social protection. Soccer balls are to be sourced only from suppliers that submit to the monitoring process. Approximately US$3 million are invested in the programmes, provided by the ILO, the UK government, UNICEF, local manufacturers, SICA and soccer's ruling body the Federation Internationale de Football Association (FIFA).[24]

The explanation for these actions by companies and sectoral representatives does not lie in a moral shift in the companies. Sporting goods companies have been at the heart of the internationalisation of production, fragmenting production across Asia (and elsewhere) between 'designer', higher cost, higher price products and mass produced, lower priced products. Nor does the explanation lie in the effectiveness of labour mobilisation. International labour organisations have campaigned long and hard against the extreme outcomes of international production fragmentation, but a sober judgement would assess their impact as at best modest. It is most pronounced in the international arenas such as the ILO. Rather, the explanation lies in two phenomena – the mobilisation of consumer attitudes and the intervention of governments. As the WFSGI explicitly notes, company and sectoral activity around the issue of child labour in the football industry was a direct response to consumer pressure and Western media coverage of the child labour in the industry. Popular mobilisation forced the sector to respond. Moreover, the response had to achieve some legitimacy if it was to divert consumer and media attention. This is equally true for Adidas–Salomon. They explicitly recognise that the advantages of a fragmented supply chain must be tempered by the creation and maintenance of an acceptable international image and reputation. Again, external validation is seen by Adidas–Salomon to be essential if international acceptance of a product is to be sustained. It is also needed to overcome what might be called the 'Nike Effect'. Nike has been subjected to sustained and implacable attack from its critics for failing to respond quickly enough or adequately to criticism of its production system. Although Nike has moved forcefully to bring itself into line with sister companies in the sector, it still bears an unenviable reputation for laxness on the standards issue. In effect, the global market has become the site of what was once primarily a domestic phenomenon of consumer response to company behaviour.

Governments and intergovernmental institutions have played a role in behavioural shifts in companies and sectors. The ILO has, naturally, been at the centre of much of this effort. We have also already noted the British government's involvement in the soccer ball standards issue. In the case of the apparel industry, including sporting goods, a major boost to standards-based activity came with the 1997 announcement by the Apparel Industry Partnership of its 'Workplace Code of Conduct' and its 'Principles of Monitoring'. Launched in the US with full support from the Clinton Administration, these measures were implemented in response to the Administration's focus on labour standards and, particularly, on its campaign against the worst abuses of child labour.[25]

The long-term impact of these company and sectoral interventions remains to be seen. There is no consensus about their importance. Supporters stress the potential of such initiatives in practical and groundbreaking terms. Critics regard them as cynical ploys to overcome consumer mobilisation and the consequent threat to revenues. From some trade union perspectives, such measures are broadly welcome as they either directly or indirectly create opportunities for labour's international influence to grow. Alternative views suggest that these opportunities are insubstantial, that the impact of these interventions may be counterproductive in terms of the creation of strong union organisations in the affected locations and sectors, and that the substance of such interventions is flimsy. We will return to these arguments below. For now, let us note the argument that the internationalisation of production may, through the internationalisation of consumption, trigger countervailing effects: global production fragmentation.

Regime fusion, social protection, regional integration and production systems: a synthesis

The four moments described above combine to present a complex picture of international labour's engagement with global governance. As we discuss below, the pressing issue for international labour has been to gain some purchase on economic internationalisation. For much of the post-war period, this has moved ahead, supported by domestic policy, in ways that have eroded domestic union strengths, yet created little obvious space for unions at the supranational level. In terms of space, the important exceptions to this have been two – the ILO and the EU. Institutionally, the emergence of the ICFTU as a strong international voice has been significant, and the continued work by International Trade Secretariats (ITSs) has been notable. Despite these institutional and regional opportunities, space and leverage has evaded international labour for much of the post-war period.

When the four moments discussed above are brought together, a potential for space and leverage is revealed to international labour. We can summarise this potential in the following way. Regime fusion suggests that labour's traditional support for and involvement in the ILO may be extended into a trade–labour standards linkage that brings a voice of labour to the heart of economic internationalisation, the global trade regime. A possible scenario is that, recognising that the demand for a linkage will not subside (despite forceful opposition from some developing states), joint activities between the ILO and the WTO on standard setting and monitoring will develop over time. In the first instance, this may take place in a 'third' location, under the guise perhaps of a 'development' agenda with broad social dimensions. As discussed above, such a development is now in discussion in WTO and ILO circles. Given the nature of the opposition to a linkage, joint actions are likely to emerge in areas of existing consensus (child labour, health and safety, environment, social protection and equal opportunity, for example). The ICFTU's concept of a joint WTO–ILO Advisory Body to implement a workers' rights clause may in time gain acceptance in some form.[26] Continued support for such activities from, for example, the US and the EU, would be an important dimension of this evolutionary mode.

International social protection agendas come into play in this process. Labour standards (and the voice of international labour) are important building blocks in the creation of an effective global social protection regime. That social protection regime is already associated in numerous ways with the international trade regime through the post-1997 crisis debate. The trade–labour standards–social protection link has two dimensions. One focuses on the protection aspects of economic development and growth and emphasises the role of standards and protective measures in social and political stability. The other focuses on the creation of conditions for high skill, high value-added growth, which depend not only on social and political stability, but also on the health, education and training aspects of labour market and social policy provision.

Regional integration adds other dimensions to this emerging scenario for international labour. If we consider the EU as an example of broad integration (that is, integration with active social and political dimensions, as well as economic), and NAFTA and APEC as examples of narrow integration (that is, primarily a simple or limited focus on the economic), broad integration clearly offers more opportunity for international labour to act supranationally than narrow integration. It does so directly, through labour and social legislation, and indirectly, in terms of the context created for the operation of firms. Certain forms of regional integration will complement the regime fusion and social protection dimensions outlined previously.

What of narrow integration such as the cases of APEC and NAFTA? In the case of APEC, the strategy of international labour is likely to take the form of work with others agencies seeking to broaden the basis of regional action, while simultaneously attempting to establish formal, effective relations between union bodies and the institutional aspects of the regional process. NAFTA, because of the side agreement, is somewhat different. In that case, the strategic goal is to operationalise and extend the existing agreement.

Finally, there is the emerging challenge to international production, launched by a combination of consumer actions, NGO information activities and campaigns, and international labour campaigns. This moment is particularly important, for the other three act at the macro-institutional level. Challenges to the ordering of international production, albeit at an early stage and still relatively narrow and inchoate, link company level strategic decision-making into the emerging scenario. As we have seen in the cases of Danone, Accor and Adidas–Salomon, for different reasons and at different times, companies operating at a global level have decided that it is strategically necessary to make an accommodation, either with international labour, or with the international standards regime. Moreover, that accommodation may involve disciplines throughout the supply chain and across an array of national boundaries. In this sense, as pointed out earlier, the nature of global integration may prefigure its own nemesis.

Taking the four moments together, an environment in which international labour is able to exert a growing presence on a global scale is feasible. It is not, however, an inevitable outcome. If it is to come to pass, it will be the effect of political organisation in a variety of regimes and institutional settings. International labour will, to a large extent, have to make its own history by facilitating the unification of the four moments.

Labour's response

In this case, we are not so much interested in the detailed examination of labour's response to the opportunities that now present themselves. Such an examination is a study in itself.[27] We are more concerned with the fundamental conceptual issue that defines the nature of that response. It engages with the perennial issue of the accommodation struck by labour with capital in any politics of accommodation or engagement. It matters little which disciplinary base one chooses to adopt in addressing this issue. The common theoretical roots of political science, international relations and industrial relations lead to similar arguments, albeit with somewhat different vocabularies. For simplicity's sake, we adopt here the industrial relations mode of analysis.

In the Oxford School and its associated discourse,[28] debate has focused on the relationships, formal and informal, between employers and employees, their institutions, and the mechanisms whereby those relationships have been sustained. Common ground exists that in the normal run of things, these relationships must be sustained. This is so for the worker, for he or she must eat and their social existence must be sustainable; it is so for the employer, who must also eat, utilise capital and maintain production. Schisms in the relationship are expected. It is the function of the mechanisms and institutions put in place to overcome these schisms and create a new accommodation. Accommodations have been understood in numerous ways: as balances of power between actors in systems; as unitary models of shared perceptions between employer and employee; as models of plural interests drawn into accommodations by necessity and, to one extent or other, trust; as contending power relationships seeking increased control over the production process and its outcome for one party or the other. A common theme across all analyses is the notion of accommodation. It may be an accommodation conceived of in terms of equality of power and participation. It may be seen as an accommodation temporarily struck in a wider environment of opposed social forces. It is often defined in terms of the bargaining process and its outcome, the collective bargain, wherein dominant thinking accepts at a minimum that, for a legitimate accommodation to be struck, the institutional power of the employer should be balanced by the collective organisation of workers.

This review of Industrial Relations also notes that collective bargaining is understood usually to take place within a national bargaining system, defined over time by institutional, legislative and cultural norms. The possibility of extending this process to a supranational level has been the site of contentious debate for many years.[29] Until the factors discussed above emerged in recent years, a context in which accommodations might be struck at a supranational level seemed unobtainable. Information and personnel exchange and education initiatives seemed destined to be the extent of supranational organisation, apart from the peculiar circumstances of the EU. The argument developed above suggests that circumstances may have changed and international labour is challenged to define its mode of operation in this emerging global landscape. What role will international labour play in emerging global governance?

This is the nub of the issue. What mode (or modes) of operation are available to international labour in this new environment? On the basis offered by the four moments, the answer seems to be a resounding affirmation of the existing national mode of accommodation, extended into, and appropriately adapted for, the supranational arena. This may be so for many reasons. To use the Oxford School terminology again, both institutional and procedural arguments can be proffered. Beginning with institutions, the centrality of the ILO and its international regime to effective international labour action is a major constraining factor. The ILO is also the forum in which the formal 'rules' of international accommodations tend to be defined. These rules must be sufficiently generic to allow national actors to operate in a globally defined context. They will, perhaps, tend to be defined by the long tradition of convention setting at the heart of the ILO. The institutions of international labour echo their constituent national elements, which, although a broad church in terms of political affiliations and organisational traditions, do adhere to certain general precepts about the nature of bargaining. Moreover, the international institutions of the labour movement (particularly the ICFTU and the ITSs) have firmly committed themselves to activity within the international context defined by regime fusion, social protection and so on. A path defined and followed is often difficult to leave.

Procedurally, the institutions of international labour are enmeshed within a bargaining framework. This framework enjoys national and, increasingly, supranational legitimacy with governments and employers. It is the dominant national discourse (even if rhetorical); it is the discourse of the beaten path. It is a discourse and practice that, because of familiarity, lends itself to adaptation to international circumstances.

Accommodation creation and bargain setting is also complemented in this framework by the representation function. If the voice of labour is to be heard globally, and if the choice made is to be effective in the framework discussed above, labour's institutions must be present in the international organisations that emerge. This is already the case for the ILO. If joint activity between the ILO and the WTO on labour standards develops, labour must hope that it will be a key participant in whatever institutions are created. This is also true for both social protection and regional integration dimensions. The IUF and other ITS activity suggests that this is also the case for company-level activity on a supranational basis. Labour is emerging into this international framework from a position of relative weakness. As a result, labour institutions may well opt to maximise levels of representation in existing institutional frameworks, rather than seeking to establish alternatives *ab initio*. In this scenario, the intention would be, presumably, to consolidate a presence and use the legitimacy thus gained to promote change in the frameworks from within.

These arguments should not be taken as an endorsement of this outcome. Nor should they be understood to exclude the emergence of new modes of activity between labour and capital in a supranational environment. It may be that in time entirely new facets of that relationship will require responses that are not reducible to the standard industrial relations analysis. At this stage, however, the dominant view has implications for trade unions and for NGOs and activists involved in the internationalisation debate. In this view, the space and leverage open to international labour involves accommodation with employers and governments in the international arena (in the ILO, for example). It is the same story for social protection and regional integration. At the company level, activity around codes of conduct, standards setting and monitoring, and incipient international bargaining, all demand similar willingness to strike bargains. Bargains and accommodations rarely achieve everything desired by the participating parties. By their nature, they involve compromise, the putting-off of some issues to a later date, the prioritisation of some issues to the detriment of others, the recognition that some issues simply will not run in given contexts, the sequencing of demands and the management of disappointment. In other words, bargaining is usually about the politics of the possible. It is also, as Alan Fox argues, about the development of trust between the parties, such that all sides understand the constraints operating on each party and are confident that, broadly, accommodations and bargains are entered into in good faith.[30] This is likely to be the terrain upon which labour's involvement in global governance will be built, at least in the current period. It will offend some NGOs, particularly single-issue campaigns. It will offend some anti-reformist union traditions. It will be portrayed by some as a compromise with capital on terms of insuperable inequality. For critics, the challenge will be to move from the criticism to the delineation of an alternative path that weans the international labour movement from its long domestic traditions and the contemporary path that it appears to have chosen.

Conclusion

This discussion began with the suggestion that, at the heart of the relationship between labour (and its institutions) and global governance, is the possibility of a global accommodation between international institutions of governance, international capital and labour. That possibility emerges in the intersection of the four developments discussed above. The accommodation proposed is substantially the extension of national accommodations into the international sphere. Emerging global governance requires such an accommodation as it seeks to encompass civil society in general, and the interests of labour in particular. Sceptics will, rightly, challenge this view. However, the history of national accommodations meets that challenge. In historical perspective, the national accommodations that emerged in the UK in the mid-nineteenth century, and later elsewhere, were unimaginable in the eighteenth century. The extension of the franchise, the social security measures, the legitimation of bargaining procedures and other measures combined to create national accommodations of some durability. They were not constructed on equitable terms, and are frequently subject to adjustment, tension and conflict. They are, as many critics point out, accommodations that have permitted the consolidation and extension of the capitalist social and production relations. Equally, they are, in the face of twentieth century experience, more durable than the alternatives that have been essayed. For labour and its institutions, they have provided conduits for representation and bargaining that, in historical terms, are superior to all pre-capitalist structures and many attempts at post-capitalist transformation. Not surprisingly, therefore, the key national and international labour institutions will identify with an international accommodation associated with the emergence of global governance. For critics of this accommodation, the task is not only to provide an effective critique, but also to lay out alternative courses of action that surpass in terms of outcome the historical experience of national accommodations and the potential offered by the international version.

Notes

1 See, for example, W. Olle and W. Schoeller, 'World Market Competition and Restrictions Upon International Trade Union Policies', *Capital and Class*, 2 (1977); N. Haworth and H. Ramsay, 'Workers of the World Untied: International Capital and Some Dilemmas in Industrial Democracy', in R. Southall (ed.) *Trade Unions*

and the New Industrialisation of the Third World (Ottawa and London: University of Ottawa Press/Zed Books, 1988); H. Northrup and R. Rowan, *Multinational Collective Bargaining Attempts: The Record, the Cases and the Prospects*, (Industrial Research Unit, The Wharton School, University of Pennsylvania, Philadelphia, 1979).

2 See for example, G. K. Schoepfle and K. A. Swinnerton (eds) *International Labour Standards and Global Economic Integration* (Bureau of International Labor Affairs, US Department of Labor, Washington, DC, 1994); G. Fields, *Trade and Labour Standards: A Review of Issues* (OECD: Paris, 1994); N. Haworth and S. Hughes, 'Trade and International Labour Standards: Issues and Debates over a Social Clause', *Journal of Industrial Relations*, 39: 2 (1997); E. Lee, 'Globalisation and Labour Standards: A Review of the Issues', *International Labour Review*, 136: 2 (Summer 1997); J. A. de Castro, *Trade and Labour Standards: Using the Wrong Instruments for the Right Cause*, UNCTAD Discussion Paper 99 (May 1995); S. Charnovitz, 'The Influence of International Labour Standards on the World Trading Regime: A historical overview', *International Labour Review*, 126: 5 (September–October 1987); S. Charnovitz, 'The World Trade Organisation and Social Issues', *Journal of World Trade*, 28: 5 (October 1994); Trade Union Advisory Committee to the Organisation of Economic Co-operation and Development, *Labour Standards and the Multilateral Trade and Investment System*, Discussion Paper (December 1994); B. Creighton, 'The Internationalisation of Labour Law', *International Journal of Comparative Labour Law and Industrial Relations*, 11 (1994); B. Langille, 'Eight Ways to Think About International Labour Standards', *Journal of World Trade*, 31: 4 (August 1997); S. Hughes and R. Wilkinson, 'International Labour Standards and World Trade: No role for the World Trade Organisation?', *New Political Economy*, 3: 3 (November 1998); R. Wilkinson and S. Hughes, 'Labor Standards and Global Governance: Examining the dimensions of institutional engagement', *Global Governance*, 6: 2 (Apr–Jun 2000); R. Wilkinson, 'Trade and Labour-Related Regulation: Beyond the Trade-Labour Standards Debate?', *British Journal of Politics and International Relations*, 1: 2 (June 1999); R. Wilkinson, N. Haworth and S. Hughes, 'Recasting Labor Diplomacy: A comment on Stigliani', *International Studies Perspectives*, 2: 2 (May 2001).

3 A comment made by both sides during discussions in Geneva in 1997. Interviews conducted in both the ILO and the WTO in that year indicated clearly that important parties in both organisations were comfortable with the distance between the two.

4 N. Haworth and S. Hughes, 'Death of a Social Clause', *Manchester Papers in Politics*, 3/00 (2000), Department of Government, University of Manchester.

5 Hansenne's speeches to the Annual Conference of the ILO during his last years in office are important statements of his desire to move the ILO forward.

6 This openness, perhaps a function of personalities and, to some extent a shared political heritage, is reported in interviews conducted in both ILO and WTO in Geneva in 2000.

7 These comments reflect discussions in the ILO and the WTO in May 2000 between senior officials and the author.

8 I draw some of the following discussion from A. Hoda, 'Imperatives for South-South Co-operation in the Multilateral Trading System', Paper to the Seminar on Interregional Co-operation in Trade and Investment: Asia–Latin America, ESCAP-UN, Bangkok, February 2000. Hoda is former Deputy Director-General of the WTO.

9 Some hardened, and perhaps over cynical, trade negotiators now openly discuss the possibility that a successful outcome in Seattle was always impossible because of pre-determined US positions dictated by domestic politics.

10 The concept of a global industrial relations regime is developed in N. Haworth and S. Hughes, 'Internationalisation, Industrial Relations Theory and International Relations', *Journal of Industrial Relations*, 42: 2 (June 2000).

11 I have used the concept of 'regime fusion' to describe the overlapping or intersection of the trade (WTO) and labour standards (ILO) regimes. It connotes the permanent conceptual and institutional integration of the two regimes. The process of fusion across these and other international regimes may usefully be conceived as underpinning the emergence of global governance.

12 See W. v. Ginneken (ed.) *Social Security for the Excluded Majority* (ILO: Geneva, 1999).

13 See, for example, N. Haworth, *The HRD Dimension of the Asian Financial Crisis: Towards the Definition of an APEC Response* (APEC Secretariat: Singapore 1998); E. Lee, *The Asian Financial Crisis: The Challenge for Social Policy* (ILO: Geneva, 1998).

14 A good example of this is the World Bank's 'Comprehensive Development Framework', created in 1998. See http://www.worldbank.org/cdf/overview.htm

15 This section is drawn in part from N. Haworth and S. Hughes, 'Internationalisation, Industrial Relations Theory and International Relations'.

16 See, for example, P. Cressey, 'European Works Councils in Practice', *Human Resource Management Journal*, 8: 1 (1998); P. Knutsen, 'Corporatist Tendencies in the Euro-polity: The EU Directive of 22 September 1994, on European Work Councils', *Economic and Industrial Democracy*, 18: 2 (1997); R. Welch, 'European Works Councils and Their Implications: The Potential Impact on Employer Practices and Trade Unions', *Employee Relations*, 16: 4 (1994); H. Ramsay, 'The Community, the Multinational, its Workers and their Charter', *Work, Employment and Society*, 5: 4 (1991).

17 See http://www.iuf.org/iuf/Danone/index.htm

18 See http://www2.icftu.org/displaydocument.asp?Index=981022043&Language=EN

19 See http://www.iuf.org/iuf/accor/index.htm

20 Recent events associated with one of the most significant claims taken up under the side agreement (the two year old Han Young dispute) have embarrassed the US Department of Labor and highlighted the problems associated with the operation of the side agreement. The case involves the establishment and operation of independent trade union organisations and has given rise to violence between competing union groups within Mexico.

21 See 'Adidas–Salomon Policy on Social and Environmental Affairs' at: http://www.adidas.com/global/custserv/soe/policy/text_c.htm

22 See 'World Federation of the Sporting Goods Industry' at http://www.wfsgi.org/

23 See 'Fair Labor Association' at http://www.fairlabor.org/

24 Other examples of this type of activity include the Rugmark Foundation, operating in India and Nepal, and companies such as Levi-Strauss, Phillips-Van Heusen, Reebok, Eddie Bauer, The Gap and Wal-Mart, which have adopted codes of conduct. On codes of conduct, see J. Murray, 'Corporate Codes of Conduct and Labour Standards', in R. Kyloh (ed.) *Mastering the Challenge of Globalisation: Towards a Trade Union Agenda* (Geneva: ILO, 1998).

25 See N. Haworth, 'Setting the Standard: APEC and the US Government's Campaign for International Labour Standards', Proceedings of the APEC Study Centre Consortium Conference 'Towards APEC's Second Decade: Challenges, Opportunities and Priorities', Auckland, May 1999.

26 See ICFTU (2000) 'Fighting for Workers' Human Rights in the Global Economy' http://www2.icftu.org/displaydocument.asp?Index=990916201&Language=EN

27 See, for example, the ICFTU webpage at http://www2.icftu.org and the associated links to the ITSs. For analysis, see Haworth and Hughes, 'Internationalisation, Industrial Relations Theory and International Relations'; Haworth and Hughes,

'Trade and International Labour Standards'; E. Lee, 'Globalisation and Labour Standards'; R. Kyloh (ed.) *Mastering the Challenge of Globalization: Towards a Trade Union Agenda*; W. Sengenberger and D. Campbell (eds) *Creating Economic Opportunities: The Role of Labour Standards in Industrial Restructuring*, (Geneva: ILO, 1994); G. van Liemt, 'Economic Globalization: Labour Options and Business Strategies in High Labour Cost Countries', *International Labour Review*, 131: 4–5 (1992), p. 457; N. Haworth and S. Hughes, 'Regime Building and its Implications for International Labour Regulation and Organisation', *Manchester Papers in Politics*, 3/99, Department of Government, University of Manchester; H. Ramsey, 'The Commission, the Multinational, its Workers and their Charter', pp. 541–66.

28 See, for example, A. Flanders, *The Fawley Productivity Agreements: A Case Study of Management and Collective Bargaining*, London: Faber & Faber, 1964); A. Flanders, *Industrial Relations: What is Wrong with the System? An essay on its theory and future* (London: Faber & Faber, 1965); A. Fox, *Industrial Sociology and Industrial Relations* (London: HMSO, 1966); Richard Hyman, *Industrial Relations: A Marxist Introduction* (London: Macmillan, 1975).

29 See, for example, R. Munck and P. Waterman (eds) *Labour Worldwide in the era of Globalisation: Alternative Union Models in the New World Order* (New York: St Martin's Press, 1999); C. Levinson, *International Trade Unionism* (London: Charles Allen & Unwin, 1972); N. Haworth and H. Ramsay, 'Workers of the World Untied: International Capital and Some Dilemmas in Industrial Democracy'; W. Olle and W. Schoeller, 'World Market Competition and Restrictions upon International Trade Union Policies'.

30 See Fox, *Industrial Sociology and Industrial Relations*.

Part V

Civil society and global governance

11 The contours of courtship

The WTO and civil society

Rorden Wilkinson

Introduction

A resurgent civil society and the gatekeeper of the trade liberalisation project, the World Trade Organisation (WTO), collided on the streets of Seattle during the Organisation's third Ministerial Meeting in late November, early December 1999. Images of the demonstrations adorned the pages of the world's media and served to focus attention on the social, ecological and, to a lesser extent, cultural impact of trade liberalisation, as well as the lack of transparency, accountability and broad-based representation in the WTO's working procedures. In what seemed to be a rising tide of global popular protest, Seattle was followed in quick succession by demonstrations during the January 2000 World Economic Forum (WEF) in Davos, and the Washington (April 2000) and Prague (September 2000) meetings of the World Bank and International Monetary Fund (IMF).

But the Seattle, Davos, Washington and Prague demonstrations are not unique, nor do they reflect a sudden and spontaneous outburst of civil militancy, as some have suggested. Less well publicised protests accompanied the second Ministerial Meeting of the WTO in Geneva in May 1998; and public shows of discontent have long been directed towards the IMF and the World Bank. Rather, they represent one stage, albeit the most spectacular, in the development of a process of dissatisfaction with the activities of the institutions of global economic governance that has evolved in tandem with the increasing penetration of the neoliberal reforms ushered in during the latter quarter of the twentieth century.

That said, this dissatisfaction has not been confined to the world bodies of the WTO, IMF and World Bank – the core intergovernmental components of contemporary global economic governance. Demonstrations accompanied the Manila (1996), Vancouver (1997), Kuala Lumpur (1998) and Auckland (1999) Ministerial Meetings of the Asia Pacific Economic Co-operation forum (APEC); the Organisation for Economic Co-operation and Development's (OECD) proposed Multilateral Agreement on Investment (MAI) met with a barrage of criticism as more than 560 non-governmental organisations (NGOs) mobilised in opposition; the social distress ushered in by the 1997–8 financial crisis in East Asia, and, to a lesser extent, the former Soviet Union, fanned public dissatisfaction with the role of world and regional bodies; and the Jubilee 2000 campaign has generated much public support for a more comprehensive approach to the extreme levels of indebtedness of many developing states.

Yet, to limit the extent of this dissatisfaction to visible popular protest would be to misrepresent the breadth of public anxiety as to the activities of world and regional bodies. The spectre of WTO-authorised US trade sanctions on certain European micro-industries (such as, for instance, Scottish cashmere) in part retaliation for perceived inadequacies in the EU's reform of its relationship with banana producers in the Caribbean, and the failure of the EU to successfully inhibit imports of hormonally modified beef from the US, have been two incidents among a growing number that have been the cause of a much less visible public concern in the industrial North. Similarly, the problems associated with a long history of structural adjustment, the very intimate consequences of World Bank sponsored microcredit and microfinance policies, and the workplace violations suffered by many in a seemingly never-ending proliferation of export processing zones, have been at the forefront of concerns fuelling anxiety in the developing South.

Whether expressed through popular protest or wider civil anxiety, a general unease has developed as to the ability of certain organisations and institutions, many of which are hidden from public view, to implement, directly or indirectly, policies that to varying degrees have a significant daily impact. In an effort to counter some of this public dissatisfaction, the most prolific world and regional organisations have embarked on a programme of courtship with representatives of what is somewhat awkwardly termed 'civil society' – in essence the realm of private activity between family and government,[1] but more often than not boiled down by the institutions of global governance to NGOs. Some, among the wider constellation of bodies that comprise contemporary global governance, have nurtured a relationship with civil society that reflects a natural symbiosis in their respective work.[2] Others have developed relations with NGOs as a means of utilising specialist knowledge and skills, or devolving responsibilities to organisations to carry out specific tasks.[3] Few, however, have sought to incorporate representatives of civil society into their decision-making structures, or implement wholesale reform directed towards increasing the parameters of representation and accountability.[4]

For those world organisations at the core of contemporary global economic governance, the story has been mixed. The World Bank began to nurture a relationship with civil society in the early 1970s through operational collaboration on particular projects – though it was not until the Bank issued a directive in 1989 that NGO involvement in projects increased significantly.[5] The wake of the Asian Financial crisis saw World Bank relations with NGOs expand further. This, however, stopped short of a commitment to civil society participation in the decision-making capacity of the Organisation or the strategic development of policy.[6] Similarly, the IMF's relationship with civil society has also been kept at arm's length. While a more inclusive approach has been noted in certain aspects of the IMF's engagement with civil society, the substantive involvement of non-state actors in the Fund's decision-making capacities or its policy development has not been pursued.

In contrast to the courtships of the IMF and World Bank, the WTO has been at something of a disadvantage. Whereas the World Bank and IMF have had some time to develop a relationship with civil society, this has not been the case for the WTO. Its creation on 1 January 1995, the result of a much protracted Uruguay round of trade negotiations and a more protracted and politically fraught process stretching back to the end of the Second World War, coincided with a step increase in the expression of public dissatisfaction at the structural inequalities of the global economy. The WTO's significance combined with this step increase ensured that it was to encounter much attention and it remains the focus of considerable public scrutiny.

Set against a tide of increasing public criticism of the activities of world and regional economic organisations, and the embarkation by these organisations on a relationship with NGOs, this chapter offers a critical examination of the emerging relationship between the WTO and civil society. It begins by detailing the significance of the establishment of the WTO and the concomitant development of public interest in the Organisation. Second, it examines the contours of the WTO's courtship of civil society. And finally, it offers some comments by way of conclusion on the future of WTO–civil society relations.

The World Trade Organisation

The WTO owes its creation to post-Second World War efforts to develop a trinity of organisations designed to manage the global economy along broadly liberal lines – the International Monetary Fund (IMF), the International Bank for Reconstruction and Development (IBRD and now, albeit somewhat differently, the World Bank) and the International Trade Organisation (ITO).[7] Each organisation was to have jurisdiction over a particular aspect of the global economy, yet all were to work together as a coherent ensemble. But there was to be one important caveat. Although the ideological disposition of this trinity was to be distinctly liberal in orientation, the memory of the economic and social distress and accompanying civil unrest generated by the highly liberalised and largely uncontrolled global economy of the inter-war period ensured that the post-war architects sought not to pursue pure *laissez-faire* policies, but to temper this with a commitment to a modicum of national interventionism – an interventionism intended to enable states to constrain, at the margins, market forces to offset adverse economic situations.

This marriage between commercial internationalism and national interventionism is most commonly referred to as the embedded liberal compromise.[8] Yet there was a further dimension underpinning the organisation

building envisaged by the post-war planners. This embedded liberal compromise was to be built upon a deeper set of social relations, wherein
national political economies – at least within those states at the core of the
world economy – were centred around a social contract.[9] This contract
brought business and organised labour into closer association with government in the management of the economy. The logic underpinning the social
contract was simple. The economic stability and concomitant producer confidence provided by government demand management policies would enable
capital to expand; and the development of a welfare system would ensure
the acquiescence of organised labour and act to forestall the emergence of
social unrest.

It was upon these foundations that the trinity of world economic organisations was to be built. The promotion of international trade was perceived to
be key to the reconstruction of the world economy. Correspondingly, the
hub of the trinity was to comprise an organisation designed to bring about
trade liberalisation. This liberalisation was to be achieved through periodic
negotiations undertaken against a backdrop of legal commitments coupled
with a means of settling disputes arising among participating states. Operating
in tandem was to be an organisation designed to assist in the restoration of
currency stability. But to enable an increase in the volume and value of trade
to come about, and to take advantage of new-found currency confidence, a
third organisation was envisaged. This organisation was to provide a much
needed lending facility to enable reconstruction, ultimately contributing to
the promotion of trade. It was out of the need for a means of promoting
currency stability and capital provision that the IMF and World Bank were
established as a result of the 1944 Bretton Woods conference.

However, the negotiations for what would have become the trade body –
the ITO – were unable to overcome residual doubts over the content of the
Organisation's legal framework.[10] Of the fifty-three states that signed the
Havana Charter (the ITO's founding document) only two sought its ratification. Indeed, it was the absence of ratification by the US that ultimately
resulted in the still-birth of the Organisation and with it the central component
of the world economic trinity.

The demise of the ITO did not, however, spell the end of efforts to provide
a source of regulation for international trade. As a means of bridging the
gap between the protectionism of the inter-war period and the designs for a
quasi-liberal commercial order centred around the ITO, twenty-three states
(known as 'contracting parties') embarked upon negotiations designed to
hammer out a preliminary legal framework (in essence, a truncated version
of Chapter IV of the Havana Charter) and begin the process of tariff liberalisation. Their efforts resulted in the drafting of the General Agreement on
Tariffs and Trade (GATT) – an agreement that was to be subsumed into the
ITO once the Organisation was up and running. However, the still-birth of
the ITO elevated the GATT from provisional status to *de facto* source of
international trade regulation, albeit without the ITO's elaborate commercial

provisions, or its interlinkages with the IMF and World Bank (though the GATT did contain provisions for some limited co-operation with the IMF).

That said, the form that the ITO would have taken has significance on two counts. First, the ITO, though reflecting the prevailing ideology of its time, provided a model trade organisation upon which the WTO was in part styled. And second, the Havana Charter, again reflecting its predication upon a deeper set of social relations, contained provisions which: (1) would have nurtured a relationship with organised labour through an inter-organisational linkage with the International Labour Organisation (ILO); and (2) would have provided the legal wherewithal for the ITO to develop relations with NGOs.[11]

What emerged after the war, then, was an incomplete trinity of organisations designed to manage the global economy. The GATT fell far short of fulfilling the role envisaged for the ITO, though it did develop a quasi-organisational form with appropriate managerial and administrative capabilities. But its status as an Agreement rather than an Organisation, the small size of its secretariat, and a correspondingly low profile, coupled with the prevailing Cold War climate ensured that relatively few outside of organised labour and the occasional NGO paid much attention to the GATT. This was in stark contrast to the attention received by the IMF and World Bank.

As public alienation increased through concerted attacks on union power and welfare provision in the early 1970s,[12] attention began focusing on the international mechanisms of neoliberalism. The unpicking of the social contract brought with it an increase in the level of public scrutiny of the GATT. But this new-found attention was to intensify markedly during the Uruguay round of trade negotiations (1986–94) held under the *General Agreement*'s auspices. During the Uruguay round a consensus emerged that the deficiencies of the GATT, coupled with growing pressure to extend the trade liberalisation project, necessitated once again that an attempt be made to create a more comprehensive organisation designed to regulate world trade. It is out of this consensus that the WTO emerged, and with it the final realisation of the trinity of organisations envisaged by the post-war planners.[13]

The establishment of the WTO did not, however, bring with it a mere formalisation of the regulation of international trade in goods. Rather, it deepened the parameters of trade regulation by revamping the GATT (now the GATT 1994) and drawing in areas previously not subject to GATT rules (such as agriculture, and textiles and clothing). It also broadened the parameters of trade regulation by incorporating rules governing trade in services (under the *General Agreement on Trade in Services* – GATS), trade-related aspects of intellectual property rights (the TRIPs), and trade-related investment measures (the TRIMs). Furthermore, it provided the wherewithal to oversee the settlement of trade disputes, and a permanent forum for the negotiation of further reductions in barriers to trade and associated areas.

Public concern and the WTO

Perhaps unsurprisingly, then, the very establishment of the WTO attracted much attention. The commencement of operations was surrounded by considerable fanfare as well as much relief that rumours that the US would once again decide not to ratify the founding agreement of a trade body failed to come to fruition. But it has been the perceived imbalances in the WTO's considerable legal framework – many of which are continuations from the GATT era – that have resulted in a large degree of public attention being directed towards the Organisation, ranging from outright opposition to calls for reform.

For certain sections of the international labour movement, the creation of the WTO proved disappointing; for others it was what had been expected. The absence of a clear linkage between trade and worker rights in the WTO's legal framework ran contrary to aspirations that the WTO would parody the ITO's labour provisions. It also, and perhaps most obviously, resulted in a clear rejection of the need to secure basic worker rights in the face of continued trade liberalisation.

The WTO has done little to ease labour's disappointment since its establishment. Recent efforts to reverse the absence of a clear linkage between trade liberalisation and the protection of worker rights by lobbying for, first, a social clause,[14] and second, a legal endorsement of core labour standards have proved unsuccessful.[15] Organised labour's plight has not been aided by WTO resistance to low level co-operation with the ILO in the form of a forum to explore further the trade–labour standards nexus. Complicating matters further are the deep-seated divisions that exist in the international labour movement about the possibility of any WTO involvement in the maintenance of worker rights. At first glance it appears that the international labour movement is split on North/South lines. The largely pro-Western International Confederation of Free Trade Unions (ICFTU) and the Trade Union Advisory Council (TUAC) to the Organisation for Economic Co-operation and Development (OECD) both favour a movement by the WTO into the area of worker rights; whereas, large parts of the Korean, Indian and Brazilian labour movement have come out against any WTO involvement in this area. Such a caricature is, however, largely artificial. Many developing country unions support the principle of a linkage between trade and labour standards; even more acknowledge the importance of this issue; but the majority fear a consolidation of Western interests and a thinly veiled medium for protectionism should the WTO move into this area.[16]

Similarly discontented are those groups purported to represent the interests of the global environment. The WTO was established with little in the way of environmental sensitivity. The Organisation's preamble commits member states merely to the 'objective' of sustainable development, rather than to any legal compunction; and a light scattering of further references to the language of environmental protection – which includes two Ministerial Decisions on trade and the environment[17] – are tempered by a commitment that the use of any such measures should not 'constitute a means of arbitrary or unjustifiable discrimination'.[18] The only legally binding provisions safeguarding the environment relate to the already existing 'general exceptions' clause of the GATT (Article XX) and a comparable clause incorporated into the GATS (Article XIV). The apparent absence of environmental sensitivity has been compounded by the failure of the WTO's Committee on Trade and Environment (CTE) – established under the authority of the *Ministerial Decision on Trade and Environment* – to make any substantive headway in its deliberations on the relationship between trade and the environment.[19]

That said, although important, neither the legal framework of the WTO, nor the lack of progress by the CTE has been the principal source of irritation for environmental groups. The WTO's dispute settlement mechanism has been highly criticised for the content of several rulings which have significant environmental consequences. An October 1998 ruling by the WTO's Appellate Body found the US to be discriminating against imports of shrimp from India, Malaysia, Pakistan and Thailand. The discrimination was deemed to have resulted from prohibitions on imports of shrimp harvested without the employment of measures designed to reduce the number of associated sea turtle deaths (by using turtle excluder devices or so-called 'tow-time' restrictions). Although the Appellate Body decision overturned aspects of a previous dispute settlement panel investigation of this issue, and was at pains to point out that its decision does not discount the need for protection and preservation of the environment,[20] the ruling angered many. It appeared yet again to privilege the trade liberalisation project over the plight of the environment, and in this case the sea turtle.

Tensions have also been exacerbated by an insistence on the part of the WTO to take 'scientific' knowledge – knowledge which is itself often essentially contested – as the ultimate source of arbitration in settling disputes. This was particularly the case during a dispute between the EU and US over imports of hormonally modified beef. In restricting such imports the EU was deemed to be discriminating against US imports. After a long and drawn-out investigation involving a series of Reports, it was decided that there was not sufficient evidence to suggest that hormonal modification in cattle presented a risk to human health.[21] As such, the EU's actions were unjustified. However, equally important is a public moral objection to hormonal modification, and an anxiety as to the wider consequences that such modification may have. Neither of these concerns appears to hold sway with the WTO.

Relatedly, the WTO has come in for considerable criticism from grassroots movements over the tension between the TRIPs and the environment. The move to patent so-called 'innovations' in biotechnology, and the codification of these patents in international law have led many to suggest that the WTO is too quick to offer legal protection to scientific 'advancements' that can have potentially damaging effects on human and animal life, as well as on the biosphere.[22] Again, this has a moral as well as a health dimension. Needless to say, however, public concerns on this issue have failed to secure much of the WTO's attention.

The inequalities between North and South have also been the source of much criticism levelled at the WTO – though media coverage of this issue has been far less pronounced than it has for labour and environmental concerns. The absence of a comprehensive approach to the issue of development has long been the source of much complaint. The residue of colonialism; the lack of adequate political representation during the negotiation of the GATT; the continuation of asymmetries in negotiating power between North and South; the failure of the 1966 addition to the GATT (Part IV) or, more widely, the New International Economic Order (NIEO) to alter the adverse trading fortunes of the developing; the crowding out of development issues by so-called new issues (intellectual property, services, investment, e-commerce); the resistance to the election of a WTO Director-General from the South by the industrial countries; and a relative disadvantage in technical and legal expertise, are among the many points of grievance. But most telling, is that the development of the global economy since 1945 has been such that the disparities between North and South, and between and across social classes, has widened considerably – a widening to which the liberalisation project first enshrined in the GATT and now the WTO is deemed to be complicit. However, the development issue is not one that sits comfortably with wider demands for a more sensitive approach to trade regulation. Rather, aspects of the post-Seattle inertia within the WTO can be attributed to tensions between civil society and the South as interested parties vie for position in an effort to shape the future trade agenda.[23]

Labour, the environment and development have not been the only areas in which the WTO is deemed to be deficient. The WTO has been much criticised for the lack of transparency and accountability in its decision-making processes – characteristics that reportedly prompted EU Trade Commissioner Pascal Lamy to liken the WTO to a medieval institution.[24] There are four distinct charges here: first, that WTO working practices are shrouded in secrecy and closed from public view; second, that the interests of various governments, particularly the leading industrial powers, are over-represented in WTO decision-making forums; third, that multinational corporations are perceived to have a disproportionate degree of access, and thus influence, in WTO decision-making; and fourth, that the broad representation of interests in the WTO does not include those who suffer most from increased trade liberalisation and accompanying changes in production processes. As Tony McGrew puts it, these charges

> sit uneasily alongside the official view of the WTO as an institution in which the principles of one state, one vote, of consensus decision-making, and of accountability through governments are considered the hallmark of its democratic credentials.[25]

Although the sources of dissatisfaction are many and varied, much cross-issue sympathy can be found among those critical of the WTO. That said, the strategies and final objectives pursued by the broad array of public groups engaged in this issue are varied, as are the ideological dispositions from which they derive influence. Crudely, and somewhat artificially, three broad types of groups can be identified.[26] First, there are those that, though critical of aspects of the WTO, are broadly supportive of the notion of a world body regulating trade on liberal lines. Among others, this group includes business associations such as the International Chamber of Commerce (ICC) and particular quasi-autonomous think tanks, such as the UK-based Royal Institute of International Affairs (RIIA).[27] Second, there are those that are critical of the activities of the WTO, but seek to engage with the Organisation in an effort to bring about change. We can count a number of trade union bodies such as the ICFTU, and NGOs such as Oxfam, Christian Aid and the World Wide Fund for Nature (WWF) among this number. Third, there are those groups that are fundamentally opposed to the WTO and seek its abolition. This group includes those that are ideologically opposed to economic liberalism as well as those that perceive the WTO as one feature of a world government; all, however, are united in their opposition to the Organisation. The groups encompassed here are People's Global Action (PGA), Globalise Resistance, GATT Watch and the Third World Network.

That said, the array of groups critical of the WTO is such that these categories are largely artificial. Some groups inhabit the hinterland between, say, those that favour some kind of engagement, and those that seek the WTO's abolition; others oppose some aspects of the Organisation's remit, but are broadly supportive of others. Nevertheless, the WTO has sought to quell some of the criticisms from those loosely inhabiting the first and second categories, and, in the process, marginalise the views of those comprising the third by pursuing a particular kind of relationship with civil society. It is to this relationship that we now turn.

The contours of courtship

In response to the seemingly never-ending stream of public interest in its activities, the WTO embarked upon a process of courtship with civil society in time for its first Ministerial Meeting in Singapore in December 1996. In order to do this it drew upon a legal provision contained within its *Establishing Agreement* – Article 5, Paragraph 2 – empowering the General Council of the WTO to 'make appropriate arrangements for effective cooperation with non-governmental organizations concerned with matters related to those of the WTO'.[28] Yet, the intended purpose of this provision had not been to enable the WTO to nurture a relationship with its critics. Rather, the utilisation of Article 5, Paragraph 2 was deemed to enable the WTO to benefit from a pool of expertise outside of that which is encompassed by the Organisation. However, the growing tide of public criticism called for innovative action.

Box 11.1 **1996 WTO guidelines for the development of relations with NGOs**

I. Under Article V:2 of the Marrakesh Agreement establishing the WTO 'the General Council may make appropriate arrangements for consultation and cooperation with non-governmental organizations concerned with matters related to those of the WTO'.

II. In deciding on these guidelines for arrangements on relations with non-governmental organizations, Members recognize the role NGOs can play to increase the awareness of the public in respect of WTO activities and agree in this regard to improve transparency and develop communication with NGOs.

III. To contribute to achieve greater transparency Members will ensure more information about WTO activities in particular by making available documents which would be derestricted more promptly than in the past. To enhance this process the Secretariat will make available on on-line computer network the material which is accessible to the public, including derestricted documents.

IV. The Secretariat should play a more active role in its direct contacts with NGOs who, as a valuable resource, can contribute to the accuracy and richness of the public debate. This interaction with NGOs should be developed through various means such as inter alia the organization on an ad hoc basis of symposia on specific WTO-related issues, informal arrangements to receive the information NGOs may wish to make available for consultation by interested delegations and the continuation of past practice of responding to requests for general information and briefings about the WTO.

V. If chairpersons of WTO councils and committees participate in discussions or meetings with NGOs it shall be in their personal capacity unless that particular council or committee decides otherwise.

VI. Members have pointed to the special character of the WTO, which is both a legally binding intergovernmental treaty of rights and obligations among its Members and a forum for negotiations. As a result of extensive discussions, there is currently a broadly held view that it would not be possible for NGOs to be directly involved in the work of the WTO or its meetings. Closer consultation and cooperation with NGOs can also be met constructively through appropriate processes at the national level where lies primary responsibility for taking into account the different elements of public interest which are brought to bear on trade policy-making.

Source: WTO, 'Guidelines for arrangements on relations with NGOs', Document WT/L/162, 18 July 1996.

In response to the need to nurture some kind of relationship with civil society, on 23 July 1996 (Decision adopted 18 July 1996) the WTO released an outline of the terrain upon which it was prepared to engage. This terrain came in the form of a set of six broad guidelines (see Box 11.1) directed at codifying the WTO's position – guidelines which reveal much about the WTO's perception of civil society as well as its perception of the legitimacy of particular NGOs. The first guideline merely restates the content of Article 5, Paragraph 2 (empowering the Organisation to develop relations with NGOs).

It does, however, have importance in that the WTO chose to reiterate at the outset that the development of relations with NGOs is an activity embarked upon at the *discretion* of the WTO's General Council, and that such activity is to be directed towards developing relations with only those NGOs that can demonstrate a concern with matters related to those of the WTO. Furthermore, in specifying the parameters within which the WTO is prepared to operationalise the provisions of Article 5, Paragraph 2, the Organisation chose to equate civil society with NGOs, rather than pursuing a broader, more inclusive and representative spectrum of public opinion.[29] The WTO has yet to determine exactly what it deems an 'NGO' to be, but recent practice points to a preference for non-profit making bodies, though a distinction is not made between groups representing business and civil interests.[30]

The second of the WTO's guidelines adds further substance to the nature of its courtship. It emphasises the role that NGOs can play in increasing public awareness of WTO activities, and uses this as the justification for improving transparency and communication procedures.[31] But while this statement was clearly included to unlock some of the inertia within a WTO membership hesitant at any movement in this direction (in that it provides justification for a move towards greater transparency and communication), it also has another function: to outline that it is principally what NGOs can do for the WTO, rather than the converse that broadly defines the relationship between the two.

The third guideline complements the second by adding a modicum of flesh to the Organisation's commitment to increasing transparency. Here we see this commitment to transparency interpreted simply as a need for greater de-restriction of WTO documents and access to these documents through the WTO's website, rather than for a more wholesale laying open of WTO working procedures.[32]

The WTO's intention of shaping the overall content of the relations developed with civil society continues in the fourth guideline. Here, though also reiterating its perception that NGOs are 'a valuable resource' particularly in contributing to the 'accuracy and richness' of public debate, the WTO outlines something of how a relationship between the WTO and NGOs is to be developed. Relations are to be developed through a variety of means ranging from the organisation of issue specific symposia, to the development of provisions to enable NGOs to submit information for the contemplation of 'interested delegations'.[33] However, as Marceau and Pedersen note, even the mention of 'symposia' in the guidelines was a fairly safe exercise. Its inclusion, they argue, is

> largely due to the success of the first symposium [on trade and environment, held in June 1994 in the run up to the formal establishment of the WTO] and the fact that Members found it to be a useful, if arms-length, exercise in NGO–WTO relations, with the Secretariat serving as 'buffer' between Members and NGOs.[34]

The fifth and sixth guidelines comprise the most telling factors shaping the contours of WTO–NGO relations. The fifth guideline states explicitly that when engaged in 'discussions' or 'meetings' with NGOs, WTO officials do so in a personal capacity, unless a previous decision has been taken to the contrary.[35] We see again an arm's-length approach to NGO relations: by requiring that officials act only in a personal capacity, NGOs are unable *officially* to influence WTO policy.

The sixth guideline contextualises the preceding guidelines. It states emphatically that under no circumstances is the development of relations with NGOs to result in the dilution of the 'inter-governmental character of the WTO', nor are NGOs to be involved in either the work of the WTO or its meetings. Furthermore, the guidelines state that the largest share of the responsibility for nurturing relations with NGOs lies with member governments, where a diversity of opinion can be reflected in national trade policy, rather than with the WTO.[36]

What arises from the WTO's operationalisation of the provisions of Article 5, Paragraph 2, then, is a framework which, though appearing broad, tightly constrains civil society interaction and ensures that the balance of power in the relationship remains firmly with the WTO. The emphasis is on the development of relations with NGOs, rather than with more informal, less well organised tracts of public opinion. And, by committing itself to court only those willing to engage with the WTO, large sections of more critical public opinion are marginalised. The resulting effect is a legitimisation of certain NGOs (and, in extension, their constituencies) and a delegitimisation of others.

The evolution of WTO–NGO relations

However, the constraints of the WTO's guidelines are not the only factors shaping the Organisation's relations with NGOs. As important in shaping the contours of WTO–NGO relations have been the WTO's first three Ministerial Meetings: Singapore (December 1996), Geneva (May 1998), and Seattle (November/December 1999). It is to these Meetings that we now turn.

Singapore

The run-up to the Singapore Ministerial Meeting was characterised by a degree of nervousness on both sides. Many within the WTO were uneasy about the development of any kind of relationship with civil society; whereas, among those NGOs that had successfully applied for official recognition at the Ministerial Meeting, few knew what to expect. For its part, the WTO, in conjunction with the Singaporean government, provided good facilities for the NGO representatives, and various proceedings were broadcast to the NGO centre. However, a number of factors served to cloud the NGO experience. In line with WTO guidelines, NGO delegations were only permitted from those organisations that could demonstrate that their interests were directly related to those of the WTO. Furthermore, NGOs were warned against any kind of public demonstration by the Singaporean government.[37]

For the WTO, the invitation to attend the Singapore Ministerial Meeting was not intended to set a precedent, nor was it to lead to a formalisation of WTO–NGO relations.[38] Nevertheless, the experience of Singapore bred a perception among the more critical members of the WTO that this first engagement with civil society had been relatively unthreatening, particularly as it had taken place against the backdrop of some limited discussion of the thorny issue of trade and labour standards.[39] As a consequence, no objections were raised to the further accommodation of NGOs at the Organisation's second Ministerial Meeting.[40]

Geneva

However, the WTO's Geneva Ministerial Meeting proved quite different from Singapore. The relative political freedom of Switzerland enabled a series of demonstrations, organised by a loose coalition of NGOs and grassroots movements, to take place illustrating a level of dissatisfaction with the WTO that had been absent in Singapore. Though it would be a mistake to suggest that a direct causal relationship existed between the protests and what took place inside the Meeting, the amount of time given over to civil society issues in the statements of key people did not go unnoticed. In a candid opening address to the Ministerial Meeting, Renato Ruggiero the first Director-General of the WTO, suggested that among the main challenges facing the WTO was the need to tackle issues of public concern. He cited financial instability, development, marginalisation, the environment, employment, health and cultural diversity as among the most pressing, and suggested that, by way of moving forward, the WTO divert some energy towards strengthening its relationship with civil society.[41] Although Ruggiero's comments did not suggest that the WTO was about to reverse its decision to exclude NGOs from the workings of the Organisation, they were followed by comparably supportive declarations from the US and EU.[42] While to some these intentions appeared largely symbolic, they were advanced in conjunction with calls for a new trade round to follow the Organisation's Third Ministerial Meeting in Seattle, raising hopes that the proposed 'Millennium Round' would take issues of public concern more seriously. Geneva, then, appeared to be a significant moment in the development of WTO–NGO relations; a point from which a deeper relationship could emerge. Such hopes were, however, short-lived.

Seattle

The run-up to the Seattle Ministerial Meeting witnessed a series of events inflame public tempers and alienate many among the WTO's membership. The election of Mike Moore to the post of Director-General was particularly messy. The member states could not agree upon a successor to Ruggierio until four months after the end of his tenure (at the end of April 1999). The political turbulence that followed witnessed the South's preferred candidate, Supachai Panitchpakdi, lose out to the US backed, and initially much unfancied compromise candidate, Mike Moore. In an effort to abate some of the ill-feeling generated among the South, Moore's tenure was limited to three years, whereupon he would be replaced with Supachai, who would serve a similar term. Combined with an historically poor record on development and the spectre of a Millennium Round designed to discuss new issues rather than to address old ones, the South arrived in Seattle in a combative mood.[43]

However, this was not the only alienation that was to have a profound impact on the Meeting. The spectre of a new round of trade negotiations resulting from the Seattle Meeting, set against the backdrop to the US presidential elections, provided fertile ground for anti-WTO protests. Fearing that those gathered in Seattle would attempt to disrupt the Ministerial Meeting, Moore gave two speeches which, though intended to have the opposite effect, contributed to much anti-WTO feeling. First, two days prior to the start of the Ministerial Meeting in an address to the ICFTU Moore announced that he believed the issue of worker rights and their relationship with the WTO to be in many ways a 'false debate'. Rather, he argued, it is poverty not trade that is the principal cause of poor working conditions.[44] Though acknowledging that work insecurity is a common feature of the contemporary global economy, he argued that more liberalisation, rather than less, was the answer. For some, Moore's comments were seen to be belittling the concerns of workers. Second, and a day later, Moore told a gathering of NGOs that the WTO is not a world government, nor does it have any intention of becoming one; it does not override national law, dictate to countries, 'kill turtles or lower wages or employ children in factories'.[45] Here Moore missed much of the nuance of NGO arguments which, while recognising that the WTO is not a formal world governing body, assert that the impact of its decision-making has governance-like consequences in that it constrains and shapes an increasingly greater part of daily life.

Unsurprisingly, Seattle proved to be a disaster. Not only was the Ministerial Meeting overshadowed by the huge outburst of public disquiet directed towards the WTO, coupled with the heavy-handedness of the US National Guard, the Meeting itself was a failure. The absence of adequate preparation in the run-up to the meeting, coupled with the political fall-out from the election of the second Director-General resulted in a collapse of the talks and a postponement of the launch of the Millennium Round.

The collapse of the Meeting saw WTO–civil society relations at their lowest level since the Organisation's creation. The relative ease with which the Singapore Ministerial Meeting had dealt with public scrutiny seemed to be a distant memory. In the wake of Seattle, the WTO has attempted to be seen as more serious in its engagement with civil society by revamping aspects of its website and inviting NGO documents for circulation. The Secretariat, however, remains a comfortable buffer-zone between those critical of the WTO and its decision-making procedures. National consultation processes have also been undertaken as a means of identifying the principal causes of the breakdown and, by extension, reformulating a more agreeable position.[46] One dimension of this process has been an invitation for NGOs to participate in a critical assessment of the EU's mandate post-Seattle; another has been for trade officials to place civil society issues further up the trade agenda; another still has seen Mike Moore offer a more thoughtful assessment of the failure of the Ministerial Meeting.[47] Nonetheless, anti-WTO feeling remains high.

Conclusion

The events post-Seattle have not shortened the distance the WTO now finds itself from public sympathy. Its position has not been enhanced by the reverberations of on-going conflicts between the principal trading powers over bananas, beef, foreign tax corporations, periodicals, alcohol and many others. All this would seem to bode well for a wholesale rethink of WTO–NGO relations and a concomitant commitment to more substantive interaction. However, one consequence of the Seattle Meeting has been the generation of much ill-feeling toward civil society by many developing countries. And current efforts to bring these states back into the fray are unlikely to be accompanied by a deepening of relations between the WTO and civil society.

There are, however, other consequences of the way in which WTO–civil society relations have evolved. The 1996 guidelines have locked the WTO into a particular kind of relationship with civil society that is, for both sides, deeply constraining. For civil society, the guidelines enable only those bodies that can demonstrate an interest in the WTO's remit to engage with the Organisation. This invariably means groups representing business and some more acceptable NGOs are included. Even then, however, the substance of this relationship is particularly shallow.

There is another, more worrying consequence. These 'acceptable' groups are among those more likely to gain access to global decision-making anyway.[48] It is those least likely to be able to exercise their voice that will again find themselves debarred. Here we are not only thinking of those bodies that do not want to engage with the WTO, such as the PGA, but also those that are unable to make representations on the international stage, particularly from the South. The sum of this legitimising/delegitimising dichotomy is that the views of those already able to be heard can quickly become reduced to a representative picture of public opinion. Without doubt, such an outcome will reinforce the Western bias already existent in the WTO particularly, and global governance more generally. Those not represented will suffer further and more acute alienation.

For the WTO, its insistence on a set of guidelines that ensure its preponderance in any relationship simply confirms its unwillingness to take account of public opinion. An increasing elaboration of its internet provisions, or the organisation of symposia which in themselves do not influence policy-making, will not alter this perception in the slightest. The task ahead for the WTO is to develop procedures that take account of the broadest range of public opinion at the core of the Organisation, rather than to continue in the dogmatic pursuit of unhindered trade liberalisation. The WTO also needs to think more critically about the intrinsic value of expanding the boundaries of its accountability. For instance, in defending the content of the WTO's courtship with civil society, Marceau and Pedersen suggest that 'some would argue that interest groups should not have "two bites at the same apple" – one domestically and one internationally'.[49] But it is precisely because of a perceived lack of representation at the national level, coupled with a widely held belief that states are losing something of their agency that civil society organisations have arisen and are lobbying international organisations. Furthermore, business groups are over-represented at national and international levels; it is in recognition of this that civil society organisations have sought to engage and redress something of the balance.

More broadly, there are as many problems with civil society as there are with the world economic organisations they seek to confront. First, many civil society organisations do not want to be seen to be getting into bed with the IMF, World Bank and WTO. But by not doing so, they run the risk of further marginalising their views from the arena of public debate. Second, while a good number of world and regional organisations resemble autocratic, oligopolistic or monarchical regimes, the same can also be said for certain NGOs. When thinking about whether or not the inclusion of NGOs in the decision-making structures of a world organisation has the capacity to counter greater concentrations of power,[50] we also need to think about the democratic credentials of civil society organisations themselves. Finally, and in many ways restating a point made above in a different capacity, we need to think carefully about the constituencies NGOs purport to represent. It is one thing to lobby for a particular approach to debt relief; it is entirely another to suffer extreme poverty, famine, personal violence and drought.

Notes

1 Nelson Kasfir, 'The Conventional Notion of Civil Society: A Critique', *Commonwealth and Comparative Politics*, 36: 2 (July 1998), pp. 4–5.
2 The United Nations Children's Fund (UNICEF) has, for instance, been actively involved with NGOs since the 1950s. See Kendall W. Stiles, 'Civil Society Empowerment and Multilateral Donors: International Institutions and New International Norms', *Global Governance*, 4: 2 (1998), p. 202.
3 NGOs have, for example, been instrumental in providing relief in zones of conflict. See Mark Duffield, 'NGO Relief in War Zones: Toward an Analysis of the New Aid Paradigm', in Thomas G. Weiss (ed.) *Beyond UN Subcontracting: task-sharing with regional security arrangements and service providing NGOs* (Basingstoke: Macmillan, 1998).

4 Willets notes that there has been some movement towards a partnership between intergovernmental organisations and NGOs within the UN system, though this has not been reflected in a legally equal relationship. See Peter Willetts, 'From "Consultative Arrangements" to "Partnership": The Changing Status of NGOs in Diplomacy at the UN', *Global Governance*, 6: 2 (Apr–June 2000).

5 Jane G. Covey, 'Is Critical Cooperation Possible? Influencing the World Bank through Operational Collaboration and Policy Dialogue', in Jonathan A. Fox and L. David Brown (eds) *The Struggle for Accountability: The World Bank, NGOs and Grassroots Movements* (Cambridge, MA: MIT Press, 1998), p. 84.

6 Stiles, 'Civil Society Empowerment and Multilateral Donors', p. 204.

7 See Rorden Wilkinson, *Multilateralism and the World Trade Organisation: the architecture and extension of international trade regulation* (London: Routledge, 2000), pp. 11–15.

8 John Ruggie, *Constructing the World Polity: essays on international institutional-ization* (London: Routledge, 1998), pp. 72–3.

9 Robert Cox, *Approaches to World Order* (Cambridge: Cambridge University Press, 1996), p. 247.

10 See William Diebold Jr, 'The End of the ITO', *Essays in International Finance*, No. 16 (International Finance Section, Department of Economics, Princeton University, 1952); J. E. S. Fawcett, 'The Havana Charter', *The Yearbook of World Affairs*, 5 (1951); Herbert Feis, 'The Geneva Proposal for an International Trade Charter', *International Organization*, 2: 1 (1948); Richard N. Gardner, *Sterling–Dollar Diplomacy: anglo-American collaboration in the reconstruction of multilateral trade* (Oxford: Clarendon Press, 1956); Jacob Viner, 'Conflicts of Principle in Drafting a Trade Charter', *Foreign Affairs*, 25: 4 (1947); and Clair Wilcox, *A Charter for World Trade*, (London: Macmillan, 1949).

11 Articles 2–7, and Article 87, Paragraph 2 respectively of the *Final Act of the United Nations Conference on Trade and Employment* (Havana Charter), Havana, 21 November 1947 to 24 March 1948. See Rorden Wilkinson, 'Peripheralising Labour: The ILO, WTO and the Completion of the Bretton Woods Project', in Jeffery Harrod and Robert O'Brien (eds), *International Trade Unions: theory and strategy in the global political economy* (London: Routledge, 2002).

12 Robert W. Cox, *Production, Power, and World Order: social forces in the making of history* (New York: Columbia University Press), pp. 373–4.

13 John H. Jackson, *The World Trading System: law and policy of international economic relations* (Michigan: Michigan University Press, 1998), second edn, pp. 44–6.

14 Nigel Haworth and Steve Hughes, 'Trade and International Labour Standards: Issues and Debates over a Social Clause', *Journal of Industrial Relations*, 39: 2 (June 1997).

15 Rorden Wilkinson and Steve Hughes, 'Labor Standards and Global Governance: Examining the dimensions of institutional engagement', *Global Governance*, 6: 2 (Apr–June 2000), pp. 262–3.

16 Rorden Wilkinson, Nigel Haworth and Steve Hughes, 'Recasting Labour Diplomacy: a comment on Stigliani', *International Studies Perspectives*, 2: 2 (May 2001), p. 210.

17 The *Decision on Trade in Services and the Environment* and the *Decision on Trade and Environment*.

18 See, for example, the preamble to the *Agreement on the Application of Sanitary and Phytosanitary Measures*, (Geneva: GATT, 1994); also the *Agreement on Agriculture* (Geneva: GATT, 1994).

19 Marc Williams and Lucy Ford, 'The World Trade Organisation, Social Move-ments and Global Environmental Management', *Environmental Politics*, 8: 1 (Spring 1999), pp. 278–9.

20 WTO Appellate Body Report, 'United States – Import Prohibition of Certain Shrimp and Shrimp Products', WT/DS58/AB/R (12 October 1998), paragraphs 161–88.

21 See WTO Appellate Body Report, 'EC Measures Concerning Meat and Meat Products (Hormones)', WT/DS26/AB/R, WT/DS48/AB/R (16 January 1998).

22 See Ian Neale, 'The WTO and Issues Associated with TRIPs and Agrobiotechnology', in Annie Taylor and Caroline Thomas (eds) *Global Trade and Global Social Issues* (London: Routledge, 1999), pp. 114–32.

23 See Wilkinson, *Multilateralism and the World Trade Organisation*, pp. 139–45.

24 Lamy is reported to have made this comment during the Seattle Ministerial Meeting, though he has since tried to distance himself from it. See Pascal Lamy, Speech to the Confederation of British Industry, 6 July 2000.

25 Tony McGrew, 'The World Trade Organisation: technocracy or banana republic?', in Taylor and Thomas (eds) *Global Trade and Global Social Issues*, p. 202.

26 See also Williams and Ford, 'The World Trade Organisation, Social Movements and Global Environmental Management', pp. 269, 276–8, 282–6.

27 See, for example, written and oral evidence presented by Duncan Brack, Head of the Energy and Environmental Programme, Royal Institute of International Affairs (Chatham House), presented to the House of Lords Select Committee on the European Union, 'The World Trade Organisation: The EU Mandate After Seattle' (10th Report), 13 June 2000.

28 *Establishing Agreement*, Article V, Paragraph 2 (Geneva, GATT: 1994).

29 See Kasfir, 'The Conventional Notion of Civil Society', pp. 4–5, 10–11; also Cox, 'Civil society at the turn of the millennium: prospects for an alternative world order' *Review of International Studies*, 25: 1 (January 1999), pp. 3–28.

30 Gabrielle Marceau and Peter N. Pedersen, 'Is the WTO Open and Transparent? A discussion of the relationship of the WTO with non-governmental organisations and civil society's claims for more transparency and public participation', *Journal of World Trade*, 33: 1 (1999), p. 14.

31 WTO, 'Guidelines for arrangements on relations with NGOs', paragraph 2.

32 WTO, 'Guidelines for arrangements on relations with NGOs', paragraph 3.

33 WTO, 'Guidelines for arrangements on relations with NGOs', paragraph 4.

34 Marceau and Pedersen, 'Is the WTO Open and Transparent?', p. 11.

35 WTO, 'Guidelines for arrangements on relations with NGOs', paragraph 5.

36 WTO, 'Guidelines for arrangements on relations with NGOs', paragraph 6.

37 For an account of the Singapore experience see Robert O'Brien, Anne Marie Goetz, Jan Aart Scholte, and Marc Williams, *Contesting Global Governance: multilateral economic institutions and global social movements*, (Cambridge: Cambridge University Press, 2000).

38 Marceau and Pedersen, 'Is the WTO Open and Transparent?', p. 13.

39 Hughes and Wilkinson, 'International Labour Standards and World Trade', pp. 375–80.

40 Marceau and Pedersen, 'Is the WTO Open and Transparent?', p. 17.

41 Renato Ruggiero, WTO Director-General, Opening Address to the Second Ministerial Meeting (Geneva, 18 May 1998).

42 See statements to the WTO Geneva Ministerial Meeting by Leon Brittan, Vice-President of the European Commission (18 May 1998), Charlene Barshefsky, US Trade Representative (18 May 1998), and Bill Clinton, US President (18 May 1998).

43 See Rorden Wilkinson, 'The WTO in Crisis: exploring the dimensions of institutional inertia', *Journal of World Trade*, 35: 3 (June 2001).

44 Mike Moore, 'Labour issue is a "False Debate" . . .', WTO Press Release, No. 152 (28 November 1999).

45 Mike Moore, 'The WTO is not a World Government . . .', WTO Press Release, No. 155 (29 November 1999).

46 See, for example, that underway in the EU's 15 member states.
47 See, for example, address by Mike Moore, 'Reflections on the global trading system' given to the Symposium on Global Economic Integration, Jackson Hole, US, 25 August 2000.
48 Scholte, in a study of the IMF's interaction with civil society, makes just this point. See Jan Aart Scholte, 'The IMF meets Civil Society', *Finance and Development*, 35: 3 (September 1998).
49 Marceau and Pedersen, 'Is the WTO Open and Transparent?', p. 43.
50 Warkentin and Mingst argue that, given the right conditions, global civil society does have such a capacity. See Craig Warkentin and Karen Mingst, 'International Institutions, the State, and Global Civil Society in the Age of the World Wide Web', *Global Governance*, 6: 2 (Apr–June 2000), p. 254.

12 Lessons from Greenham Common peace camp

Alternative approaches to global governance

Lucy James

The protests in Prague during the September 2000 meetings of the World Bank and International Monetary Fund (IMF) were an immediate and forceful reminder of alternative political claims and approaches to world governance. Seeking to repeat the considerable global impact made in Seattle in 1999 during the World Trade Organisation's (WTO) Ministerial Meeting, these diverse, diffuse and at times inchoate groups of protestors offered a powerful critique of the dominant, liberal consensus on globalisation, and, in doing so, bring attention to those who are marginalised, excluded and impoverished. Environmentalists rallied with activists from the left; protestors from the South marched with Western trade union delegates. While the protestors' immediate concerns may have differed – and even conflicted to some extent – together they constitute not only a wide-ranging critique of contemporary global capital, but also create a forum, or space, where links between issues are made, and active opposition organised.

This chapter focuses on the construction and organisation of such a space, where political issues are linked to form a clear oppositional platform for grassroots politics and the role that this can play when considering questions of governance. The example looked at here is that of the Greenham Common peace camp, a women-only camp during the 1980s which primarily existed to protest against the deployment of ground-launched Cruise and Pershing II missiles in Europe, but where links were made between the issue of nuclear defence policies with environmental politics, women's rights, queer politics, social justice and so on.[1] What Greenham offered was a bottom-up approach to governance, similar to that demonstrated in Seattle and Prague, where the political agenda is publicly and volubly contested by individuals and groups outside established mechanisms of power – the establishment being embodied by such institutions as national ministries of defence or the World Bank, the North Atlantic Treaty Organisation (NATO) or the IMF. Following Cox, the underlying premise here is that taking inter-state multilateralism as the central model for global governance is misguided, and that we also need to look at social forces and social movements, as it is in this arena of civil society that the effects of decisions made by elite institutions are really felt, and the liberal, state-centric consensus is challenged.

As well as moving away from the traditional, state-centric apparatus of governance, this chapter argues that we need to take gender seriously when looking at bottom-up processes. This is because, by using a gender-aware analysis we can begin to challenge the hierarchical nature of many established forms of governance, develop alternatives, and question and reconstruct dominant patterns of power. Many feminists, such as Peterson, argue that the central gender hierarchy that stems from the public–private dichotomy is naturalised and extended to justify other hierarchies based on difference.[2] If, then, we seek to pursue a critical approach to governance, exposing and transforming inherent power relationships based on dominance and subordination, then using gender as a means of delineating new forms of governance is crucial.

What is particularly important here is the way in which the concept of power is used. Power is generally understood to denote a form of dominance, of A getting B to do something against his/her will. But a key problem with such an absolute understanding of power is that it is linked to controlling others, and effectively renders the majority powerless – and this is something that a bottom-up approach to governance needs to take seriously, as it clearly implies a reversal of the traditional, hierarchical model of power dynamics. If we instead understand power in terms of empowerment, which is about controlling oneself rather than others, and link this to the ability to accomplish certain goals, then we can move to a model of power that rejects a hierarchical model of dominance and subordination.[3] When considering issues of global governance, this recognition of the value of grassroots politics is crucial, as it introduces the politics of the immediate and the local, and the real issues that motivate and activate protest. And it is this that needs to be recognised and embraced in any attempt to construct global governance, in order to avoid the trap of over-bureaucratised hierarchies with little connection to people's lives (as will be seen later, in the slow and sclerotic structures of the British security establishment). Looking at grassroots movements is also valuable in terms of harnessing their power and energy; the will for change in contrast to cynical apathy.

When looking at Greenham, the most obvious defining organisational feature of the camp was the fact that it was women-only. However, while for radical feminist separatists this might be perceived as a viable and necessary option for bringing about an alternative form of governance, because of the limited nature of this principle's wider application (and for reasons of space) I will not focus primarily on this aspect here. Instead, we will look at other, more general running principles of organisation that were operative at Greenham, such as the determinedly consensual decision-making process, skill-sharing, the sense of spontaneity, and the non-hierarchical structure. We will then look at Greenham's broader organisational base, reaching out beyond the camp itself, to local peace and women's groups. This was a two-way link, with ideas, contributions and inspiration travelling in both directions, helping to support and sustain the camp itself, as well as stimulating and encouraging local action. This can be linked to feminist models of organisation, which may in turn be helpful in understanding and developing alternative arenas of governance.

The strengths of this framework will then be examined, seeing how the methods and structure of Greenham were felt to be empowering, liberating, healing and personally enriching as well as politically effective. This will be followed by a section on what were perceived to be the camp's structural weaknesses, seeing how – for all its claim of mass appeal – it was a predominantly white, middle-class interest; how the single-sex policy could be seen to work to its disadvantage, alienating potential groups of support; and how the lack of formal structure tended to stoke inter-personal conflict, with ultimately fatal consequences for the camp itself. Finally, the chapter will look at what emerged once the camp itself had finished: how the processes of Greenham, the ethos and methods of organising lived on both on a political level, in terms of continued projects and action, and on a personal level, in terms of individual and collective empowerment.

Structure: 'You don't go round telling people what to do and how to do it'

A striking feature of Greenham was the sense of spontaneity underlying the actions and organisation, the apparently unstructured nature of events. One woman remembered her first visit as being in response to 'some sort of call for women to go down on December 12th, something like that'.[4] While another felt these calls seemed to come out of nowhere: 'I could never understand how it all happened anyway, who organised these demonstrations, they just seemed to happen [laughs] – I think that was what impressed me about it, nobody said "this is what we're going to do", just "it's next week", it just happened'.[5] All the actions at Greenham shared this air of spontaneity, lacking rigid organisation or structure, allowing the women to follow their instincts, rather than orders from above.

This system created its own sort of order, based on general principles rather than fixed rules and hierarchy, and there were no fixed roles or expectations of anyone:

> The only rule was no violence; and you had to sort of pick it up, that you did the washing-up voluntarily – no-one would come and ask you to; if you were there for about a month and you still hadn't done the washing-up you might find someone coming up to you and saying 'I'd like to get into town to do some shopping' or they might say 'I feel a bit like a housewife' [laughs] and put it to you indirectly without making an accusation of any sort.[6]

Women chose to do domestic tasks – there was no rota – and these chores were allocated as little time as possible. According to Roseneil, this 'challenged the popular fetishisation' of housework, and countered arguments that Greenham was essentialist and maternalist, as if it had been, housework would have been given a higher priority.[7] And by working together on the everyday, contributing as they could, without excessive expectations, the women forged a sense of collective identity.[8] The structure and nature of Greenham changed, according to its composition: by consciously embracing differences, Greenham developed a style and approach that was heterogeneous, open and flexible, as embodied in the different coloured gates around the base, which women could live at and move around according to mood.

Just as the atmosphere of each gate shifted over time, so did the make-up and feel of the camp as a whole, with the emphasis moving from a broad church of protest against nuclear weapons to a more focused, women-centred organisation. In this way the camp was reflective and dynamic rather than solid and immobile: 'It wasn't a "one thing" that Greenham was, in my opinion; it just was growing and changing all the time, depending on who was there, and always shifting and changing'.[9]

This flexibility meant that there were few restrictive rules or expectations as to the women's own contributions to the camp – for example, there was no demand that all women cut fences or take part in direct action – rather, there was an acceptance that, whatever level each woman wanted to work at was fine. Similarly the actions themselves were flexible and adaptive, according to the women there, the situation on the base and so on. This gave the women a distinct advantage over the military, which they saw as a very solid, tied institution, unable to camouflage its intentions or movements. In contrast, the approach adopted by the women at Greenham operated as an antithesis to military methods:

> I felt very strongly, with some women that I worked closely with, that we didn't have to join their games, but we could undermine them because we could work completely differently, they could never predict what we were doing the way that we could predict what they would do. They were – well, still are, really – three months behind in changing any of their working practice, so we can do something for three months before they get their act together to actually change it.[10]

One woman saw this slowness of the Establishment's response as a product of its structure:

> I think patriarchal structures tend to be more pyramidal than, say, weblike; and so you've got the people doing the real work, and they're in the majority but they have very, very little power; and then they report to a level of management who reports to a level of management, and then the people at the top of it, really, are the people who hold the purse strings, and the people who hold the purse strings are still largely men or male-dominated organisations. And so you have this quite heavy

sort of structure and there's some movement between levels but it's not all that much, and you can see very clearly where the decision-making lies. The interesting thing about the web structure too is that it's not very clear immediately where the decision-making lies; and there's a reason for that, and it's that the central level of decision-making has to be with each strand, with each individual. There are other levels, and it would be naive to say that you don't, at the same time, have people who are maybe looking a bit in the longer term, and making more long-term plans and things like that, you have got that, but you've got that always balancing out.[11]

The women therefore believed that the authorities tended to be so hidebound by structure and regulation that they were unable to overcome the women's actions and protest, which operated in a completely different form and medium: the Greenham camp consisted of a large, leaderless network of women, with only a few of them in one place at any one time. Thus, the movement was not tied down to any restrictive demands or structures, whether organisational or physical. This enabled Greenham to retain a physical flexibility, as the women learnt to adapt to the environment and materials available, and a structural malleability, with women only staying for as long as they wanted, and only participating in actions they were happy with. The constant ebb and flow of new arrivals provided a stream of new energy and ideas, preventing any one individual from dominating, and giving each woman the chance to take initiatives and exercise personal responsibility.[12] This deliberate anti-hierarchical structure can be clearly mirrored against the fixed hierarchies of the state and, especially, the military that were on the opposite side of the fence. While hierarchies are often valued for their apparent efficiency, Iannello points out that hierarchical structures tend to be inflexible – as the women themselves noticed above – and that they take away any focus on human needs, demotivating those without a direct role in decision-making. An alternative framework, similar to that pursued by the camp at Greenham, is one of consensual organisation, whereby authority belongs to the whole rather than just the elite; and social control is exercised by peer pressure rather than supervision from above.[13]

There was a sense of freedom engendered by the lack of hierarchy: 'We were making decisions, as individuals, of how to behave; and nobody was passing judgement on anybody else, unlike in a hierarchical society where those at the top tell you what to do, and there are sanctions if you don't . . . the freedom of individual action was empowering, and very significant'. While Greenham sought to avoid set, hierarchical power relationships, it was not rigidly egalitarian either. The camp accommodated and embraced differences – such as the length of time spent at Greenham, articulacy with the media, how far each woman took direct action – yet these differences were the basis of an incipient structure that evolved.

I think Greenham itself had its own kind of hierarchy, but it was a more fluid one, and to some extent you could change it. Part of the hierarchy was how long you'd been there, or how many times you'd been to prison; now I personally found those a bit unpleasant although I scored quite well on them, because I felt that that was missing the point, and that itself was a kind of macho thing. But there was a fluidity ... frankly, if you'd been at the camp for about three months you'd already moved into a position where, you knew how things were going, and you understood where things were, and you could work out where you wanted to put your work in, and so in terms of your effectiveness, you could be as effective after three months as somebody could after two or three years, and in fact sometimes you could be more effective, because you often had more energy. So, although there was an element of that sort of hierarchy, in some ways it was in the minds of a very small number of women rather than an actual set of boundaries.[14]

While how long individual women had been at Greenham was bound to be important – long-term residents were well-equipped to teach newcomers about the camp's ethos and operation; and being at Greenham often brought about a greater self-confidence, which can at least give the impression of power – there was a great awareness of the possibility of an incipient hierarchy, and a conscious, collective attempt was made to counter it.[15]

This suggests that, by virtue of their commitment and experience, some women were viewed as 'natural leaders'. Yet while they were often the focus of media attention, it was more the case that they simply used their abilities to present Greenham's case publicly, while others did not see that as their own priority, and had the space to make their own contributions to the camp without necessarily feeling themselves to be less important. To some extent, therefore, that form of hierarchy which emerged was externally constructed, by the media, who tended to home in on those they pinpointed as eloquent 'leaders'.[16] This suggests that the camp was more susceptible to dominant patterns of power and hierarchy than it would have liked, especially given that those who were targeted as 'spokeswomen' or 'leaders' did in fact respond to the attention of both the women at the camp, and the media.

Even so, determined efforts were made to overcome such patterns of hierarchy, for example by skills-sharing:

I think that one thing was really important, the skill-sharing aspect of Greenham, and that we rotated; and it meant that sometimes we had people going out to do speaks – which is our kind of language for talks, speaks ... that really weren't good enough, on one level, or talking to the media. But how are you going to learn, you only learn by doing, and you can't just rely on two or three people to do it, because when they're not there who's going to do it?[17]

Again, for Iannello this is consistent with a consensual model of organisation, and was used in the peace group that she studied. There, having individuals permanently in certain roles was seen as threatening the underlying idea of empowerment that informed the structures and processes of the group, as others were prevented from learning. Thus, it was felt that specialisation would inevitably result in hierarchy, so it was avoided – as at Greenham – through concerted skill-sharing.[18]

As well as being demonstrated in the sharing of tasks, the striving to avoid hierarchy was perhaps most in evidence when decisions had to be made:

> We would sit round in a circle, we would have a facilitator, which would be different on any different occasion, and the facilitator's task was not to contribute to the debate but to assist and be sure that everyone who wanted to speak had space to speak and that no-one was . . . dominating and intimidating other women. So, we would go round, in turn, saying our name, because it was open to anybody who happened to be there at the time, and then we'd go round and say what we thought about the issue, whatever it was; and it would become clear from that that some people knew a lot, and had interests in the issue, and other people were more observers, and more going to weigh up the situation and decide what they thought after they'd heard the debate. And we'd go round one by one, and if someone didn't want to speak they would just say they didn't want to say anything; and then after that there would be more of an open exchange, across the circle if necessary, and sometimes it would get very heated. And if at the end, probably about an hour and a half, it didn't look as though we were getting towards a conclusion, there would be a break for tea, and stoking the fire; we'd do this sitting round the fire most of the year, though in the heat of summer we'd just sit round in a circle, not round the fire. But also, it wouldn't be round the camp fire, we would move the venue to a different space so that anyone who didn't want to take part in the discussion still had the home base . . . and then we would reconvene, some people very much groaning about meetings, and some people enjoying it, and some people interested, and some people very concerned and determined that they made clear to women what they said and thought was something that needed support. And then we would continue, and if after about another hour, hour and a half, couldn't come to a conclusion there'd be another break, and it might be decided to leave it till the next day. Quick decision-making was something else again, and we did try – not particularly there, to some extent, but in various places – in working in small groups, and making quick decisions, which during direct actions you have to do.[19]

Camp decisions were, therefore, the result of a shared consensus, with everyone in the group given an opportunity to voice their opinion. While this method had a clear structure, and process, there was no predetermined concentration of power, as all the participants had access to the decision-making.

Thus, the Greenham model is in marked contrast to the decision-making process of a pyramidal model of power, or where the majority rules absolutely, and only a limited number of competing points of view are aired, with the most forceful proponent 'winning'. Although, as we have seen, there was a perception of some women being 'natural leaders', this was most common in the area of dealing with the media. In the actual process of decision-making, there was time and space for the less confident and less eloquent to make their points, and all arguments were heard equally. At Greenham the discussion was continually redefined to assimilate new ideas, rather than polarising into distinct, rigid options; in such a process there was greater openness, producing a sense of unity and trust, as all the women could participate on equal terms.[20] By choosing consensus rather than voting as a method of making decision, Greenham could involve some women losing out, as although the process was clearly slow, at least all members ultimately agreed to the final decision.[21]

Thus, the day-to-day running of the camp observed certain, feminist principles, following on from the practice of groups formed during the rise of the Women's Liberation Movement (WLM) in the 1970s: the structure was decentralised, enabling people to exercise their own responsibility; in meetings, space was given to all who wanted to speak, others were listened to and the chair was rotated; the validity of *emotional* responses was recognised – this was something that many women felt was overlooked in the mixed peace groups they attended; different opinions were listened to and taken on board in the eventual decision-making process, and accommodated if possible; and 'male sparring techniques' arguing to win points, just for the sake of it, were given short shrift.[22] There were no institutionalised procedures, formal membership, or committees – instead, there were patterns of working which were supple, and dynamic.[23]

Women at Greenham came together to challenge nuclear weapons, but discovered and developed ways of working that helped overcome their political inexperience and lack of confidence – for example, the decentralisation and democratisation of decision-making processes gave everyone the space to listen and contribute to the running of their own environment, through co-operation rather than competition, and using consensus and compromise over conflict and confrontation. Yet Greenham's organisation extended well beyond the camp itself: its impact and longevity relied on a broad and intricate network of local groups and peace activists who publicised the camp and its aims. We will now look at how these groups were influenced by the methods of Greenham, and how they reciprocated, helping to shape the actual camp.

Local outlets: 'The women at Greenham were the visible side of the network'

The local groups and interests that acted as access points to Greenham and the peace movement as a whole were diverse: while many women made a first move via the Campaign for Nuclear Disarmament (CND), others became involved through a local group or church interests. For some, their first moves into organised peace politics therefore began with applying the arguments on an immediate, local basis, questioning the impact of nuclear policy on their own environment. Local, small-scale groups articulated the nuclear threat in accessible, comprehensible and immediate terms, avoiding the language of abstract high strategy. This low-level approach, seeking to inform and inspire on a local level rather than intellectually intimidate was carried through to Greenham itself. Such an approach is helpful when considering bottom-up processes of governance, linking the local with the global. In this case, the global issue of nuclear deterrence policy was filtered out from the military base at Greenham, to small local groups utilising a creative and wide-reaching network, mobilising many women who had not previously been politically active.

Greenham spawned dozens of autonomous local groups, which maintained links with the camp through visits, newsletters and friendships. Like the actual peace camp, these groups often lacked a set structure, and overlapped with other activist networks (such as rape crisis, or CND) which helped to broaden and revitalise the protest.[24] Thus, through a broad local network, the issues that Greenham raised were voiced and spread; and the same network provided support and supporters for the camp itself. The extent and effectiveness of the network gave Greenham a strong base of resources and ideas.

Major events at Greenham – which attracted huge numbers of women from across the country – illustrated how these broad networks operated:

> I think one of the big moments was the Embrace the Base demonstration where you had over 30,000 women holding hands around the base, that was an extraordinary moment historically. But it didn't just come from nowhere – women 'phoned up women who were on 'phone trees, who were already in networks, who were already in groups.[25]

As well as providing sheer numbers, Greenham's support base helped replenish more material resources as and when required. Small, local support groups came together and responded as and when they were needed, perpetuating the core Greenham structural qualities of informality and flexibility.

As the impact of Greenham boosted CND membership, smaller groups flourished; and the voice that women were learning to develop in the women-only space of Greenham, was able to grow and articulate itself on a local level. Through processes such as this, the women-only nature of Greenham began to define and shape the network of groups that supported it, through changes taking place within the women themselves in terms of awareness, and self-realisation. Greenham provided a focal point for the women's movement, and offered an accessible entry point into a certain feminist consciousness and method, which offered an alternative to traditional, male-dominated political activism.[26]

The local peace groups also drew from Greenham a strong sense of purpose, and solidarity, that sustained and renewed them, without endangering the flexibility and informality of their structure. A sense of solidarity was engendered by inter-personal contact with Greenham women, and through working at the grassroots, reaching out to talk and explain to people, debates were brought back down to earth from the abstractions of high-level politics. Moreover, local-level groups followed the same general principles of organisation and method as Greenham. For example, on a practical level, one woman's group was given seminars on direct action and non-violence, so that protests could be conducted locally.[27] Another local peace group sought to skill-share and work as consensually and democratically as possible, as well as maintaining the sense of flexibility that Greenham had:

> I did all the mailing, so in a sense, sometimes I felt that was quite a powerful position to be in, having the mailing list, and sending everything out, but I suppose it would have been really difficult to have more than one person doing that, maybe we could have swapped it round. But we did try, in our groups, to make it work on a very equal footing, and we used to meet at different houses, all over the county.[28]

As the cause of Greenham was taken up by women across the UK, and the approach and organisational methods were applied at a local level, so the term 'Greenham women' covered not just the women living at the camp, or a formal, set membership. Instead, it embraced all those who chose to take part in non-violent action for peace, connected with each other by common ways of working, and communicating largely by word of mouth.[29] And women moved out from Greenham itself to form other peace camps, based on the same methods and principles. By means such as this, the Greenham network spread outwards from the actual base, to cover more issues and reach more women. This weblike structure and flexibility helped sustain and innovate the camp, strengthening it. Another way of understanding this structure is, as Iannello describes, of intersecting circles, moving outwards from a core of more 'hardline' activists, to those who are less able to commit time, to 'sponsoring' members who help provide the funds. All levels are involved in critical decision-making.[30] We now look at its other structural and organisational strengths in more detail.

Strengths: 'It seemed like you could get through so much more dross'

The essential flexibility of Greenham and its lack of rigid structure meant that women had the space to make of the camp what they wanted, without having to fit into the rules and regulations dictated by others. In this way, the camp lacked the sense of military rigour or strict hierarchy that some women found other in peace camps. Yet while Greenham lacked precise order, it had more space and flexibility to explore and create; one woman felt that Greenham could focus more on what it was trying to achieve: at Fairford (a mixed peace camp), 'they got so internally wound up about whether there'd be somebody there to hoe the weeds, they forgot what they were there for in the end, and it became a burden'. And while Greenham may have been less neat and outwardly attractive, 'it functioned. People were lying around in the sun, having a happy time; nobody was worrying about hoeing the beans, or anything like that. And there were women who did try, from time to time, to plant vegetables and do all sorts of things when they wanted to, but they didn't feel that they had to impose that on others, or form a support network for the beans [laughs]'.[31]

The women themselves never treated each other as secondary, and Greenham was seen as their place first and foremost, rather than solely as a location for an anti-nuclear message. As well as providing space for women who needed a place to heal, Greenham was a space for those who felt uncomfortable in the usual confines of society, providing an environment of safety, trust and tolerance that they were usually denied. This space was taken by women to re-assess and recover, and to determine their own lives: many women felt able to explore their sexuality for the first time at Greenham and, in an all-women environment, felt able to come out.[32] Even for women who felt less troubled, the space at Greenham proved value as 'a retreat, a time to strengthen your feelings and come out strengthened'.[33] In this sense, the lack of formal structure in the camp gave the women a sense of legitimate, autonomous power and a sense of consciousness which they lacked in a world where gendered, hierarchical patterns of power predominated.[34] Through these experiences, many of the women began to develop a stronger sense of their own identity, and hence a sense of self-confidence that many had previously lacked. At Greenham they had an arena to think, explore and conjecture without the constraints of gendered power relations or competitive game-playing.

Women were given the emotional space to articulate their instinctive reaction to the nuclear issue, which could often be deadened by the bureaucratic politics of the mainstream peace movements. A woman quoted in Cook and Kirk felt in shock, angry and fearful after attending a local CND meeting, as while the discussion was dominated by talk of SS-20s, missiles, demonstrations and so on, her own feelings were given no space, crowded out by 'all kinds of political things that I don't understand. They don't seem to *feel* about it. All they seem to do is work with their heads'.[35] This sentiment was shared by others: 'it seemed like you could get through so much more dross when you were at Greenham, or actually talking to women who were actually right on the front line there; and you went to these endless meetings with CND when you used to stir round and round – I used to find it frustrating at times'.[36]

Some of the women had other roles which restricted their participation at the camp, yet Greenham's flexibility meant that these differences in contributions were accommodated and even welcomed, rather than denigrated. This contrasts with the macho tendency of high expectations, constantly pushing the self to the limit and tending to overlook the private realm while devoting maximum energy to the public. Greenham was not dominated by the media-articulate, or the most fervid proponents of direct action. Instead, by accepting diversity, the camp achieved a balance that worked: 'It was interesting how very intelligent and lucid some people were, while others were there because of their emotions. Some can speak, others can move and act, but between them it's a whole'.[37] Thus, skills and contributions which were not readily quantifiable, or marketable, represented significant contributions to the camp as a whole:

For many women, this was the first time that they felt themselves to be worthwhile, or to be given the space to develop and appreciate these skills.

Weaknesses: 'We ended up tearing each other apart'

A key element of Greenham's approach – the determination to empathise with the oppressed, thereby overcoming traditional, polarised power structures of the dominant and the subjugated – could be seen to go too far, and ultimately led to the split of the camp, as it allowed a destructive faction too much power within the camp. In addition, the 'balancing out' that Greenham attempted, and the looseness that aimed to give women maximum space, contributed to its structural vulnerability:

> As the Women's Movement found in the '70s, so Greenham found in the late '80s – where you have this very decentralised structure, where you haven't got any specific leadership, you can be vulnerable to attack from an organisation that uses male power, whether it's women running it or, or men . . . like Wages for Housework; using men's way of doing things, so taking the answers from a leader, where you've got your leader and you've got the acolytes, and you drive a wedge, and you set up a leadership and you flatter or bully, or whatever a certain small group and you set them up in leadership; you can do a lot of damage.[38]

The blatantly conflictual nature of the camp'a product of its openness, and of giving women space to voice their opinions and speak their minds – could be seen as a possible weakness, as it could be misinterpreted as unfriendliness:

> There were so many humdinging rows, it was a very conflictual place, on one level, but I think that's partly the living conditions as well, because you got so grumpy sometimes that you weren't about to be polite; which I think was difficult because sometimes people forgot what it must be like for visitors, who didn't know that you'd just woken up in a puddle, or you hadn't had a break for weeks.[39]

Thus, while Greenham's diversity was a key source of its appeal and dynamism, as the camp grew older, the tensions and differences such diversity implied were exacerbated, to the point where they could become damaging. And the non-hierarchical structure of the camp could actually exacerbate the emotional intensity of the experience – with every member responsible, and equal, so disagreements can begin to matter far more than in a hierarchical structure where only a few are responsible.[40]

In addition, there was a sense of difference and inequality between short-term visitors and long-term residents, which seemed in-built and inevitable, as long as Greenham remained open to all women for as long or as short a time as they wanted. This made some feel uncomfortable and guilty, and they found it hard to feel accepted there. As well as inter-personal tensions between residents and visitors in terms of their relative contributions, differences developed about the groups' political direction, with some women disliking the drift towards increasingly feminist and global issues, which they felt detracted from Cruise.[41]

Another source of tension was the adamant exclusion of men, a stance some found simply incomprehensible: 'Most of them were not, I don't like to say men-haters, but absolutely singled themselves out from the other sex, and I couldn't understand that . . . Some of the women were so anti-men, and I thought how can you be anti-men when you've got to have children, you know, you've got to have a partner to have children, haven't you?'[42] Others felt that the dismissing of all men who came to help merely perpetuated the divisive, destructive categorisation that was practised in the outside world, which was antithetical to the sense of community and equality that Greenham preached.

Thus, while Greenham's women-only organisational basis was central to the movement in terms of providing a forum for a traditionally marginalised perspective, and giving space for views and feelings to be expressed in a way that established political debate did not usually allow, some individual women at the camp were uncomfortable with the consequences of its separatist principles. Yet this apparent contradiction between Greenham's avowed cosmopolitanism and diversity, and its women-only status, was perhaps inevitable, and for most of the women at Greenham the sense of space and discovery in an all-women environment effectively counterbalanced the risk of alienating male support.[43]

Another way in which Greenham effectively forsook its own policy of inclusion and acceptance was the inescapable bias of class and race within the camp: simply the logistics of participating at Greenham could be impeded by background:

> There was a real class problem, and an ethnic problem . . . if you were a single mother in a working-class community it would be more difficult to get somebody to look after your children, if you didn't want to bring your children, if there were problems there. If you were black, or a woman of colour, the vast majority of women there were white. Very often the people who spoke, or appeared to speak for the movement

were very middle-class; and I think this defined who went; I think that was a very serious problem, right from the beginning.[44]

This effectively skewed Greenham towards being middle-class right from the outset, and the camp had little success in changing this, or broadening its appeal: 'We'd have talks about including more working-class women, and women of colour but you'd find yourself getting very irritated, because we were very privileged, in the main'.[45] Thus, whole groups of women were denied the chance to participate in a camp that was designed specifically for them, resulting in an inherent divisiveness.

A further problem with the way Greenham functioned was, for some, the lack of organisation – while individually freeing, and making the movement flexible and adaptable, it could also prove frustrating on an immediate, personal level, in terms of rapid communication. Also, as Iannello has pointed out, organisations based on a consensual model can be very, very slow at making decisions.[46]

However, for one woman, the really fatal flaw for Greenham was not within the camp itself, but in the reactions of others: 'We lost the argument due to the disgraceful behaviour within the peace movement of men, which was dreadful: they really wanted to be at Greenham, and if they couldn't be at Greenham, then they wanted to run it down. Internationally men supported it, because they recognised how important it was; here, in this country, within the peace movement, they let it down'.[47] This reluctance of men within the mainstream British peace movement to support Greenham as a women-only enterprise echoed their disinclination to take seriously the rapes at the Molesworth peace camp, or the significance of women's issues within a broader understanding of security. This view suggests that while Greenham was effective to a limited extent, gendered patterns of power relations out-side the camp (as well as the eventual replication of these relations within the camp itself) had a destructive impact. This view is echoed by Spike Petersen, who argues that women's struggles – such as women-only peace marches 'are denied the status of political behaviour'; that they are inter-preted as domestic issues and dismissed as politically insignificant in a patriarchally determined political arena.[48]

Yet while Greenham clearly did not bring about a revolution in terms of how we are governed, or how security policy is decided, its impact beyond the confines of the camp itself are undeniable, albeit at a more gradual pace and more subtle level than the original protest seemed to demand. We will now look at Greenham, in terms of the women who went there, the ideas they picked up, and the organisational principles they adopted after the actual life-span of the camp itself.

Post-Greenham: 'It seems to have permeated everything'

In terms of the long-term impact of Greenham, some women felt that it had a real impact, permeating through politics, bringing about a new and dynamic culture of process of change; while others were more cynical about what it had achieved. Aware of this cynicism in themselves and others, many women felt that after Greenham there was no real cause any more, that there was little point to activism. Without Cruise, Greenham was felt to have lost its driving sense of purpose, and began to disintegrate, as the camp on its own was not enough to motivate and draw women together. And after the removal of Cruise missiles, the intensity and aim of protest faded, as other, related issues seemed to lack the same urgency. This is certainly a weakness of many social movements, and one of the difficulties in delineating an effective bottom-up process within governance: how to make the leap from local to global while maintaining the momentum that a single-issue campaign embodies. While, as we shall see, many of the women's own political activism proliferated through the issue-related links that Greenham made, a single-issue group may be too parochial to be effective at a global level; and if it expands beyond its single issue, it may become too general and vague to survive as a coherent group.[49]

Perhaps, then, ultimately Greenham was unsuccessful. It had offered a clear social and political alternative in terms of structure and values to the dominant set, and yet nuclear weapons remained in the world, politics was still hierarchical and unequal, and conflict seemed a more potent force than co-operation. Moreover, the camp itself dissipated into conflict. Yet although some felt that their political energies had been used up by Greenham to no effect, for others it heralded an era of activism which carried on after the camp itself faded from view, campaigning with the issues they had picked up there. In this way, Greenham acted as an important, politicising catalyst, inspiring women to pursue certain political threads of activism they had encountered at the camp, and take them further. For some women, the removal of Cruise from Greenham did not dilute the urgency of the anti-nuclear campaign in general, and they continue to obstruct nuclear convoys to draw attention to the continuing defence policy, using Greenham methods, such as climbing onto warhead carriers and so on.[50] Thus, Greenham women continued with direct, non-violent action, for a variety of causes: 'All those women that were there before are still out there doing things, perhaps not directly related to nuclear weapons, but they're involved in environmental issues, health issues, education, they're out there doing all sorts'.[51] Because of this, the demise of the camp itself did not mark the end of its purpose, and the very way in which the camp was organised – the decentralisation, the individual empowerment and liberation – helped its spirit survive beyond the camp's physical life-span.

Greenham therefore lives on with the women who had been there, not only in direct, political ways but in terms of the women's personal lives as well. So, while it could perhaps be argued that Greenham's international political role was marginal, its impact nonetheless resounded in multiple personal arenas, and from there outwards. Greenham often acted as, if not a direct causal factor, then a catalyst for change. Several of the women interviewed went on to college, 'and I think that says something in a sense about the confidence that Greenham gave a lot of women'.[52]

Thus Greenham often acted as a powerful motivating and educational force with a far-reaching personal impact for many of the women who went there. And women continued their activism in different ways: some tried to work from within the system instead, to try to address the issues that Greenham left unresolved; others found that traditional politics seemed stifling and began working in pressure groups, such as Amnesty, finding that having been at Greenham, no other traditional, institutionalised political approach addressed issues in a way that appealed. Others retained the camp's principles of organisation, and managed to apply them elsewhere, to other concerns and in other environments, such as challenging traditional procedure: 'All Greenham women are doing this, automatically, so you can't help yourself, you're saying what on earth do we want a chairperson for? And why can't we take it in turns, and why do we have to have this sort of figurehead? And you're asking questions like this all the time'.[53] Another woman sought to enmesh the personal with the political, as Greenham did – 'there's no organisation, no chairman, it's just informal . . . when we do it, we do it; there's no minutes, or agenda or anything. And people share parts of themselves, rather than taking on a position; the meetings have been quite personal'.[54] In terms of governance, this has significant potential in terms of the kind of momentum that a grassroots organisation can have, in terms of transforming political structures and processes from below. Thus there are certain principles that Greenham articulated and used, in everyday situations, that are being applied to the world outside the camp itself. Through challenging and changing ways of thinking, beginning with the individual, Greenham offered a different perspective and approach: 'I still think there is an alternative way of structuring society, I don't think that it has to be run in the way it is now; I still think that those kinds of thoughts are really important if we're going to change things'.[55]

Conclusion

Through the arguments and actions of women, Greenham as an ethos, and a set of applicable and practical principles continued to exist and impact on the political arena beyond the heyday of the camp itself. Greenham deconstructed the traditional, male-dominated approach of International Relations, and how it was conducted. With its own form and methods the camp offered an alternative, web-like structure which was able to be one step ahead of the more cumbersome, pyramidal, military structure; and which was able to survive beyond the central issue of Cruise and the physical location of Greenham itself. The organisation of Greenham worked politically – by galvanising networks of women, spreading awareness – and personally, through providing a flexible, all-women environment within which many women developed a sense of autonomy, empowerment and security for the first time. And through the camp's personal impact, it continued to resonate politically, as the women applied what they had learnt in terms of non-violent methods, and their own self-confidence, to other areas of their life. The women were not uncritical of the camp's form: its lack of structure could be frustrating, and allowed for the abuse of power; the fact that Greenham was women-only was potentially alienating to a wider, mixed group of supporters; the diversity the camp engendered entailed disagreements and conflict; and despite the camp's egalitarian stance, it retained a middle-class bias, and nascently hierarchical patterns developed. However, there is much less critical data within the interviews conducted that inform this chapter than there are accounts of finding the structure empowering and instructive. And these contradictions that Greenham contained do not in themselves negate its impact both individually and politically, as an empowering agent of protest. Rather, it points to a healthy ambivalence rather than a new panacea of a clear, alternative political structure. And at least the structure offered by Greenham clearly helped, through processes of empowerment, to overcome the sense of political alienation that concerns many writers in the field of global governance.[56] This clearly links to feminist understandings of power, which critique a competitive hierarchy, that is 'the longest running system of organised bullying ever to arise on earth'.[57] In this way, the feminist principles and processes enacted at Greenham and elsewhere can help us rethink the nature of political authority, linking existing naturalised gendered hierarchies to other power inequalities; and using alternative, consensual models of organisation to radically challenge existing systems of governance in an attempt to link the personal to the political and global.

Notes

1 This chapter is based on original doctoral research. Twenty women who had spent time at Greenham during the 1980s were interviewed about their experiences; this data was then used to develop a distinctly feminist approach to understanding security. The quotes used in this chapter are taken from a series of interviews conducted between 1994 and 1995; the names of the interviewees are concealed to ensure anonymity. For further explanation of the methodology and results of the research, see L. James, *Greenham Common: the Development of Feminist Security Ideas in Britain in the 1980s*, unpublished PhD thesis, University of Birmingham, 1996.

2 V. S. Peterson, 'Seeking World Order Beyond the Gendered Order of Global Hierarchies', in R. Cox (ed.) *The New Realism: Perspectives on Multilateralism and World Order* (London: Macmillan, 1997), p. 40.

3 K. Ianello, *Decision Without Hierarchy* (London: Routledge, 1992), pp. 43–4.

4 James, *Greenham Common*, p. 179.

5 James, *Greenham Common*, p. 179.

6 James, *Greenham Common*, p. 181.

7 S. Roseneil, *Disarming Patriarchy: Feminism and Political Action at Greenham* (Buckingham: Open University Press, 1995), p. 83.

8 Roseneil, *Disarming Patriarchy*, p. 87.

9 James, *Greenham Common*, p. 182.
10 James, *Greenham Common*, p. 184.
11 James, *Greenham Common*, p. 184.
12 L. Jones, *Sanity*, December 1984, p. 38.
13 Iannello, *Decision Without Hierarchy*, pp. 21–9.
14 James, *Greenham Common*, p. 188.
15 Roseneil, *Disarming Patriarchy*, pp. 94–5.
16 Roseneil, *Disarming Patriarchy*, p. 93.
17 James, *Greenham Common*, p. 190.
18 Iannello, *Decision Without Hierarchy*, p. 66.
19 James, *Greenham Common*, p. 191.
20 A. Cook and G. Kirk, *Greenham Women Everywhere* (London: Pluto Press, 1983), pp. 72–3.
21 Iannello, *Decision Without Hierarchy*, p. 120.
22 M. Beresford, 'Women and Disarmament', *Sanity*, 1/1981, p. 7.
23 Roseneil, *Disarming Patriarchy*, p. 72.
24 Roseneil, *Disarming Patriarchy*, pp. 73–4.
25 Roseneil, *Disarming Patriarchy*, p. 4.
26 B. Harford, 'Greenham: Four Years Later', *Peace News*, 4 October 1985, p. 8.
27 James, *Greenham Common*, p. 201.
28 James, *Greenham Common*, p. 201.
29 L. Jones, *New Statesman*, 16 and 23 December 1983, p. 9.
30 Iannello, *Decisions Without Hierarchy*, p. 75.
31 Iannello, *Decisions Without Hierarchy*, p. 50.
32 James, *Greenham Common*, p. 208.
33 James, *Greenham Common*, p. 208.
34 See J. Rosenau, 'The Person, the Household, the Community and the Globe: Notes for a Theory of Multilateralism in a Turbulent World', in Cox (ed.) *The New Realism*, for the empowering subtext of social movements.
35 Cook and Kirk, *Greenham Women Everywhere*, p. 83.
36 James, *Greenham Common*, p. 211.
37 James, *Greenham Common*, p. 212.
38 James, *Greenham Common*, p. 216.
39 James, *Greenham Common*, p. 217.
40 Iannello, *Decisions Without Hierarchy*, p. 30.
41 Roseneil, *Disarming Patriarchy*, p. 74.
42 James, *Greenham Common*, p. 219.
43 It is worth noting that both these women, while being critical of Greenham's women-only status here, in other statements endorsed this principle.
44 James, *Greenham Common*, p. 220.
45 James, *Greenham Common*, p. 220.
46 Iannello, *Decisions Without Hierarchy*, p. 29.
47 James, *Greenham Common*, p. 222.
48 Petersen, 'Seeking World Order Beyond the Gendered Order of Global Hierarchies', p. 45.
49 M. Smouts, 'Multilateralism from Below: a Prerequisite for Global Governance', in M. Schechter (ed.) *Future Multilateralism: the Political and Social Framework* (London: Macmillan, 1999), p. 301.
50 James, *Greenham Common*, p. 228.
51 James, *Greenham Common*, p. 229.
52 James, *Greenham Common*, p. 229.
53 James, *Greenham Common*, p. 231.
54 James, *Greenham Common*, p. 231.

55 James, *Greenham Common*, p. 233.
56 For example, see R. Cox, 'Introduction', in Cox (ed.) *The New Realism*, p. xxi.
57 See Petersen, 'Seeking World Order Beyond the Gendered Order of Global Hierarchies', p. 52.

Index